RECONNECTIONS

EUROPAN 11 RESULTS

WINNING PROJECTS

The first part of the catalogue is a presentation of the 95 winning projects from the eleventh session, classified into site families (Identity/Uses/Connectivity). It provides access to all the session results with the points of view of the team and the jury.

ANALYSIS OF A SESSION

The second part of the catalogue formulates interpretations around the most emblematic winning projects, based on 5 hypotheses of "reconnection", accompanied by the perspectives of a number of European experts.

CONTENTS

WINNING PROJECTS
95 projects, 41 winners and 54 runners-up

Introduction 4
DIDIER REBOIS, ARCHITECT, TEACHER, EUROPAN EUROPE GENERAL SECRETARY

Map of sites 8

Identity 11
From a marginal status to a significant image 12
- LEEUWARDEN (NL) 12
- WIEN (AT) 17
- PEJË / PEĆ (KO) 20
- SIMRISHAMN (SE) 25

From a question to a new character 30
- AMSTERDAM (NL) 30
- DUBLIN (IE) 34
- DUBROVNIK (HR) 38
- IBBENBÜREN (DE) 42
- SESTAO (ES) 46
- WITTSTOCK (DE) 49

From obsolete identity to new identity 53
- GRAZ (AT) 53
- REIMS (FR) 56
- OSLO (NO) 60
- EINDHOVEN (NL) 64
- NEUILLY-SUR-MARNE (FR) 68
- DEVENTER (NL) 70

Uses 77
From fallow lands to city life 78
- ALMERE (NL) 78
- INGOLSTADT (DE) 82
- MONTHEY (CH) 86
- SAMBREVILLE (BE) 90
- SZEGED (HU) 93
- WARSZAWA (PL) 96

From isolation to social integration 100
- MALMÖ (SE) 100
- CAPELLE AAN DEN IJSSEL (NL) 103
- WÜRZBURG (DE) 106
- CLERMONT-FERRAND (FR) 109
- LINZ (AT) 112

From in-between places to shared spaces 116
- AIGLE (CH) 116
- KØBENHAVN (DK) 120
- NYNÄSHAMN (SE) 124
- RØDOVRE (DK) 128
- SELB (DE) 132

Connectivity 137
From border to seam 138
- ALCALÁ DE LA SELVA (ES) 138
- MARCHE-EN-FAMENNE (BE) 143
- ALLERØD (DK) 146
- SAN BARTOLOMÉ (ES) 150
- TOULOUSE (FR) 154
- TURKU (FI) 158

From void to link 162
- HAUGESUND (NO) 162
- CERDANYOLA DEL VALLÈS (ES) 165
- GETARIA (ES) 169
- NORRKÖPING (SE) 173

From place to territory 177
- SAVENAY (FR) 177
- ALCORCÓN (ES) 182
- GUIMARÃES (PT) 186
- PORVOO (FI) 190
- ROMAINMÔTIER (CH) 194
- SKIEN-PORSGRUNN (NO) 198
- STAINS (FR) 200

54 honourable mentions 206

Backstage at a session 213

Index 221
- WINNING TEAMS 222
- JURIES 234

ANALYSIS OF A SESSION

Reshaping shared spaces 242
CONVERSATION WITH **OLIVER SCHULZE**, ARCHITECT, TEACHER (DK)

Linking with uses 249
CONVERSATION WITH **JOSÉ MARÍA EZQUIAGA**, ARCHITECT, URBANIST, TEACHER (ES)

Cultural interferences 256
CONVERSATION WITH **ENRIQUE SOBEJANO**, ARCHITECT, TEACHER (ES)

Common resources and mutation 263
CONVERSATION WITH **MATHIEU DELORME**, ENGINEER, LANDSCAPE ARCHITECT, URBANIST, TEACHER (FR)

Rhythms and timeframes 269
CONVERSATION WITH **CHRIS YOUNÈS**, PHILOSOPHER, ANTHROPOLOGIST, TEACHER (FR)

Europan secretariats 275

Credits 276

INTRODUCTION
BY **DIDIER REBOIS**
GENERAL SECRETARY OF EUROPAN

4

Reconnections
Connecting the separate and linking the divided

In the "principle of ecology in action", the philosopher Edgar Morin writes: "Our civilisation separates more than it connects. We are lacking reconnection, which has become a vital need; it is not only a complement to individualism, it is also the answer to the worries, uncertainties and anxieties of individual life. Because we have to accept uncertainty and worry, because there are many sources of anxiety, we need forces to hold us and reconnect us. We need reconnection because we are on a venture into the unknown. We have to accept the fact of being here without knowing why."…

"The notion of reconnection fills a conceptual void by giving a substantive nature to what was known only adjectivally, and by imparting an active character. The substantive: 'reconnected' is passive, 'reconnecting' is participatory, 'reconnection' is activating. Is it not still about 'connecting the separate and linking the divided'?"

An act of reconnection is about connecting what has become isolated, separated, disjointed, disconnected. It is about creating connections between things, to be used by human beings to generate a social bond.

Sites in need of "reconnection"

In the era of sustainable development, an urban project that regenerates existing neighbourhoods becomes a project of reconnection. Functionalist urban planning was based on the spatial separation of functions and focused on territorial division through large transport networks and the establishment of mono-functional the zones. Thus each site proposed for the Europan 11 competition can be seen as a state of disconnection caused by now obsolete urban planning principles. The participating European municipalities face the same problem and are keen to correct the effects of social division generated by planning based on spatial separation. Each site is like a question to the competitors about how to recreate a spatial connection that can generate a social bond.

The first problem of contemporary urbanisation is that of **Identity**. As the session theme suggests, it is about linking local and global, which raises the question of identity and its visible and symbolic components, which constitute the character of a place. Indeed, it often happens that the more identifiable cities become at the global scale, the more they risk losing their identity at local level. Certain Europan 11 sites need to be regenerated and reintegrated into the city, either by reconnection to an existing structure or by the creation of a new identity that residents can embrace, in order to avoid creating new enclaves. What existing elements should be retained and what legacy protected, whilst introducing new elements, whether uses or spaces?

The second question is how to allocate new **Uses** to a site, which will have a multitude of impacts in very varied domains, from architecture itself to social or economic life. Underused land encourages cities to introduce new programmes, but is this enough to restore the richness of urban life to these sites? Sometimes a localised operation may change a much wider environment, like a missing piece that completes the urban puzzle. In other cases, there may be intermediate places which lack communal uses, transit spaces primarily suitable to cars. How then do you turn a space that is empty or has been emptied of inhabitants into a shared space?

The third group of questions raised by the sites relates to the theme of **Connectivity**, which is about ways to interconnect the spatial and temporal scales, the natural and social environments. These may be sites at boundaries (transport networks, topography, etc.) that create divides, where borders (between town and country, between suburb and city, between

SAMBREVILLE (BE), RUNNER-UP – *QCM* > SEE MORE P.91

SAN BARTOLOMÉ (ES), WINNER – "RURBAN" GEOLOGY > SEE MORE P.152

districts, etc.) can be changed in multiple ways to create new urban connectivities. Urban environments are the outcome of processes of all kinds, which inject new dynamics into local contexts will and transform local micro-activities into regional activities. New links with metropolitan networks are created or reinforced to generate connections and adjust this relation between global and local.

In order to give the catalogue clarity, we have presented the winning and runner-up projects under these three themes, in other words in terms of the questions of "reconnection" raised by the 49 sites located in 17 different European countries.

Projects as ideas on connectivity

In their in-depth meetings, the 14 juries analysed more than 1800 submissions, some 45% of which were submitted by teams for sites outside their own country. This huge output of "project ideas" shows, if that were necessary, the importance that young professionals of urban, architectural and landscape design attribute to formulating proposals that in most cases go beyond the purely formal level, and seek to formulate ideas about the potential life of the sites concerned.

The 95 selected projects (41 winners and 54 runners-up) presented in this catalogue can therefore be seen as stimulating visions of the future of urban situations. In order to identify the key emergent themes, we asked a committee of experts made up of young professionals and researchers (some of them former competition winners), all teachers, to classify these winning projects in terms of the way they effect a "reconnection" by combining spatial formalisations and ideas on the social and cultural future of these areas.

Five "reconnection" themes emerged from this process, themes that structure the second part of the catalogue. Each of these themes is linked with a group of emblematic projects, which are discussed in interviews between the members of the technical committee and outside experts with recognised expertise in the relevant field. These interviews together encompass the multiple forms of "reconnection" brought about by the winning projects.

The first theme asks the question: **What if the focus were placed on shared resources?** This session of Europan marks the growing role of nature in urban project design. The presence of natural elements is refined to the point of becoming an essential element of the project. The awareness that natural resources are finite, although perhaps still abstract at the local level, is nevertheless more clearly recognised by this session's urban designers. And many winning projects can be understood as a new quest for compatibility between urban development and the value of existing resources. It is the landscape engineer Mathieu Delorme who answers Europan's questions and responds to the main themes associated with this issue. Here, reconnection can work in different ways.

6

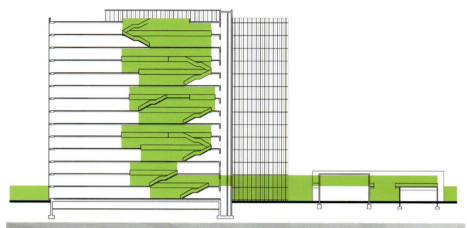

EINDHOVEN (NL), WINNER – *COMPOSITION IX, OPUS 18* > SEE MORE P. 66

By protecting the resource but allowing access whilst minimising intervention; or conversely, by artificially adding a missing resource to a site. By reactivating and reinforcing existing resources in order to link the heterogeneous elements of a site, or by juxtaposing built spaces with a protected resource to create interactions. Finally, by substantially transforming the context by reshaping resources, in order to create a hybrid inhabited landscape.

The second idea takes the opposite perspective, placing the emphasis more on the cultural than the natural: **What if we could reconnect to a place through cultural references?** It is apparent that references emerge as a significant generator of strategies in the winning projects, sometimes based on the physical features of the site or its surroundings, sometimes based on more spiritual elements, such as mental images or even a narrative of social practices projected into the context of the site. The projects here seem to explore solutions that go beyond the traditional meaning of cultural reference by incorporating different interpretations. According to Jens Metz, the expert on this theme, they are transformed into "cultural interferences". Enrique Sobejano, a well-known Spanish architect and former Europan winner answers his questions through several sub-themes associated with "reconnections" effected through references. This can be done by reactivating and updating traces present on the site, by giving them a new meaning, by revealing the collective memory associated with the area, or by revisiting a local archetypal symbol. Other projects inject external references by reinventing an iconic image that will make sense in a given context, or by describing potential social practices that could metamorphose the site.

The third idea applies to projects in which uses play a more important role than form: **What if we created new links through an intensification of uses?** In the contemporary understanding of urban phenomena, the possibilities of the concept of connection need to be amplified. And beyond physical connections, the idea of what might be called social connection sometimes seems more relevant. This can refer not only to the structure of relations established between the inhabitants of a neighbourhood or a city, but also to the urban connectivity that occurs as a result of new social dynamics and of relations between spaces where social life takes place, according to David Franco, the expert on this theme for Europan. And it is the famous Spanish urbanist José María Ezquiaga, who was asked to respond to the projects that proposed new forms of social relation, for example by introducing focal points or a variety of programmes to create more widespread dynamics. This reconnection can also be achieved by programming urban space to reconnect fragments or by injecting programmes that give a new identity to the site.

Less programmatic but focused more on practices, the third idea reminds us of a strategic issue: **What if shared spaces were reshaped?** One could even say "shareable spaces", given the number of potential places that could be shared in the modern city. A sustainable approach to urban development encourages the urban authorities to incorporate "community" spaces with a social purpose, where individuals can share values. The term "shared" implicitly suggests the concept of "public space", but

SELB (DE), WINNER – *DORNRÖSCHEN* > SEE MORE P. 134

for the architect Bernd Vlay who analysed the projects in this group, this term is historically loaded and profoundly embedded in the history of cities. However, through the Europan projects we are seeing the emergence of teams that have chosen to think of new forms of collective space, which do not necessarily have the defined character of traditional public spaces, but nevertheless offer places of urban community, open to the encounter with others. This is the group of winning projects assessed by Oliver Schulze, one of the directors of the famous Danish office, Gehl architects, which designs new shared spaces in many of the world's cities.

Some Europan 11 projects propose modifying the hierarchy of spaces to explore coexistence between citydwellers, others propose modifying the street network by creating multiple, interconnected networks. Others move into the linear corridors created by modern urbanism to provide socially dynamic spaces. And finally, others encourage the emergence of community practices by linking the local and territorial scales so that the former can share in the dynamics of the latter.

Reflecting the multiple timeframes of uses, of nature, of flows in the project is a recurrent feature of a number of winning ideas. They all formulate one idea: **What if we reflected the rhythms and timeframes of the city?** All the projects in this group use the dimension of time as an instrument of reconnection. The proposals seek to develop relations between people, or between urban and natural rhythms. Integrating time and rhythms means thinking about how to make urban spaces hospitable so that people feel at home in them. For the philosopher Chris Younès, who responds to some of the emblematic winning ideas on this subject, this can be achieved by means of an urbanism which reconnects by creating, through urban metamorphoses, spaces that are open to multiple uses at different times. It is about creating urban processes by deciphering the existing character of a place and capturing its strengths, but also by imagining other possible relationships, transitions and porosities.

Creating a better osmosis between city and dynamics in urban metamorphoses depends primarily on three attitudes: interweaving flows with the city and architecture, introducing eco-rhythms to enhance urban quality and opening up the urban project to change.

So around these five outlines of the themes of an urbanistic renewal, this session proposes a range of stimulating positions and perspectives. They are embodied in projects, which, whilst connecting to precise situations, offer us visions of the future, like a morphing process in which we see the transition from the actual to the possible.

We therefore invite the reader to treat the catalogue as a flexible tool, making use of its two separate but interlinked parts. The first, a presentation of all the winning projects classified into site families (Identity/Uses/Collectivity) provides access to all the session results with the points of view of the team and the jury. The second part formulates interpretations around a number of the most emblematic winning projects, based on these 5 hypotheses of "reconnection", accompanied by the different perspectives of European experts.

From these visions of possible urban metamorphoses, the task now is to encourage the emergence of actual processes of change, by engaging multiple partners and the winning teams in the pursuit of the ideas. The key to success therefore begins with sharing on the way to better reconnection.*

ALCORCÓN (ES), WINNER – *ARBOLÓPOLIS* > SEE MORE P.184

* published in parallel with this Europan 11 Results Catalogue is IDEAS CHANGING, a book that presents some sixty implementation processes from previous sessions developed between 2008 and 2012, illustrating how the winning visions become active processes of metamorphosis in the world.

EUROPAN 11
MAP OF SITES

#	City	#	City		
1	AIGLE (CH)	116	25	MONTHEY (CH)	86
2	ALCALÁ DE LA SELVA (ES)	138	26	NEUILLY-SUR-MARNE (FR)	68
3	ALCORCÓN (ES)	182	27	NORRKÖPING (SE)	173
4	ALLERØD (DK)	146	28	NYNÄSHAMN (SE)	124
5	ALMERE (NL)	78	29	OSLO (NO)	60
6	AMSTERDAM (NL)	30	30	PEJË/PEĆ (KO)	20
7	CAPELLE AAN DEN IJSSEL (NL)	103	31	PORVOO (FI)	190
			32	RØDOVRE (DK)	128
8	CERDANYOLA DEL VALLÈS (ES)	165	33	REIMS (FR)	56
			34	ROMAINMÔTIER (CH)	194
9	CLERMONT-FERRAND (FR)	109	35	SAMBREVILLE (BE)	90
10	DEVENTER (NL)	70	36	SAN BARTOLOMÉ (ES)	150
11	DUBLIN (IE)	34	37	SAVENAY (FR)	177
12	DUBROVNIK (HR)	38	38	SELB (DE)	132
13	EINDHOVEN (NL)	64	39	SESTAO (ES)	46
14	GETARIA (ES)	169	40	SIMRISHAMN (SE)	25
15	GRAZ (AT)	53	41	SKIEN-PORSGRUNN (NO)	198
16	GUIMARÃES (PT)	186	42	STAINS (FR)	200
17	HAUGESUND (NO)	162	43	SZEGED (HU)	93
18	IBBENBÜREN (DE)	42	44	TOULOUSE (FR)	154
19	INGOLSTADT (DE)	82	45	TURKU (FI)	158
20	KØBENHAVN (DK)	120	46	WARSZAWA (PL)	96
21	LEEUWARDEN (NL)	12	47	WIEN (AT)	17
22	LINZ (AT)	112	48	WITTSTOCK (DE)	49
23	MALMÖ (SE)	100	49	WÜRZBURG (DE)	106
24	MARCHE EN-FAMENNE (BE)	143			

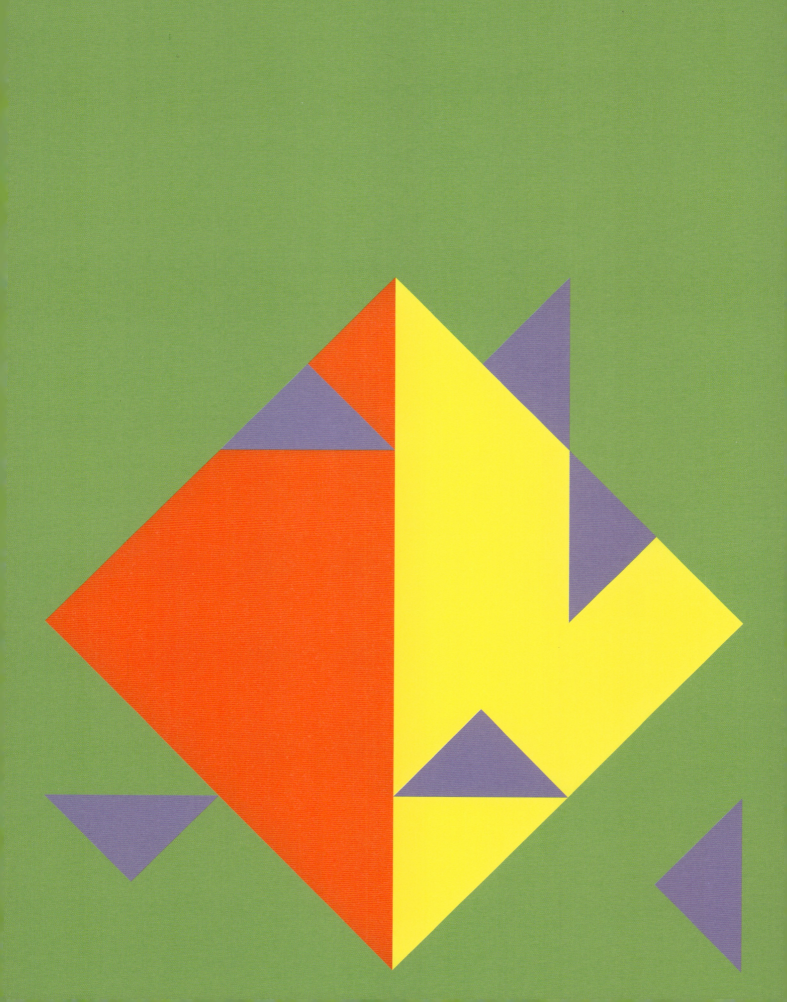

EUROPAN 11
WINNING PROJECTS

THEME 1

11

Identity

Linking the local and the global addresses the question of identity – its visible and imaginary components, and what constitutes the character of a place. But we are confronted with a paradox: while cities become more identifiable in a global context, they risk losing identity on a local level. How can we resolve this conflict, reconcile scales, and simultaneously create a contemporary image of European urbanity?

From a marginal status to a significant image — 12

Some sites require imagination to be transformed into meaningful places, as they are currently unoccupied, lacking specificity or tangible meaning. These sites need to be reclaimed as part of the city, either by connecting them to the existing fabric or by defining a new identity that citizens can appropriate, in order to avoid creating new enclaves. But in this change of identity, there is nevertheless the question of retaining existing remnants and protecting a heritage.

LEEUWARDEN (NL)	12
WIEN (AT)	17
PEJË / PEC (KO)	20
SIMRISHAMN (SE)	25

From a question to a new character — 30

Although the sites are not unoccupied, their current state is rather unsatisfactory and there is a strong wish for improvement and greater visibility. Through new programs to be developed in certain cases, the existing structures could be made more dynamic by introducing new urban spaces and landmarks.

AMSTERDAM (NL)	30
DUBLIN (IE)	34
DUBROVNIK (HR)	38
IBBENBÜREN (DE)	42
SESTAO (ES)	46
WITTSTOCK (DE)	49

From obsolete identity to new identity — 53

As the current occupation is obsolete, inappropriate or simply underused, there is a desire for a new spirit, brought about by new programs, additional values and better connection to the surroundings. All of the sites have to resolve their cultural heritage, either physically where there are remaining buildings, or indirectly by way of a collective memory from the past.

GRAZ (AT)	53
REIMS (FR)	56
OSLO (NO)	60
EINDHOVEN (NL)	64
NEUILLY-SUR-MARNE (FR)	68
DEVENTER (NL)	70

IDENTITY
FROM A MARGINAL STATUS
TO A SIGNIFICANT IMAGE

LEEUWARDEN
(NL)

12

LEEUWARDEN - KANAALZONE
POPULATION: 94,000 INHAB.
STRATEGIC AREA: 46 HA
PROJECT AREA: 19 HA
SITE PROPOSED BY: CORPORATIE
ELKIEN AND MUNICIPALITY
OF LEEUWARDEN
SITE OWNER: MUNICIPALITY
OF LEEUWARDEN

Living with water
Water is an important element in the Kanaalzone area. The objective is a unique residential area adjacent to the water in the tradition of waterside housing in Leeuwarden. Kanaalzone is situated along the Van Harinxmakanaal on the southern side of Leeuwarden. The site forms the transition area from the existing town to the new residential and working area, De Zuidlanden. The spatial relationship with the northern bank is part of the brief. The programme for the study area comprises an urban remit for 400-500 residential units. The site is adjacent to open water and openings into the area can be introduced at two places. A short-stay harbour with small-scale catering facilities is an optional part of the programme.

ALINA LIPPIELLO (IT)
LEONARDO ZUCCARO MARCHI (IT)
ARCHITECTS

VESNA MARKOVI (SRB)
ARCHITECT
PIERRE BERTRAND GUYOT
DE LA HARDROUYERE (FR)
ANNALISA ROMANI (IT)
LANDSCAPE EXPERT-ARCHITECTS
FAUSTO CUZZOCREA (IT)
FABIO DE CIECHI (IT)
MANUELE MOSSONI (IT)
FILIPPO ZORDAN (IT)
STUDENTS IN ARCHITECTURE

RUNNER-UP

EUROPEAN RESULTS
**FROM A MARGINAL STATUS
TO A SIGNIFICANT IMAGE**

LEEUWARDEN (NL)

Floating Blocks

Team point of view The new residential area, hosting up to 500 houses, merges into a water landscape and is well connected with both the existing urban structure and the countryside. All apartments have direct view and contact with water (almost 40% of the total area), which is conceived as useful infrastructure space. The whole site is then integrated through ecological management. The master plan is divided into three main sectors, built in three different phases: "San Francisco bay" in the east, the first part of the development; the "Tokyo bay" in the centre, where small islands between narrow housing strips, become sustainable wetlands; "Venice bay" in the west, designed with high flexibility with a texture of public voids that recall the urban structure of Venice.

Jury point of view Floating Blocks… thanks to its flexibility, can be easily adapted to changing insights or circumstances… The way in which the water is used to create a special residential area is convincing… Thanks to its scale, the large floating block fits in well with its surroundings. At first sight the architecture looks intriguing, but it is insufficiently elaborated to be assessed properly.

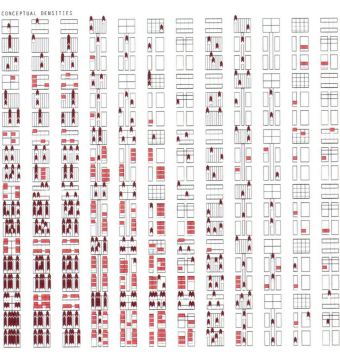

EUROPAN RESULTS
FROM A MARGINAL STATUS TO A SIGNIFICANT IMAGE

LEEUWARDEN (NL)

★ WINNER

PALOMA BAQUERO MASATS (ES)
JAVIER CASTELLANO PULIDO (ES)
TOMÁS GARCÍA PÍRIZ (ES)
LUIS MIGUEL RUIZ AVILÉS (ES)
JUAN ANTONIO SERRANO GARCÍA (ES)
ARCHITECTS

JUAN BACHS RUBIO (ES)
ALEJANDRO CARLOS GALINDO DURÁN (ES)
CRISTÓBAL ADRIÁN GARCÍA ALMEIDA (ES)
JOSÉ ENRIQUE INIESTA MOLINA (ES)
MARÍA DE LARA RUIZ (ES)
ALEJANDRO PEDRO LÓPEZ FERNÁNDEZ (ES)
ELENA MARÍA LUCENA GUERRERO (ES)
ARCHITECTS

14

Landscape, memory, tradition and water for the future

Team point of view NIEU WAter gaRDEN, a new landscape of water, meeting between urbanity and agriculture.
The proposal proposes Niwu Water Garden through the encounter of three main materials: water, city and farmland. In a scenic enclave of particular importance to the city of Leeuwarden an appropriate balance between these materials creates a hybrid landscape which establishes a transition between rural and urban. This gives rise to a new environment in which elements of the city (historical and modern) establish a proper dialogue with the existing agricultural plot and its associated infrastructure. The scale of the proposal permits research on the development of an urban layout model based on the relation between houses and water in Leeuwarden. NIEU WAter gaRDEN becomes a landscape designed for true water lovers. The place is the outcome of a technological, constructive and typological tradition and a space for collective memory, where the city's past emerges to support the present.

Jury point of view An intelligent design that is well conceived on all scale levels. The urban design incorporating a great deal of water is clear and allows for phased planning. The blocks with housing create an interesting intermediate scale. The Boksumerdyk dyke is a strong element which, as a separate cycle and footpath, does it justice as a cultural-historical relic…

Linked with the article *Cultural interferences*, p. 256

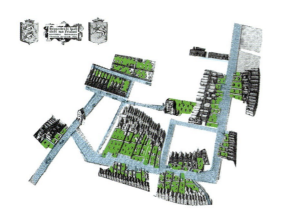

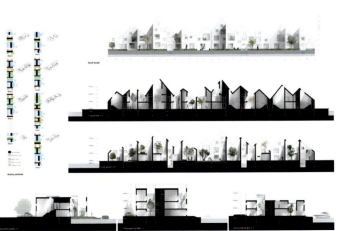

16

WIEN
(AT)

IDENTITY
**FROM A MARGINAL STATUS
TO A SIGNIFICANT IMAGE**

17

Urban gravity for a historical suburb

The City of Vienna has set ambitious inner-urban development goals in order to achieve sustainable use of land and infrastructure. Growth in "grown-up" and developed areas is therefore a central interest for modernizing the city. Being a "leftover" of the construction of the new railway tunnel, the site marks an important spot for the surrounding area which is dominated by historic suburban housing types with extensive green spaces. The city is seeking a development which will be an architectural and programmatic "landmark", including a breadth of social services, small-scale commercial uses, intermodal facilities (bike and ride) and high quality public and green spaces. The question of whether housing is possible in conditions of increased noise and vibrations has to be explored.

WIEN-HIETZING
POPULATION: 2,000,000 INHAB.
STRATEGIC AREA: THE PUBLIC
PATHWAYS OF THE WHOLE AREA
PROJECT AREA: 2.2 HA
SITE PROPOSED BY: WIEN HOLDING
GMBH (REAL ESTATE DEVELOPER
OF THE CITY)
SITE OWNER: CITY OF VIENNA,
RAILWAY COMPANY

EUROPAN RESULTS
**FROM A MARGINAL STATUS
TO A SIGNIFICANT IMAGE**

WIEN (AT)

★ WINNER

ARTUR BOREJSZO (PL)
ARCHITECT

LEENA CHO (US)
LANDSCAPE ARCHITECT,
URBAN PLANNER
JASON HILGEFORT (US)
URBAN PLANNER, ARCHITECT
ANDREAS KARAVANAS (GR)
ARCHITECT, URBAN PLANNER

18

Dreiecksplatz

Team point of view Currently dominated by houses with large areas of private green space, the site lacks a transition from private to public use that will enable diverse community groups to gather, live and work. The triangular plaza is conceived as a binding agent fundamental to our site strategy: it brings together multiple housing needs, commercial and social amenities, and various community profiles without compromising structural, cultural and aesthetic integrity. The railway line slope is transformed into an anchor point in the plaza together with improved stops for other major mass transit forms. The invisible networks on the site – Lainzer tunnel, ORF satellites, underground parking and Lainz River – are further revealed via the use of local materials, highlighting the site within a regional context.

Jury point of view The jury underlines the quality of the simple resolution of the traffic problem. The proposal seems both obvious and convincing, creating different sub-areas by the simple gesture of the triangular central square. It then develops these sub-areas with very different housing qualities… The solution seems easy and effortless…

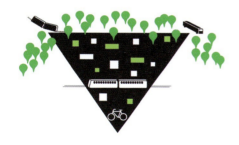

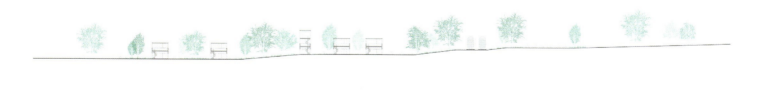

Regional - Network Society

Regional - Housing Community

Regional - Urban Health

Regional - Shared Ecology

Site - Network Society

Site - Housing Community

Site - Urban Health

Site - Shared Ecology

IDENTITY
FROM A MARGINAL STATUS
TO A SIGNIFICANT IMAGE

PEJË/PEĆ
(KO)

20

PEJË/PEĆ - FORMER KOSOVO
FORCE MILITARY CAMP
POPULATION: 95,000 INHAB. (CITY),
122,000 INHAB. (CONURBATION)
STRATEGIC AREA: 42.60 HA
PROJECT AREA: 12 HA
SITE PROPOSED BY: MUNICIPALITY
OF PEJË/PEĆ
SITE OWNER: MUNICIPALITY OF PEJË/
PEĆ AND KOSOVO FORCE (KSF)

A new education, sport and tourism area
Peja town is located in the Dukagjini Plain in the western part of Kosovo, and is one of the main cities in this young country. It envisions its growth based around a landscape of learning and leisure, and the proposal calls for a mixed used area for education, sports, and tourism facilities, reflecting a striking location on the edge of the Rugova Mountains, and tying sustainable economic development to real sustainability in the civic, communal and environmental life of the town.
This new area should take the role of a major public space for education (a university campus) and recreation (a cable car station) that can enliven and dynamise Peja, a threshold to the Rugova Valley, and act as a model for adapting and re-inhabiting military installations in the region.

SANTE SIMONE (IT)
LAURA FABRIANI (IT)
GIOVANNI ROMAGNOLI (IT)
ALESSANDRO ZAPPATERRENI (IT)
ARCHITECTS

RUNNER-UP

EUROPAN RESULTS
FROM A MARGINAL STATUS TO A SIGNIFICANT IMAGE
PEJË/PEĆ (KO)

Diana's Ring

Team point of view The project operates simultaneously through measurement and interpretation. It builds the necessary relationships with the setting through the character of the buildings. The project is pre-existence unveiled. We believe that Kosovo should measure the loci of its own independence through architectural construction – along the natural bar that defines its orographical boundaries – in the most important urban settings, which serve both neighboring cities and the nation as a whole. For Pejë we plan a courtyard building for the college campus that take a portion of the ecological corridor and defines the community dimension, with the construction of library towers in a happy interchange between the loci of knowledge and of day-to-day existence. The size and the structure of the building restores to the city's form a kind of architecture that has always been there.

Jury point of view The project proposes one large square block and a green central space… What is appreciated is the clarity and strength with which the project positions the university at the heart of the site and claims for it to be an independent entity. It also questions the tendency to create a hybrid between nature and architecture, creating a clear sense of inside and outside…

Linked with the article *Cultural interferences*, p. 256

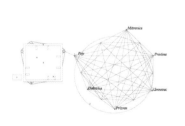
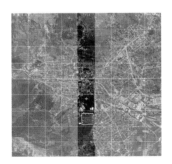
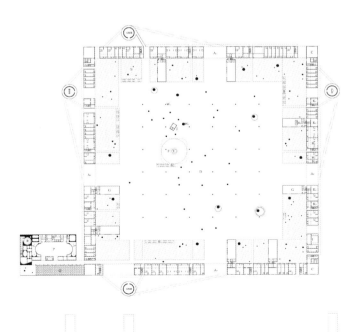

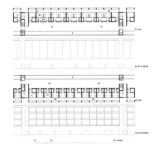

EUROPAN RESULTS
**FROM A MARGINAL STATUS
TO A SIGNIFICANT IMAGE**

PEJË/PEĆ (KO)

★ WINNER

HECTOR ARDERIUS SALVADOR (ES)
ROBERTO GARCIA FALLOLA (ES)
ARCHITECTS

22

Fratres

Team point of view The plot where the university area is located is the boundary between the city of Pejë and the untamed nature of Rugova mountains, and the aim of our proposal is precisely to emphasize that reality, operating a reconnection between the organic of nature and the artificial of the urban.
Whilst on the large scale, this boundary is intensified by the rhythmic repetition of singular elements that the small residential towers imply, a continuous but human scale action is what configures the different areas of the campus from an inner perspective. The serpentine structure that houses the shared facilities of the residence reconfigures the contour lines holding the ground, liberating a long green corridor across the city revealing the university zone – a complex volume of smaller parts carved out of the natural topography.

Jury point of view The project proposes megastructures instead of single objects ... The most important drawing is the diagram that shows how the building creates an edge towards wild nature. This line also suggests the formation of a retaining wall to the soft and earthy structure of the hills. The space in between buildings seems to suggest an idea of open nature rather than a park...

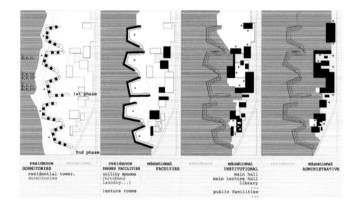

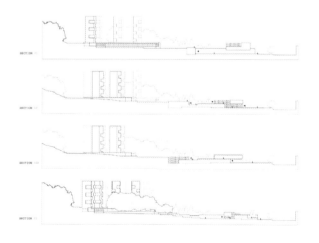

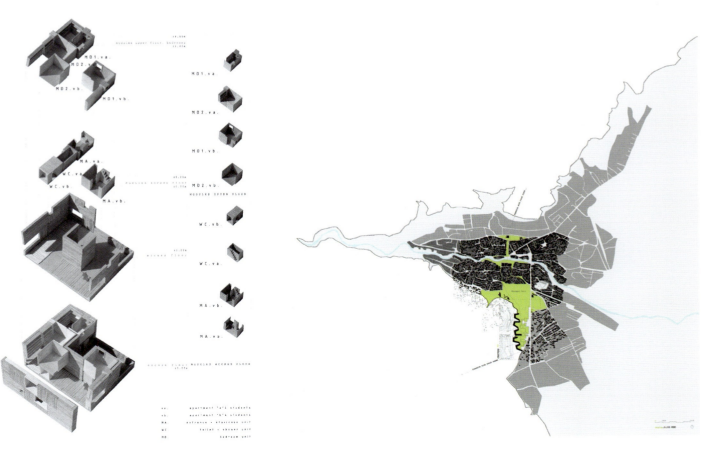

24

SIMRISHAMN
(SE)

IDENTITY
FROM A MARGINAL STATUS
TO A SIGNIFICANT IMAGE

25

Sea town extension

Simrishamn is a coastal town with a small, compact and picturesque structure. The town centre surrounds the main square, where many of the municipal facilities are located. The site at present is a park, located directly northwest of the town centre.

The main goal is to develop a comparatively dense housing scheme with demarcated green qualities and sea contact, which exploits the existing characteristics of the town. Besides residential buildings and green spaces, it should provide good public spaces and be well integrated into the local communication network in terms of pedestrian, bicycle and motor traffic.

SIMRISHAMN - KVARTERET LASARETTET
POPULATION: 19,400 INHAB.
STRATEGIC AREA: 7 HA
PROJECT AREA: 2.5 HA
SITE PROPOSED BY: MUNICIPALITY OF SIMRISHAMN
SITE OWNER: MUNICIPALITY OF SIMRISHAMN

EUROPAN RESULTS
**FROM A MARGINAL STATUS
TO A SIGNIFICANT IMAGE**

SIMRISHAMN (SE)

★ WINNER

MIGUEL HUELGA DE LA FUENTE (ES)
IRIA DE LA PEÑA MÉNDEZ (ES)
ARCHITECTS

26

Wear out

Team point of view The proposal is a response to the special characteristics of the plot, adjacent to the sea and crossed by a stream with a serious flood risk for part of the year. The original basin is modified, creating new streams which determine future constructions by eroding them. Wetland areas will appear in the urban fabric, coexisting with wildlife and controlling the risk of overflow. New ways to coexist with water are proposed.

This aspect is transposed to the typologies. The housing volume literally rests on the ground through extremities filled with program functions, with the capacity to connect public space while incorporating protected areas outside the home. The use of the outside space is extended, in an area characterized by an extreme climate, with small pavilions directly related to the garden. This creates more vivid interiors and a unique appearance at the urban level.

Jury point of view This project is a sophisticated experiment in new housing typologies. It is an exciting prototype that, if developed further, could play a role in the strategic future of Simrishamn in terms of living, water management and its image as a town ... The jury felt that there was a connection between the proposed housing and the intimacy, density and proximity of the historic fishing village of Simrishamn, achieved in a contemporary idiom that does not ape the historic urban pattern…

Linked with the article *Rhythms and timeframes*, p.269

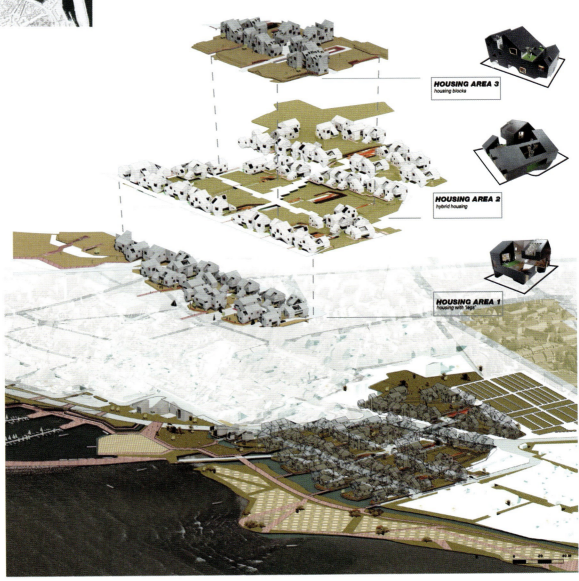

HOUSING AREA 3
housing blocks

HOUSING AREA 2
hybrid housing

HOUSING AREA 1
housing with 'legs'

EUROPAN RESULTS
**FROM A MARGINAL STATUS
TO A SIGNIFICANT IMAGE**

SIMRISHAMN (SE)

★ WINNER

ANDERS ERIKSSON (SE)
ARCHITECT

EGIL BLOM (SE)
HANNES HAAK (SE)
DANIEL LINDBERG (SE)
ARCHITECTS

28

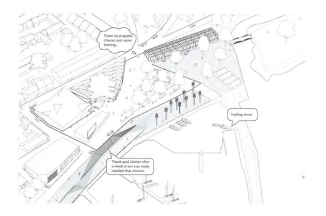

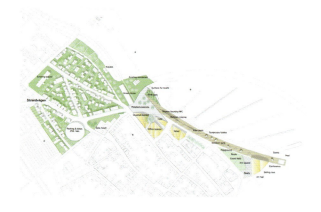

Strädde

Team point of view "Strädde" is a regional word for small lanes that run perpendicular to the sea and connect the main roads in coastal villages. As passages they are tight and narrow and interrupted by unexpected garden niches and house facades.

This interpretation provides a composition where a dense and varied urban plan offers unique possibilities for thriving intimate public spaces. When walking through the dense city, glimpses of the sea can be seen from different vantage points. "Strädde" aims to create a contrast between the close proximity of urban life and the open sea. "Strädde" shows the site as one part of a loop running within the city and promotes a continuation of the "harbour walk" in the south and the preservation of the allotment gardens north of the site.

Jury point of view This project was founded on a very sensitive analysis of the existing conditions of Simrishamn that displayed an all-too-rare sympathy for the site... The observations made by the architects were developed into tools that proved effective in creating small scale urban spaces – new versions of the 'Strädde' – while still proposing a plausible neighbourhood of density and variety…

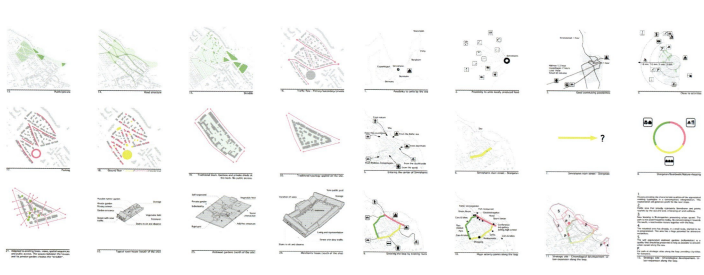

IDENTITY
FROM A QUESTION
TO A NEW CHARACTER

AMSTERDAM
(NL)

30

AMSTERDAM - AMSTEL III
POPULATION: 750,000 INHAB.
(REGION 2.5 MILLIONS)
STRATEGIC AREA: 250 HA
PROJECT AREA: 16 HA
SITE PROPOSED BY: MUNICIPALITY
OF AMSTERDAM, PROJECTBUREAU
ZUIDOOSTLOB
SITE OWNER: MUNICIPALITY OF
AMSTERDAM (PLOTS ALLOCATED
UNDER LONG LEASE)

Urban strategies for transformation
Amstel III is a "promising problem area". Approximately 30 % of the office area is structurally vacant, ownership is fragmented, the investment climate has deteriorated. There is a lack of vibrancy and public and private external space is designed primarily for the car. The city is looking for innovative ways to transform a mono-functional business park into a lively urban district. This requires a strong development strategy, one that is appropriate at every scale. The objectives are to introduce new functions, including housing, and to improve the quality of the external space. The municipality's preference is for an integrated area-focused approach including financial instruments in collaboration with the leaseholders.

MATTEO BETTONI (NL)
YONG CUI (CN)
SARAH WOLFF (DE)
ARCHITECTS
MILENA ZAKLANOVIC (NL)
PETAR ZAKLANOVIC (NL)
ARCHITECTS, URBAN PLANNERS

RUNNER-UP

EUROPAN RESULTS
FROM A QUESTION TO A NEW CHARACTER

AMSTERDAM (NL)

Basic City

Team point of view A matrix of key strategies is at the heart of our proposal. It interlinks the realms of infrastructure and urban conditions with the three different scales of intervention: city, neighbourhood and architecture. The existing spatial framework on the city scale links the site both to the old city and to nature at the perimeter. Public space is articulated through the improvement of the existing urban grid.

A new hybrid city quarter is generated by several small-scale key urban regeneration projects and added to Amsterdam's rich collection of distinct urban neighbourhoods. Transformed vacant office space is mixed with voluminous new residential typologies, enriched by private and communal outdoor space. The proposed plan reveals the latent qualities of AMSTEL_3 and similar areas Europewide. Change in the perception of those qualities leads to a truly alternative yet realizable development model that reflects the current attitudes of the key players in the urban development.

Jury point of view The runner-up also demonstrates how, with a package of relatively modest and well-organised interventions, developments can be started in Amstel III. An intelligent analysis of the – often hidden – qualities in the area leads to a number of well-substantiated interventions... One of the interesting ideas is the proposal to use as many of the upper floors as possible of the half-vacant office blocks so that the plinths become available at street level to activate new programmes…

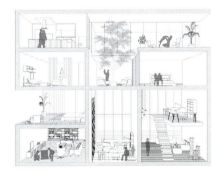

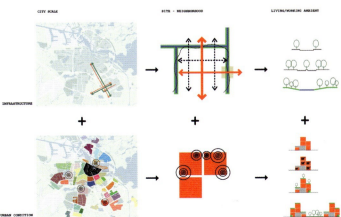

EUROPAN RESULTS
FROM A QUESTION TO A NEW CHARACTER

AMSTERDAM (NL)

★ WINNER

SARA REICHWEIN (DE)
ARCHITECT, URBAN PLANNER

32

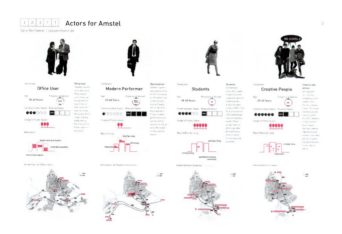

I Amstel 3

Team point of view I AMSTEL 3 is a process that transforms the vacant mono-functional non-place of Amstel 3 into a multilayered and vibrant district. The project is based on a definition of its future user groups and their needs. Starting with the creation of three initial points, Amstel 3 will be transformed punctually. These public spaces are coded for different user and usage groups to encourage a self-driven characterization of the district. Contiguous vacant office spaces are transformed into residential flats, tailored to the specific needs of the pioneer groups. Whilst the rest of Amstel remains almost untouched, the initial points will send impulses into the area through small constructional interventions. In addition, it attracts new users and types of usages from the city by creating hotspots of activity.

Jury point of view The designers began by giving careful consideration to the relevant target groups. On the basis of that analysis they developed a clear and convincing strategy for a gradual transformation of what is now still a mono-functional office area. Their proposal I AMSTEL 3 is complete on several levels (buildings, public space)… The clear presentation of the plan also suggests that they may be expected to communicate well…

Linked with the article *Rhythms and timeframes*, p. 269

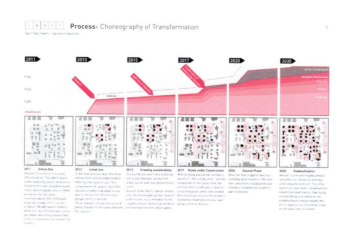

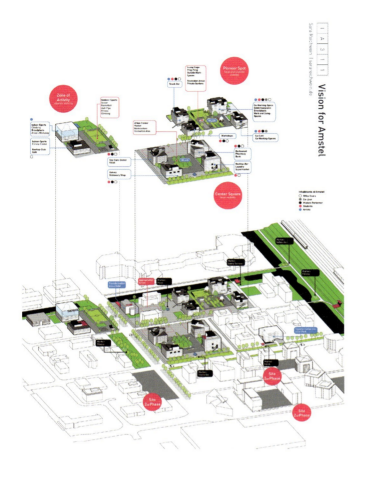

Vision for Amstel

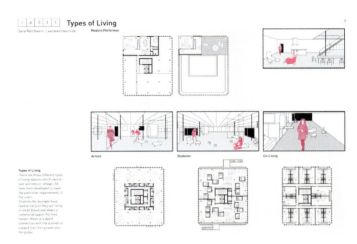

Types of Living
Modern Performer

There are three different types of living spaces, which vary in size and interior design. All have been developed to meet the particular requirements of the users. Students for example have least privacy as they are living in small boxes and share a communal space. For this reason, there is a direct connection with the outside to expand their living room into the public.

Center Square

Pioneers Spot

Zone of Activitiy

Section Pioneer Spot

Modern Performers · Co-Living · Students · Artists · Co-Working

IDENTITY
FROM A QUESTION
TO A NEW CHARACTER

DUBLIN
(IE)

34

DUBLIN DOCKLANDS
POPULATION: 45,000 INHAB.
STRATEGIC AREA: 526 HA
PROJECT AREA: 62 HA
SITE PROPOSED BY: DUBLIN DOCKLANDS DEVELOPMENT AUTHORITY
SITE OWNER: DUBLIN DOCKLANDS DEVELOPMENT AUTHORITY

Gateway to the docklands

Until a decade ago Dublin Docklands did not for most citizens, constitute part of the 'mental map' of the city, despite the fact that it is located within ten minutes' walk of the city centre. This isolation was in part due to extreme social and physical degeneration, which had befallen the area following the relocation eastwards of the port activities with the coming of containerisation. The Dublin Docklands Development Authority (DDDA) and Master Plan were launched 1997 and the development of the area has been guided since then by a series of Masterplans, most recent of which is the Dublin Docklands Area Masterplan 2008. The primary objectives for the Docklands area set by the Authority are a social and economic regeneration on a sustainable basis and a continued improvement of the physical environment of the Area.

JANE LARMOUR (GB)
PATRICK WHEELER (GB)
ARCHITECTS

HUGH MAGEE (IE)
STUDENT IN ARCHITECTURE

RUNNER-UP

EUROPAN RESULTS
**FROM A QUESTION
TO A NEW CHARACTER**

DUBLIN (IE)

East Wall Lot

Team point of view The resonance between territories and the question of what architecture is necessary for sustainable cities opens up questions of character, identity and appropriateness. The most positive global identity of urban Dublin living is arguably a nostalgic Georgian Dublin of tall elegant townhouses overlooking green squares. Our proposal responds to that domestic familiarity and the modest positive qualities of the traditional stock of Dublin while meeting the challenge of increasing the potential density of the site. Our new collection of buildings proposes a mix of residential, community, educational and commercial uses which can promote and support a sustainable new community, contribute to the existing surrounding community life and relink the site to the city.

Jury point of view Simple, clear and resonant this project aspires to a commonality, which underlies all good urban housing. The confident use of building profile and silhouette, the making and rhythm of opes, the deployment of elements on the site and the calm formation of private and shared spaces constitutes design of a high order. The visualisations are beautifully rendered.

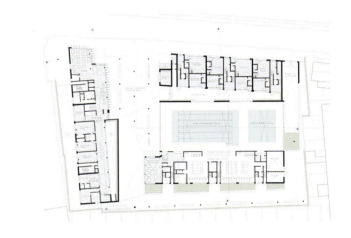

EUROPAN RESULTS	★ WINNER	CAROLINE O'DONNELL (IE)	LESLIE MIGNIN (US)
FROM A QUESTION TO A NEW CHARACTER		ARCHITECT	STUDENT IN ARCHITECTURE
DUBLIN (IE)			

36

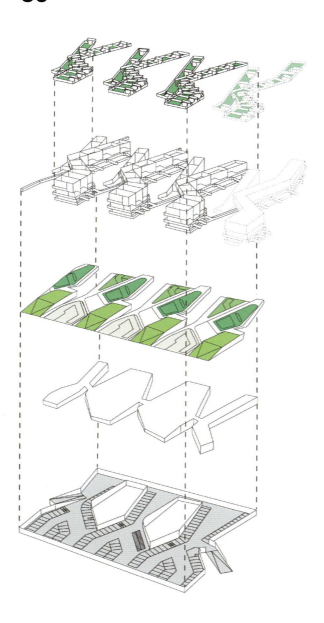

Counterspace

Team point of view Counterspace is a proposal for an assertive and tough architecture for a tough industrial, yet ambivalent, site. The scale and aesthetic of the Docklands industrial history is interwoven with the scale of the housing rows beyond. The row character of the urban fabric is maintained but pulled apart and the ground is doubled to create green areas and play spaces in-between the rows and above the street-level community programmes. The housing units themselves are a rethinking and recombination of the elements of the rowhouse—stair, chimney, garden, stoop—in order that there is continuity but radical reuse and recontextualisation of the elements. The deep understanding and manipulation of the site at both an urban and an elemental scale, allows for the project's meaning to emerge from the site. And through the experience of the project, an understanding of the greater context is achieved.

Jury point of view This dreamlike scheme is rooted in an idea of layering public and private space across the depth of the site. Poetically imagined and drawn, its robust, rhythmic form-making is softened by vertical landscaping. It is a bold, generous and compelling vision of a different urbanism, maybe even a different time.

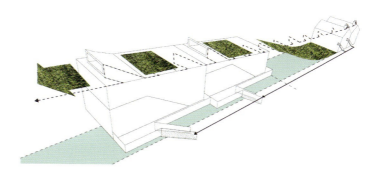

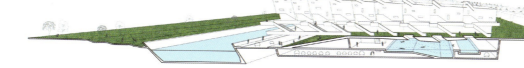

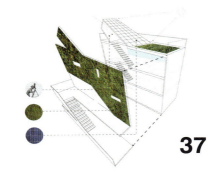

37

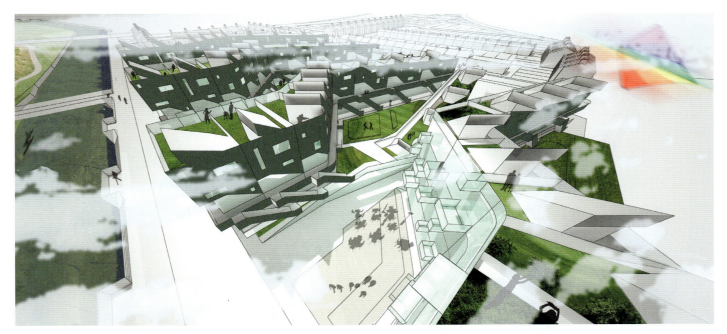

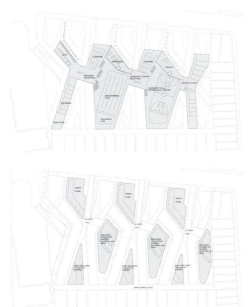

IDENTITY
FROM A QUESTION
TO A NEW CHARACTER

DUBROVNIK
(HR)

38

CITY OF DUBROVNIK
POPULATION: 30,436 INHAB.
WITHIN THE CITY WALLS
STRATEGIC AREA: 4.5 HA
PROJECT AREA: 1 HA
SITE PROPOSED BY: CITY OF DUBROVNIK
SITE OWNER: CITY/PRIVATE

Infrastructure behind the city
The city of Dubrovnik is a tourist mecca, attracting large numbers of visitors throughout the year, but especially in summer. One of the main problems in the old city is lack of space. Parking and storage space for businesses within the city walls should be planned on a maximum of 5 underground levels, and a tourist bus terminal with complementary public facilities at ground level, in order to improve the inhabitants' quality of life. The city walls should be free from parking, and offered as a view, being one of the iconic features of the city's image.

ANTONIO BRAVO RINCÓN (ES)
MARÍA CARMEN RUIZ IBÁÑEZ (ES)
ARCHITECTS, URBAN PLANNER

SALVADOR APARICIO MASSÓ (ES)
ARCHITECT
CLAUDIA CABALLERO MOYA (ES)
STUDENT IN ARCHITECTURE

RUNNER-UP

EUROPAN RESULTS
**FROM A QUESTION
TO A NEW CHARACTER**

DUBROVNIK (HR)

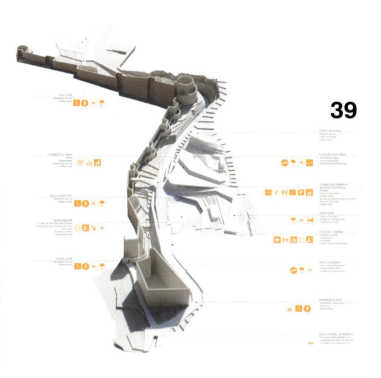

Play Topography

Team point of view The main aim of the proposal is to build an habitable route, where underground car park roofs are used as squares where urban life take place. Car traffic burial: the historic city's connection with the shoreline has a high-quality landscape value. We want to reclaim this space for pedestrians and cyclists and move cars underground.
"Behind the City Centre" will concentrate a number of services, with varying schedules and degrees of use: the tourist bus terminal will create abundant pedestrian traffic in Dubrovnik's historic town centre, the system of free spaces with its terraced squares has great potential as a stage for different events: concerts, plays, dances and festivals. Commercial, cultural and office uses that take place daily below the roofs of the centre will generate continuous activity that will make the terraced squares lively places, for use as playgrounds, flea markets, food stands, kiosks, terraces, etc.

Jury point of view The project responds to the infrastructural problems by burying the traffic in tunnel from Ploce to Pile gate. This underground connection provides access to parking lots and releases surface space for pedestrian use, thereby creating a park that extends the old city traffic free zone to its surroundings…

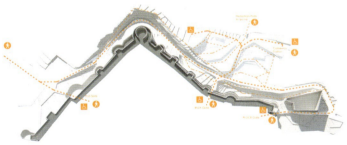

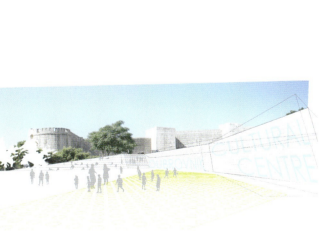

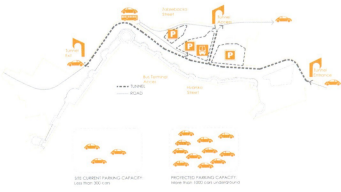

EUROPAN RESULTS
FROM A QUESTION TO A NEW CHARACTER

DUBROVNIK (HR)

★ WINNER

JAIME FONT FUREST (ES)
ARCHITECT

JORDI ESPINET ROMA (ES)
JORDI PARCET COMAS (ES)
MARCOS PARERA BLANCH (ES)
STUDENTS IN ARCHITECTURE

40

Back to citizens!

Team point of view The ancient World Heritage Wall in Dubrovnik acts as a physical barrier, isolating the interior of the Old City, which is gradually becoming purely a tourist attraction. Local citizens are being driven out because of the lack of proper amenities and reasonable prices.

Our proposal goes a step further than the initial remit for a large new central square outside the Wall, which would become a new core of activities and parking hub, and instead opts to create three smaller squares linked by a three-level promenade. The three city gates are all included in the strategy, giving the city wall the role of a main structuring and space-defining element. These new urban spaces create an interesting tension between the old city walls and the newly established programme in a high density structure.

Jury point of view The proposal – Back to citizens – does not directly solve the competition brief within the site boundary. The project is rather understood as an urban transformation strategy utilizing the existing city wall as a reflective element. The three city gates are all included in the strategy, giving the city wall the role of a main structural space-defining element. This winning entry is successful in terms of quality of public space, and the jury finds the design strategy convincing…

Linked with the article *Cultural interferences*, p. 256

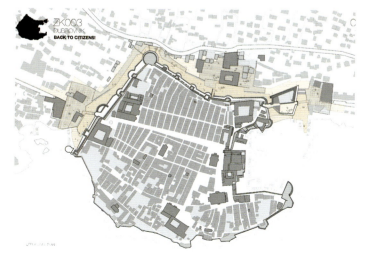
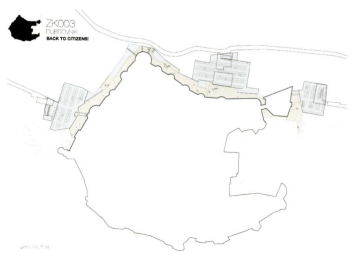

FIRST SQUARE   SECOND SQUARE   THIRD SQUARE

41

ZK003
DUBROVNIK
BACK TO CITIZENS!

01_08

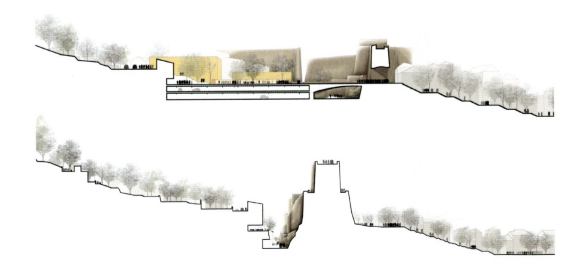

IDENTITY
FROM A QUESTION
TO A NEW CHARACTER

IBBENBÜREN
(DE)

42

IBBENBÜREN - WERTHMÜHLEN-PLATZ, DIEKWIESE
POPULATION: 52,000 INHAB.
STRATEGIC AREA: 11 HA
PROJECT AREA: DIEKWIESE 2.8 HA, WERTHMÜHLENPLATZ 7 HA
SITE PROPOSED BY: IBBENBÜREN TOWN COUNCIL
SITE OWNER: IBBENBÜREN TOWN COUNCIL

Regeneration of inner-city wasteland

The competition in Ibbenbüren focuses on two derelict sites in the town centre which are connected by the river Aa and separated by a major road access. In exploring the site, it is essential to take into account a layered development, to maintain existing and develop new connections with the surroundings and to revitalize an urban space that has so far been underused. New usage concepts need to be developed which are suitable for a middle-order centre. The aim for the future is that the areas should gain strong meaning as joints and connecting elements within the urban fabric. Their visibility needs to be increased to enhance the perceived image of Ibbenbüren. The goal is to maintain, develop and revitalize local identity in a contemporary way.

GIOVANNI SANTINI (IT)	ANDREA KARIMKHAN (IT)	RUNNER-UP	EUROPAN RESULTS
ARCHITECT	ALEXANDROS LIASKOVITIS (GR)		**FROM A QUESTION TO A NEW**
	ROSA ROMANO (IT)		**CHARACTER**
	ARCHITECTS		IBBENBÜREN (DE)

Ianus

Team point of view The two project areas are located on the boundaries of a natural belt, an important naturalistic system which determines the conditions for rethinking the rapport between Ibbenbüren and its surroundings, building a strong element of identity on the border between the city and nature.

The project proposes a new urban model that revolves around public space, connecting nature and architecture. This new city derives its identity from the boundary, which is precisely the place where innovation and hybridization are naturally accepted. This becomes a constructed and inhabited border that winds through city and country like an architectural ribbon, facing the city on one side and open space on the other, reminiscent of Ianus, the two-faced god seen on doors and pathways.

Jury point of view The project outlines lively meandering "architectural ribbons" which create well-dimensioned courtyards in the urban interior with a feel for the landscape situation and the scale of the adjacent residential buildings. These courtyards could provide the structural potential for diverse appropriation options by the residents… The project provides a remarkable contribution to the issue of living between the city and green space.

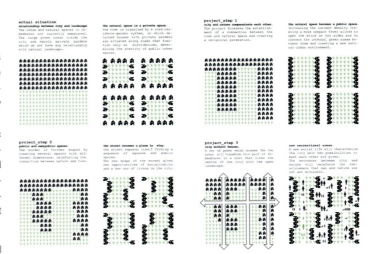

EUROPAN RESULTS
FROM A QUESTION TO A NEW CHARACTER

IBBENBÜREN (DE)

★ WINNER

MEHDI MOSHFEGHI (DE)
ARCHITECT

LILIJA BARTULI (DE)
ARCHITECT

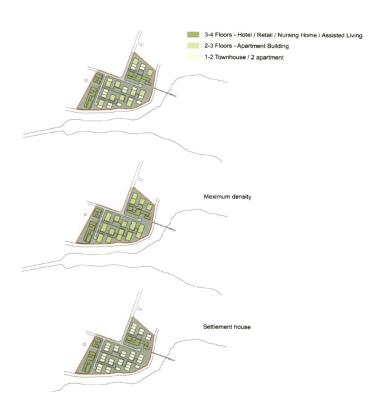

Between the courtyards

Team point of view Reorganising the two areas in Ibbenbüren provides the opportunity of creating high quality forms of housing to meet the demands of a constantly changing society and at the same time to preserve and strengthen their specific conditions. The identity and peculiarity of the new neighborhood is not characterised only by the new building structures. It will probably find its definition by the use of networked spatial sequences and urban spaces which are open to the landscape.
The main purpose of the area is integration with the nearby Lake Aa. The two new districts are characterized by an orthogonal structure that can flexibly respond to the remit by type and density of usage. Alternating public and semi-public basis, culminating in the Aasee cycle and footpaths, the districts connect in a public recreation space.

Jury point of view … The jury appreciated the project's approach, as the position of the development sites provide for a clearly recognisable boundary with the coherently developed public park space at the Aa River and/or Lake, and at the same time, the street space on Werthmühlenstrasse is redefined and upgraded by the new buildings. The emphasis on the junction created by additional buildings is also seen as a good opportunity to clarify the fragmentation of the existing entrance to the city…

Linked with the article Reshaping shared spaces, p. 242

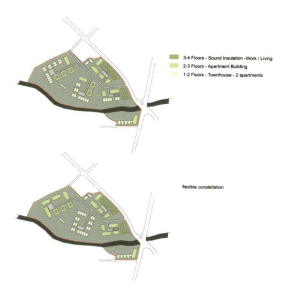

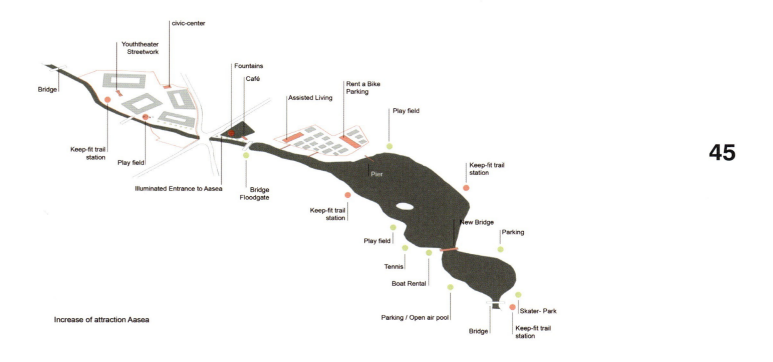

Increase of attraction Aasea

Diekwiese

Werthmühle

IDENTITY
FROM A QUESTION
TO A NEW CHARACTER

SESTAO
(ES)

46

SESTAO - U.E. 2 PAU VEGA GALINDO
POPULATION: 29,684 INHAB.
STRATEGIC AREA: 210 HA
PROJECT AREA: 10.67 HA
SITE PROPOSED BY: BASQUE GOVERNMENT, SESTAO MUNICIPAL COUNCIL
SITE OWNER: PRIVATE

Re-founding a city

The "Vega Galindo" area currently suffers from considerable socio-economic degradation and a lack of basic urban services. The aim for this site is to convert and revise degraded areas, and also to release land for social housing, with two objectives: to build affordable housing and, in the process, to facilitate the relocation of residents in the renovation zones. The Master Plan provides for a link between the new zone and the city centre by extending Gran Via along the Ballonti axis to Punta del Carmen. Zone U.E. 2 is proposed as a Europan competition site in the hope of identifying planning alternatives, given that Zone U.E.1 is now under construction.

CARLES CROSAS ARMENGOL (ES)
JOAN SOLÀ FONT (ES)
ARCHITECTS

ÁLVARO PÉREZ OTÍN (ES)
ARCHITECT
GUILLEM MARTÍNEZ PIERA (ES)
STUDENT IN ARCHITECTURE

RUNNER-UP

EUROPAN RESULTS
**FROM A QUESTION
TO A NEW CHARACTER**

SESTAO (ES)

Con la falda remangá

Team point of view The public transport network (Urbinaga) intersection gives this site amazing character. The old industrial periphery of Sestao is today apparently isolated, despite its privileged position next to the Nervion River. The project adds a new programmatic intensity to the transport junction: a mixed-use district well situated in the context of a city population of 1 million (Metropolitan Area of Bilbao). Offices, shops and stores, parking lots, hotel, gardens and facilities are merged together, above, between and below the new and old infrastructures. In order to achieve this, the predesigned layout is reconsidered. A new axis is defined at a single stroke: the new avenue (Gran Via) is the station street, defining full and empty spaces and organising the new dwellings on the Galindo bank.

Jury point of view This proposal contemplates a regional strategy, linked to transport infrastructure and alignment, which sketches out the project's main argument. It minimizes work on the Ballonti axis and presents an interesting alternative alignment for Gran Vía with a direct link to the new intermodal station, including a proposal for the latter's infrastructure…

Linked with the article *Rhythms and timeframes*, p. 269

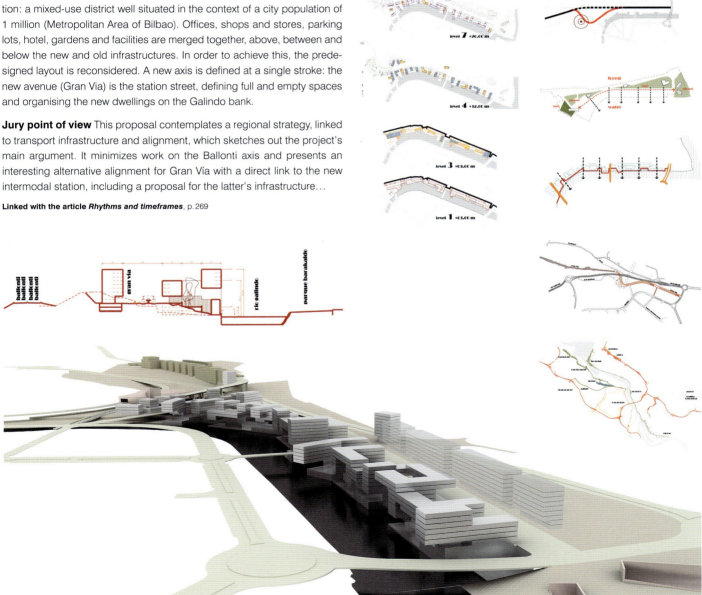

EUROPAN RESULTS
FROM A QUESTION TO A NEW CHARACTER

SESTAO (ES)

RUNNER-UP

RAQUEL BÁSCONES RECIO (ES)
ARCHITECT

MIGUEL JIMÉNEZ SÁNCHEZ (ES)
ITXASNE LÓPEZ GOITI (ES)
SUSANA RODRÍGUEZ JIMÉNEZ (ES)
SARA ZUGASTI ROYUELA (ES)
STUDENTS IN ARCHITECTURE

48

La Punta in state of transition

Team point of view Founded in REHABILITATION and REUSE, our proposal builds on the existing topographical conditions that divide the space into three terraces.
The building system is based on horizontal and vertical stacking which, resting on the different levels, gives it physical and programmatic connection. The area is unified by a unique architectural language, which includes an iconic tower, containing the social housing programme.
This enables the existence of a permeable riverbank, which opens onto small squares with public uses, thus avoiding a continuous facade to the river. An urban park is located in the central part, exploiting the strategic position that offers an elevated view over the estuary. The park and the river promenade are connected by urban elevators and public amenities.

Jury point of view This proposal suggests a respectful attitude to the territory. It acknowledges and enhances the natural green spaces, the trees and the retaining walls that outline the boundaries of the existing terraces… It also recognizes the pre-existing industrial fabric, salvaging the potentially most valuable parts for new community uses, attractively illustrated, which will prompt an interesting relation between the existing park, the estuary and waterside pathway…

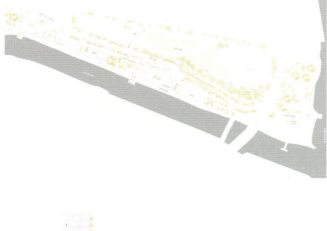

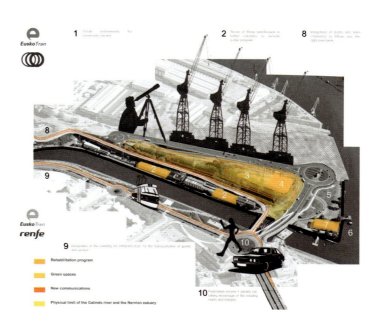

WITTSTOCK
(DE)

IDENTITY
**FROM A QUESTION
TO A NEW CHARACTER**

49

Revitalising the town centre
Wittstock town council regards the shrinking process and associated changes as an opportunity for regeneration. The essential planning goal is to revitalise the old town and its surrounding areas in order to strengthen the inner-city's function as an "anchor in a rural zone" by offering a variety of social and cultural uses. The strategy entails a functional consolidation and enhancement of the town centre by offering innovative residential buildings on inner-city wasteland as well as improved links between the historic centre and the edges of town in terms of space and design and a clear accentuation of the town entrances. The future design of the railway station and surrounding area as an entry to the town is particularly important in the process.

WITTSTOCK - DOSSE
POPULATION: 15,400 INHAB.
STRATEGIC AREA: OLD TOWN 26 HA
PROJECT AREA: STATION AREA
(4.3 HA), KYRITZER STRASSE
(1 HA), EMPTY BUILDING LOTS
WERDERSTRASSE (0.7 HA)
SITE PROPOSED BY: WITTSTOCK
TOWN COUNCIL
SITE OWNER: WITTSTOCK TOWN
COUNCIL, PRIVATE OWNERS

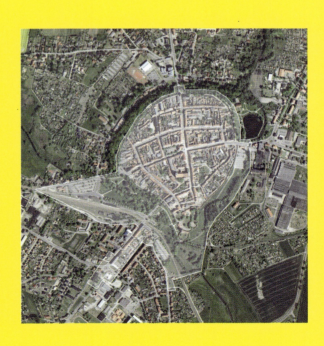

EUROPAN RESULTS
FROM A QUESTION TO A NEW CHARACTER

WITTSTOCK (DE)

★ WINNER

STEFFEN BARNIKOL (DE)
STEFFEN BURUCKER (DE)
ARCHITECTS

50

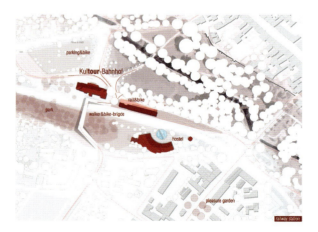

Bahnrad

Team point of view Wittstock has a mediaeval centre that is almost completely preserved. Outside of this, it is a heterogeneous urban entity. The town structure, which has been maintained for centuries, is the motive for dealing with processes of growth and shrinkage within.
The Deutsche Bahn buildings are currently idle. The aim is to reactivate the homogenous historical area while preserving its substance. So the railway building will become the location for cultural events to boost the area supra-regionally. The Berlin-Wittenberge railway optimizes public transit flows. A network of bicycle lanes not only links with the surrounding municipalities, but also connects to national bicycle routes and therefore strengthens the Brandenburg region's tourist appeal. The historic core town, dominating the inner part of the city, creates clear street-walls, which are also recreated in the Werderstrasse by construction along the streets. The diverse building in the inner area not only generates a new quality of usage, but the identified intra-urban spatial reserves also offer great potential for enlargement.

Jury point of view The authors develop excellently thought-out approaches to a "continuation" of Wittstock's strong urban structure, based on a sound analysis of the city as well as its relations and distances to the countryside. Emphasis is placed on development of the city centre, through adaptations to existing conditions… Overall, the authors succeed in setting well thought out priorities in dealing with the location. Solutions are presented that may initiate development which will be appropriate and sustainable in the existing context.

Linked with the article *Rhythms and timeframes*, p. 269

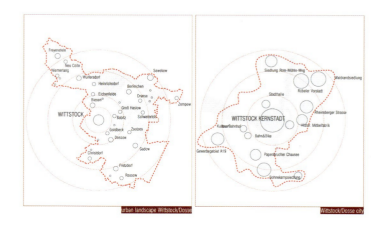

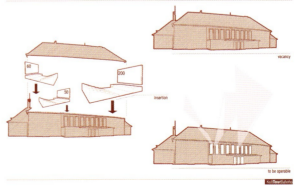

EUROPAN RESULTS
FROM A QUESTION TO A NEW CHARACTER

WITTSTOCK (DE)

RUNNER-UP

JANNA HOHN (DE)
ARCHITECT, URBAN DESIGNER
JOSHUA JOHN YATES (GB)
ARCHITECT

ANNA BUCHWALD (DE)
LANDSCAPE ARCHITECT

Inner Gardens, Outer Gates

Team point of view Our project seeks to give relevance to Wittstock's strong urban form, connecting its current role as home and destination with its historic identity.

Three urban elements are identified and the nature of each is strengthened by a site proposal: in the compact medieval city heart the historic housing typology is adapted to create inner gardens, each with a small community of garden lofts. In the cradle of green outside the city walls the station is incorporated into the old landscape of rivers and meadows. Radiating arteries act as spines to the periphery, reinforced with outer gates that complete them in the currently fragmented townscape. Each site's solution reinforces the character of one of the three urban elements whilst helping to integrate them with the city as a whole.

Jury point of view The authors develop their approach from the definition of a strong city centre, the green belt including the station environment, as well as from three important "suburban streets" that lead out of the city. Detailed and well thought out interventions are proposed for the further development of each of these structural elements… In general, the authors succeed in presenting very appropriate and well considered proposals on all scales for both the buildings and the open spaces. These proposals may seem cautious and unspectacular, but their quality lies in the opportunity to create strong and sustainable solutions on an almost individual level…

2 room Gardenlofts (1 Person)
2 room Gardenlofts (2 Person)
3 room dwellings
4 bedroom townhouses

GRAZ
(AT)

IDENTITY
FROM OBSOLETE IDENTITY
TO NEW IDENTITY

53

Visionary sustainability: wooden highrise & connective base
The issue of inner urban growth constitutes one of the main focuses in the city's development concept. Above all, it faces the challenges of the coexistence between infrastructure, mixed uses, public space and living programmes. Important sites will be developed as radiating urban hubs using a comprehensive evaluation strategy, ranging from progressive concepts for sustainability to the creation of a strong visual identity. As one of the most important entrance points of the city, the project site will create a new landmark for the city, on the physical as well as the programmatic level. The project will create an urban topology resulting in the best possible framework for the area's urban activation, including the possibility of further developments along the strategic area's N-S axis.

GRAZ - LIEBENAU
POPULATION: 210,000 INHAB.
STRATEGIC AREA: 9.09 HA
PROJECT AREA: 3.38 HA
SITE PROPOSED BY: CITY OF GRAZ
SITE OWNER: CITY OF GRAZ, PRIVATE INVESTOR

EUROPAN RESULTS	RUNNER-UP	STEFAN GRUBER (DE)	GILBERT BERTHOLD (AT)
FROM OBSOLETE IDENTITY TO NEW IDENTITY		ARCHITECT	ARCHITECT
GRAZ (AT)			PHILIPP SOEPARNO (AT) STUDENT IN ARCHITECTURE

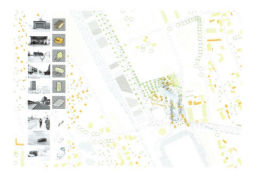

54

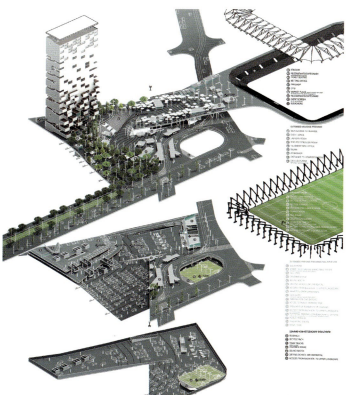

Magnetic Urban Field

Team point of view The project reconfigures 'found objects' in Graz's sprawling streetscape – kiosks, street lamps, parked cars – and condenses them into a new artificial landscape: a field condition blending the notion of landscape, architecture and infrastructure. Their intricate aggregation acts as a catalyst activating the latent space of a parking lot (scaled for occasional peak events) and re-imagines it as a public space for a variety of formal and informal urban activities. A clockwise spiral organizes flows of cars, public transport, bicycles and pedestrians through a unifying topography while offering shortcuts and oblique perspectives. Here, the spectacle of the arena is transposed to its urban setting: the props of everyday suburbia turn into a stage for the "choreography" of traffic and re-frame it as an attractive urban setting.

Jury point of view The project approaches the issue of traffic flow quite differently, suggesting an amalgam of movements with a maximum of compression and proximity… The clear idea of creating a "theatre" of traffic can be seen as the primary condition for an attractive urbanity. This is a most valuable "message" for the urban planning strategy, offering an alternative response that includes the potential of the existing fabric and poetically extrapolates its qualities…

Linked with the article *Rhythms and timeframes*, p. 269

JUAN PEDRO DONAIRE BARBERO (ES) ARCHITECT

IGNACIO NÚÑEZ BOOTELLO (ES)
JESÚS NÚÑEZ BOOTELLO (ES)
DELIA PACHECO DONAIRE (ES)
PABLO BARUC GARCÍA GÓMEZ (ES)
ARCHITECTS

RUNNER-UP

EUROPAN RESULTS
FROM OBSOLETE IDENTITY TO NEW IDENTITY

GRAZ (AT)

Yeswebridge

Team point of view The goal is to reclaim the street level in Graz for pedestrians, for activities like sports and social and cultural events, with the option of being outside or under The Bridge, and to create a visual reference. The strategy is to create a green corridor extending towards the centre of Graz, with a reference point, a focus of local activity around a building, with commercial and cultural activities that will promote community life in Graz. The ease of shifting between different transport modes will make it a reference point for access to the city. The Bridge envisages a change in the way of accessing the city, connecting to the city centre via a green corridor. This reference point is defined by a building with a Residential tower, and it is recognizable from any point of the city.

Jury point of view … The project's large scale clearly reflects the conflict between big events and the urban everyday, both spatially and programmatically. At the same time this carpet-like transformation of the linear public space can be seen as a centre of a development whose potential existence can be introduced through the very fact of its large scale…

IDENTITY
FROM OBSOLETE IDENTITY
TO NEW IDENTITY

REIMS
(FR)

56

REIMS - MOULIN DE LA HOUSSE
POPULATION: 181,500 INHAB. (CITY);
220,000 INHAB. (CONURBATION)
STRATEGIC AREA: 75 HA
PROJECT AREA: 30 HA
SITE PROPOSED BY:
AGGLOMERATION COMMUNITY
OF REIMS MÉTROPOLE AND THE CITY
OF REIMS
SITE OWNER: CITY OF REIMS,
RÉSEAU FERRÉ DE FRANCE,
UNIVERSITY OF REIMS

A new district on an abandoned university site
Once the Moulin de la Housse campus is empty, a single-function 1960s university complex, Reims municipality wants to build a new district. It plans to promote new ways of living here, with a programmatic mix (housing, businesses and services), high-quality public spaces and a wide variety of housing typologies (dense individual housing, intermediate housing, small apartment buildings). Taking a new public railway service as its starting point, it wishes to begin a process of eco-responsible urbanisation, extending to the whole campus site and the areas around Avenue Farman, by developing a neighbourhood with an innovative urban character, which will become a distinctive element of the metropolis.

AMÉLIE FONTAINE (FR)
ARCHITECT, URBAN PLANNER
CÉSAR VABRE (FR)
ARCHITECT

MADELEINE CLAVEL (FR)
STUDENT IN ARCHITECTURE

RUNNER-UP

EUROPAN RESULTS
FROM OBSOLETE IDENTITY TO NEW IDENTITY

REIMS (FR)

Landscape beyond limits

Team point of view The architectural and urban composition is structured on the View. The topography and the university campus, designed as a new open space, are used to establish the view with the Large Landscape. The composition full/empty permits to create new links with the existing context. The former university enclave is integrated in the network of open spaces of the city of Reims. The dwellings are used as structuring mass. The housing typology forms a spread, its modularity permit to adapt the densities. Flexibility and evolution possibilities generate a sustainable design. In order to protect the site from the cars, the motorized displacements are contained on the site limits. Slow and collective traffic are enhanced. The mobility system will connect the site on different scales.

Jury point of view…The approach to different ways of life are interesting and the architectural typology, with its dense, low-level layers, respects the nature of the site and the existing distant views. The jury liked the sensitivity of the proposal and its work on the ways of inhabiting a periurban site.

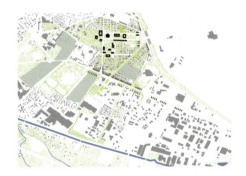

EUROPAN RESULTS
FROM OBSOLETE IDENTITY TO NEW IDENTITY

REIMS (FR)

★ WINNER

TADAS JONAUSKIS (LT)
URBAN DESIGNER, ARCHITECT
JUSTINA MULIUOLYTE (LT)
URBAN DESIGNER
LUKAS REKEVICIUS (LT)
ARCHITECT

Multitalented city

Team point of view Multitalented city is the proposal for an old modernistic university campus on the edge of Reims. The introverted and disconnected campus, with large open spaces, is isolated from its surroundings. A new network of coherent public space created by clearly defined new squares brings clarity and spatial organization to the site. Five squares guide users through the sequence of individual places. Cycle and footpaths are the main tools linking with the squares in between and the immediate surroundings. Public transport is spatially embedded into the squares, which link the site with the city and the region. The squares create a continuous network of places and new stopovers linking the peri-urban landscape in the north to the green/blue belt of the city centre in the south.

Jury point of view … This is a project that conveys great conceptual and programmatic clarity. The jury liked the urban qualities of the project, which seeks to define a new urban fabric from the urban polarities formed by clearly characterised public squares. The project works in an interesting way on these living spaces, which are the enduring elements of the urban project… The project is at the same time realistic and highly original.

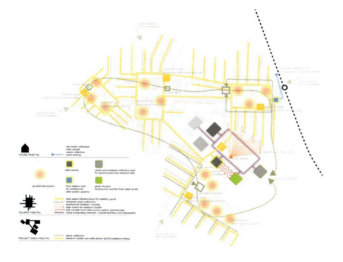

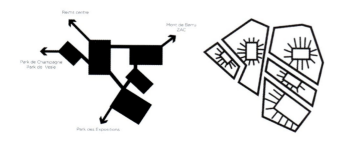

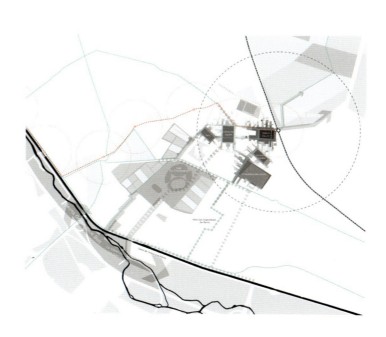

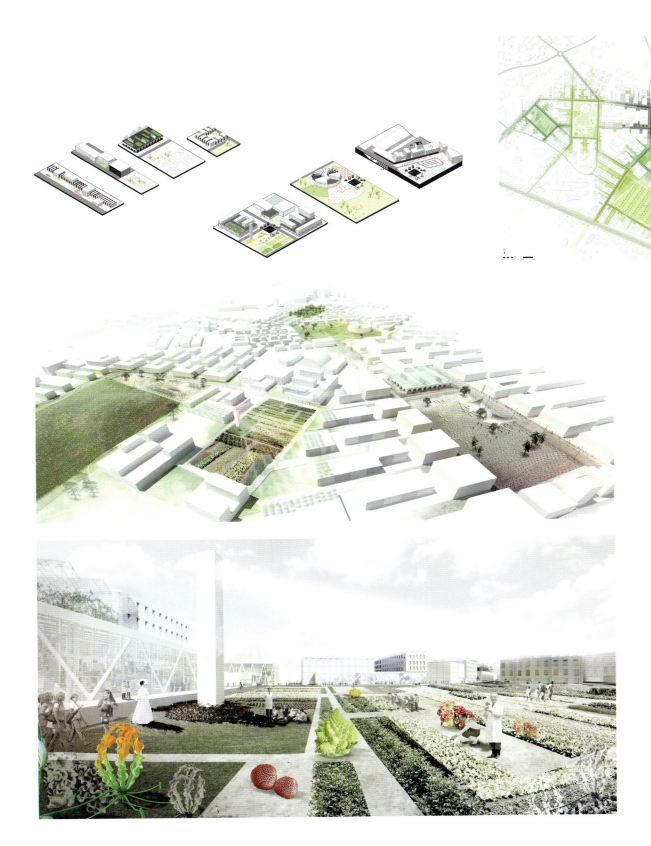

59

IDENTITY
FROM OBSOLETE IDENTITY
TO NEW IDENTITY

OSLO
(NO)

60

OSLO - SØNDRE NORDSTRAND
POPULATION: 600,000 INHAB.
STRATEGIC AREA: -
PROJECT AREA: 52 HA
SITE PROPOSED BY: MUNICIPALITY OF OSLO
SITE OWNER: MUNICIPALITY OF OSLO

Exploring wastespace

Historically, landfills have been the commonest form of organized waste disposal, and remain so in many places around the world. But as more and more waste is recycled, composted or incinerated with energy recovery, opportunities arise for these spaces to be put to new use. In its heyday, the Grønmo landfill was the largest in Northern Europe. Having functioned as Oslo's main spot for the undesirable since 1969, Grønmo contained over 8 million cubic metres of trash when it closed in 2009. The objective is to transform this place into something positive and to give it new uses and new identity. For it to become a future attraction and meeting place.

JUAN BERASATEGI (ES)
LANDSCAPE ARCHITECT
ELI GRØNN (NO)
ARCHITECT

RUNNER-UP

EUROPAN RESULTS
**FROM OBSOLETE IDENTITY
TO NEW IDENTITY**

OSLO (NO)

In return

Team point of view In return proposes a link with the larger scale (fjord-Grønmo-forest) and a new cycle for the Grønmo area. 5 layers of circuits structure the programme and meet, making Grønmo work as one complete circuit.
1. A rotating vegetation matrix will help to decontaminate the soil.
2. A recycling facility, composting area and pick up point are integrated along the park.
3. A basic layout of activity circuits and meeting places.
4. A participation process, with target collectives, that determines its (3) final use and programme.
5. A learning arena: an outdoor educational circuit that connects relevant points on the other circuits.
In return weaves past and present, existing and new functions into a whole, contributing to a holistic understanding of the cycle of waste and matter.

Jury point of view This scheme expands programmatically on the flows and loops of material and energy that are inherent in the historical – as well as present and future – conditions of the site ... The project deploys a range of 'recycling' processes across the entire field of the site through a variety of landscape "circuits" and meeting points ... Furthermore, the scheme suggests a strategy for deploying a diversity and density of programs across the site...

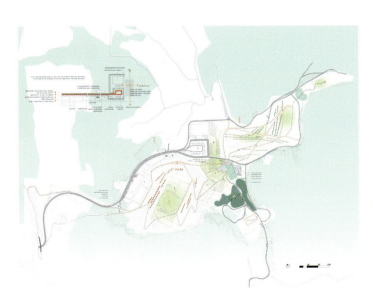

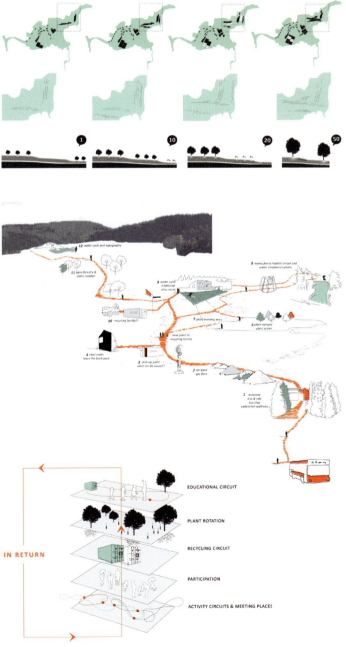

EUROPAN RESULTS
FROM OBSOLETE IDENTITY TO NEW IDENTITY

OSLO (NO)

★ WINNER

SILKE VOLKERT (DE)
MAGNUS WEIGHTMAN (GB)
ARCHITECTS

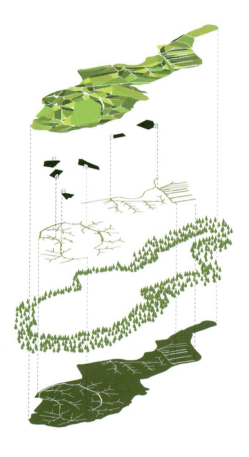

FLEXIBLE INFILL
different plot sizes according to demand

FIXED FRAMEWORK
gas control station & farm yards

FIXED FRAMEWORK
main path system

MARKA
growing until the 'waste line'

INHERITED CONDITIONS
under the top cover: waste areas & gas pipes

The gardens of Grønmo

Team point of view Situated on the edge of Oslo, the Grønmo landfill is now regarded as a scar in the Marka forest. But Grønmo's apparent weaknesses can be turned to strengths through urban farming; heat from the waste, a composting and recycling facility and clean top soil are ideal ingredients to support cultivation. We propose a range of gardens which will grow with demand, within a fixed framework that is defined by a path system following the landfill's gas piping network. The path system features educational and recreational layers and 'farm yards' acting as social and functional hubs. The gardens are assigned to three groups: local inhabitants, schools from Oslo and agronomists. In this way the gardens will engage and integrate communities on the district, city and global scale.

Jury point of view This scheme offers a persuasive proposal for 'doing more with less'. It suggests an appropriate and resource-efficient approach to the contemporary challenges of Grønmo. The proposal is singular and coherent in its introduction of the program of allotment gardens... It presents a relatively coherent development from concept to program to structure and spatial elements – suggesting a range of gardens, from private, and communal, to public and institutional...

Linked with the article *Cultural interferences*, p. 256

MARKA

SCARS-LANDFILLS

GOLFCOURSE

GARDENS

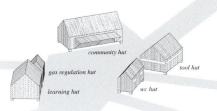

RECYCLING

COMPOSTING

ENERGY EXTRATION

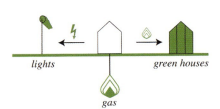

IDENTITY
FROM OBSOLETE IDENTITY TO NEW IDENTITY

EINDHOVEN
(NL)

64

EINDHOVEN - POTENTIAAL BUILDING TU/E
POPULATION: 216,000 INHAB.
STRATEGIC AREA: 70.4 HA
PROJECT AREA: +/- 1.75 HA
SITE PROPOSED BY: TECHNISCHE UNIVERSITEIT EINDHOVEN
SITE OWNER: TECHNISCHE UNIVERSITEIT EINDHOVEN

Re-use of sixties architecture
With regard to spatial developments, the TU/e and the municipality of Eindhoven have agreed on a cautious approach to the cultural heritage of the campus. The Potentiaal building is part of an ensemble of buildings designed by architect S.J. van Embden for the first construction phase (1957–1965) of the campus. It used to house the Electrical Engineering Faculty and with the redevelopment of the campus into TU/e Science Park it has a new designated use: a University College, a cultural function and some three hundred residential units. The redesignation of Potentiaal incorporates low-rise, high-rise, "Corona" and the immediate surroundings. The architectural brief requires a solution that correlates with the urban, landscape and cultural historical qualities of the surroundings. In addition, in technical terms Potentiaal should be sustainable and energy neutral.

TIBOR KIS (NL)
FLORIS VAN DEN BIGGELAAR (NL)
ARCHITECTS

DOROTA KOLEK (PL)
THIJS VAN SPAANDONK (NL)
ARCHITECTS

RUNNER-UP

EUROPAN RESULTS
**FROM OBSOLETE IDENTITY
TO NEW IDENTITY**

EINDHOVEN (NL)

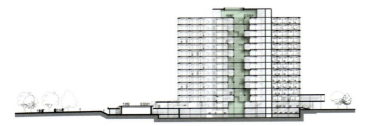

Volt

Team point of view
The current campus model of the TU/e used to be a solitary spatial element within the urban fabric of Eindhoven. With the current regeneration of the Dommel valley, its cultural programme and the University acting more as an open society, opportunities arise to develop a new connection with the city.
The old modernistic master plan of the campus consisted of a flexible grid placed in a beautiful landscape with omni-oriented buildings. To give direction and to create a sense of place we propose a scheme of three volumes. The biggest volume, based on a flexible design strategy, facilitates the needs of a changing programme. On ground level, two smaller volumes respond to the specific conditions of the public programme and to the environment. The volumes connect in the lobby.

Jury point of view
After renovation, the Potentiaal building remains recognisable as a member of the "family" of buildings on the university campus. One of the ways this is achieved is by applying a new curtain wall, closely related to the existing façade. The other components of this entry were also well received. The student rooms, grouped differently each time, create a pleasing impression…

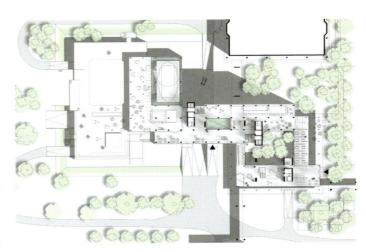

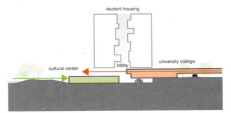

EUROPAN RESULTS
FROM OBSOLETE IDENTITY TO NEW IDENTITY

EINDHOVEN (NL)

★ WINNER

DANIEL ZARHY (PL)
ARCHITECT

Composition IX, opus 18

Team point of view The project deals with redesign rather than design, reinvention rather than invention.

We maintain the original principles of S.J Embden's campus master plan: free-standing pavilions connected by elevated public walkways and a clear rectilinear morphology.

We want to reconnect, to introduce social spaces into an existing structure by subtraction rather than addition. Public space is our design tool, the generator of the building's new organisation and form.

We propose to build a new cultural centre, to define an open plaza and to extend the public space, not only in plan but in section as well. We create a series of voids that generate the social heart of the building, linking the different floors and forming interaction zones. Pushing the rooms to the column line generates, achieving environmental and social sustainability.

We recreate the infrastructure for social interaction.

Jury point of view …The winning prize is one of the few entries that succeeds in combining the renovation of the building with a sound approach to the surrounding space – both at ground floor level and at the (+1) level of the walkways that connect the buildings on the campus with each other. Inside the building the public space is extended upwards in an inventive way…

Linked with the article *Reshaping shared spaces*, p. 242

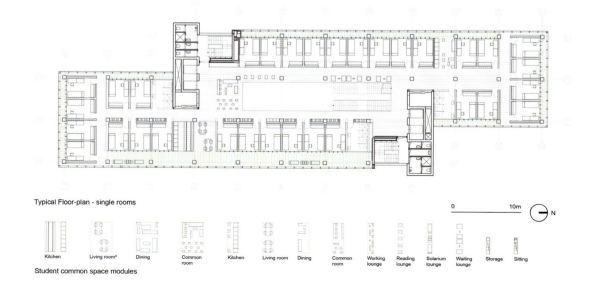

Existing floor plan → Creation of communal living rooms → Private balconies

Existing situation

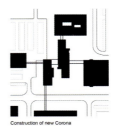
Construction of new Corona

New public space

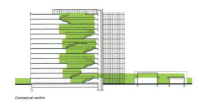
Conceptual section

Public space as a design tool

New Corona Concept - City like organization

IDENTITY
FROM OBSOLETE IDENTITY
TO NEW IDENTITY

NEUILLY-SUR-MARNE
(FR)

68

NEUILLY-SUR-MARNE - LA POINTE DE GOURNAY
POPULATION: 32,000 INHAB.
STRATEGIC AREA: 50 HA
PROJECT AREA: 7 HA
SITE PROPOSED BY: CITY OF NEUILLY-SUR-MARNE, ETABLISSEMENT PUBLIC D'AMÉNAGEMENT DE LA VILLE NOUVELLE DE MARNE LA VALLÉE (EPAMARNE)
SITE OWNER: ÉTABLISSEMENT PUBLIC DE SANTÉ VILLE-EVRARD, CONSEIL GÉNÉRAL DE SEINE SAINT-DENIS AND PRIVATE

A lakeside estate

Neuilly-sur-Marne is recognised as one of the 5 central nuclei of the "Descartes Cluster". This makes the town a primary location for the development of an eco-activity project, reflecting the Cluster's goal of becoming an acknowledged global centre for sustainable urban construction, management and services. The site of the former Ville-Evrard psychiatric hospital is earmarked as an eco-neighbourhood that will attract more than 7500 inhabitants and 2000 jobs. Nearby is the "Pointe de Gournay" Europan site located in a flood area. However, recent ideas about "urban water" and the ability to design flood-resilient urban projects, mean that it is now possible to consider combining the future psychiatric hospital district with a Lakeside Estate.

ANDREA BELLODI (IT)
MICHELE PASCUCCI (IT)
CARLOTTA MAZZI (IT)
ARCHITECTS

MARCO LOMARTIRE (IT)
STUDENT IN ARCHITECTURE

RUNNER-UP

EUROPAN RESULTS
FROM OBSOLETE IDENTITY TO NEW IDENTITY

NEUILLY-SUR-MARNE (FR)

Cartilaginous

Team point of view Strategy. The project concept is based on an analogy with the medical practice in the case of joint repositioning.
It works on two distinct elements which are put in relation: a cartilage meant as an empty urban fabric, elastic and permeable with an high degree of malleability and resistance detected on the administrative boundaries; and a rigid plate meant as the well-established urban fabric out of the cartilaginous stripe. The relationship between cartilage and plate is fixed by inserting pins into the key points of friction between administrative perimeters. These govern the cartilage being in fact strategic connections of strengthening of the joints.

Jury point of view The jury liked the project's large-scale interpretation, integrating the site into a chain of market garden areas. It is one of the few projects to work on a large scale.
The approach protects the natural area and the existing biotope to the maximum, whilst allowing for local crops. Green walkways are integrated into the potentially flood-prone site, offering the possibility of a wetland landscape such as that of Haute-Île…

Linked with the article *Common resources and mutation*, p. 263

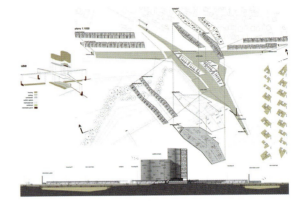

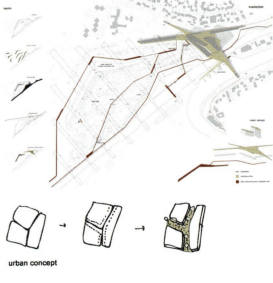

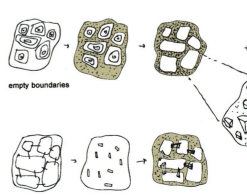

IDENTITY
**FROM OBSOLETE IDENTITY
TO NEW IDENTITY**

DEVENTER
(NL)

70

DEVENTER - HAVENKWARTIER,
"DE SILO'S" SUB-AREA
POPULATION: 100,000 INHAB.
STRATEGIC AREA: 8,600 M2
PROJECT AREA: 3,600 M2
SITE PROPOSED BY: MUNICIPALITY
OF DEVENTER
SITE OWNER: MUNICIPALITY OF
DEVENTER AND DEVELOPER

Harbour district transformation
Once you pass the silos at the lock, you are really in Deventer. These buildings are not officially listed, but are well-known landmarks for the local population. This is why it has been decided to preserve and re-use them. The assignment focuses on the transformation of the "Hoge Silo" and new development on the wharf as a contemporary extension of the industrial ensemble. The programme is mixed use: innovation and production, culture, entertainment and housing. The municipality of Deventer has opted for gradual transformation: existing industrial and maritime functions are not pushed aside, but complemented. Its strength lies in spontaneous creation. Character needs to be developed.

MARIEKE KUMS (NL)
ARCHITECT

EUH YONG KIM (KR)
YONG IL KIM (KR)
ARCHITECTS
YUKA TAKEUCHI (NL)
STUDENT IN ARCHITECTURE

RUNNER-UP

EUROPAN RESULTS
FROM OBSOLETE IDENTITY TO NEW IDENTITY

DEVENTER (NL)

Bricolage

Team point of view The City of Deventer is in search of ideas for the re-generation of the old harbour area: how to update the outdated industrial parts of a city?
Before proposing new interventions we began with a careful study of the dynamics of the existing situation. We organized spaces, places and activities not by age or type, but by the way people use them today. We identified and mapped all areas and investigated the potential of un(der)used spaces. After that we started a study of a possible distribution of the varied programme and activities: (traditional) work spaces, student housing, a cafe, car parks, spaces for artists, a waiting area for boats, a public toilet, outdoor cinema area, etc. To accommodate these programmes, adding a single volume, as proposed in the original master plan, seemed to make it difficult to interweave and integrate with the existing context. Strangely, we felt that to connect, we needed to disconnect, to fragment. Our proposal thus became a closely-knit collection of single volumes. The ensemble allows various identities to co-exist naturally and for existing elements to be easily incorporated. It allows users to move on site in multiple directions and activities to take place simultaneously. Not everything needs to be built at once; it can grow over time and mutate parallel to the needs and wishes of its users. The old surrounding silos will maintain their dominant historical appearance and position, but will be re-programmed to connect better with the new conditions on site.

Jury point of view *Bricolage* proposes a flexible design that allows for a gradual transformation. Because it is based on a continuation of the existing fabric with small-scale development, it fits in with its surroundings. The concept of raised construction volumes that appear to be suspended above the transparent ground floor is interesting…

Linked with the article *Cultural interferences*, p. 256

EUROPAN RESULTS
**FROM OBSOLETE IDENTITY
TO NEW IDENTITY**

DEVENTER (NL)

★ WINNER

ERWIN SCHOT (NL)
BAS MEIJERMAN (NL)
ELMAR HAMMERS (NL)
ARCHITECTS
ELOI KOSTER (NL)
GRAPHIC DESIGNER

72

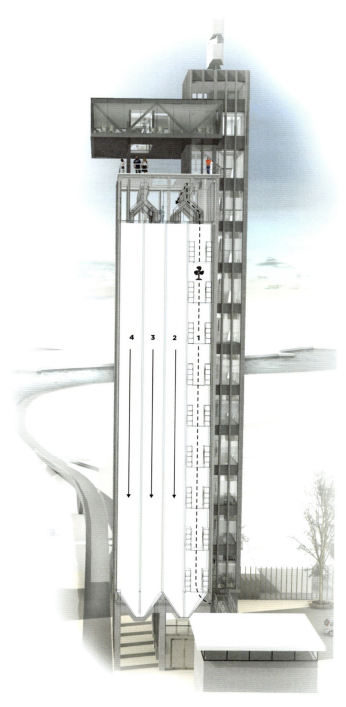

Planting havenkwartier

Team point of view… In search of social cohesion. The new urban design for the area focuses on the preservation of the genius loci. It emphasizes the existing qualities of the built environment and searches for a new social cohesion for its new inhabitants: entrepreneurs, students, artists or starters. The Hoge Silo, as a sole object in the public realm, is regenerated with new program. The existing tower will be used as a vertical gardening silo based on innovative LED technology. The top floor and the existing roof will be used as a panorama deck. A new glass volume is positioned on top of the silo, housing a new restaurant. All functions are allocated in the Hoge Silo with the aim of generating more activity in the area. A new bridge for slow traffic connects the harbour area with the city of Deventer. An eco-market, festivals and other spontaneous activities can take place in the rough, industrial public realm. The proposal also aims to boost the regeneration of the Havenkartier as a whole. The chosen angle could be an inspiration for other, future developments in the harbour district.

Jury point of view *Planting Havenkwartier* is a clever plan that demonstrates the makers' sensitivity to the special character of the Havenkwartier area and that they can subsequently continue building on this with their interventions. The urban design, the architecture and the functions that are added, fit in well with what is already there…

Linked with the article *Linking with uses*, p 249

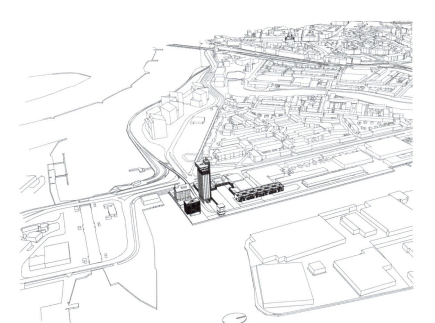

INTERVENTION AREA
ASSIGNMENT CLUSTERED PROGRAM

CONCLUSION: UNDEFINED SQUARE

NEW PROGRAM
EDGES OF THE INTERVENTION AREA

BUILDINGS REFER TO THE EXISTING URBAN STRUCTURE

URBAN MOBILITY
CONNECTING THE CITY

SLOW TRAFIC

SUGGESTION
BUILDINGS MOVED TO EDGES OF THE AREA

RESULT: REDEFINED SQUARE FOR URBAN INTERACTION

BACK BECOMES FRONT
URBAN RIBBON

PRIVATE WHEN NEEDED
OPEN IF WANTED

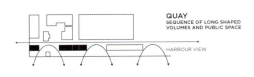
QUAY
SEQUENCE OF LONG SHAPED VOLUMES AND PUBLIC SPACE

HARBOUR VIEW

SILO
PRESERVED IN CENTRE SQUARE

NEW PROGRAM MOVED TO EDGES OF THE AREA

SQUARE
REDEFINED

ENLARGEMENT OF PUBLIC SPACE

APARTMENTS
SHIP ON DOCK VERSUS HANGAR UPSIDE DOWN

HANGAR APARTMENTS ELEVATED LIKE A SHIP ON DOCK

PRIVATE / PUBLIC

CURRENT SITUATION
KEEP BUILDINGS AS THEY ARE

GENIUS LOCI

FESTIVAL
STAGE

POSITION CREATES BACKSTAGE AND GOOD VIEW TO STAGE

dB

STUDENT ACCOMMODATION
IN REFERENCE TO ZWARTE SILO

INSIDE LOOKING OUT

BLACK SILO REPETITION OF MASS GALLERY / CAFE / ETC. ON GROUND FLOOR

HOUSING CLOSED
TRANSPARANT

EUROPAN RESULTS
FROM OBSOLETE IDENTITY TO NEW IDENTITY

DEVENTER (NL)

RUNNER-UP

FERDY HOLTKAMP (NL)
J-P WENINK (NL)
ARCHITECT

KEVIN CLAUS (NL)
STUDENT IN ARCHITECTURE

DHK, a new history

Team point of view DHK a new history continues the rich harbor history of Deventer. The ground level dominates the design, with a large checkerboard of public space covering the site. The square is defined by the addition of three new buildings, with the silo remaining freestanding and converted into apartments. Every addition to the area has its own identity, but meshes in naturally with the existing industrial character of the area. A corresponding architectural element that is added to the new buildings are shutters. If there is little activity, the area will have a closed character, but when it's busy the new buildings can represent themselves as completely transparent. This open/ closed concept shows the dynamics of the area! Just like it did in the buildings of the old Deventer docks.

Jury point of view *DHK, a new history* is a well-balanced and complete design that meshes in naturally with the existing situation. It can be developed in stages and is remarkable for its reserved and traditional character. One strong element is the way in which a plaza is created with new construction volumes that do justice to the site's potential…

EUROPAN 11
WINNING PROJECTS

THEME 2

77

Uses

Introducing a new use to a site is a strategic move with a wide array of implications in very different areas, from the purely architectural to the social or economic. The program is the main concern in redefining the relation between global and local. The starting point for each site is different, but three subgroups can be identified according to the relation between the components and the context, and their relative sizes.

From fallow lands to city life — 78

Fallow land is land that is currently unproductive. Whether greenfield (agricultural), brownfield (industrial) or greyfield (asphalt), underused areas invite municipalities to inject new programs. What strategies can bring a rich city life to these sites? How can new urban areas be designed for maximum quality of life while minimizing their footprint? What are the contemporary ways of living together?

ALMERE (NL) — 78
INGOLSTADT (DE) — 82
MONTHEY (CH) — 86
SAMBREVILLE (BE) — 90
SZEGED (HU) — 93
WARSZAWA (PL) — 96

From isolation to social integration — 100

A collection of fragments, an isolated segment, a clearing in a forest — a small local initiative could offer an opportunity to alter the whole context. What kind of programme could enhance the surrounding areas? How can design provide an open platform for social and economical integration? What missing piece could help make sense of the whole puzzle?

MALMÖ (SE) — 100
CAPELLE AAN DEN IJSSEL (NL) — 103
WÜRZBURG (DE) — 106
CLERMONT-FERRAND (FR) — 109
LINZ (AT) — 112

From in-between places to shared spaces — 116

Here, the in-between space may just be empty space, with no sense of place or belonging that might prompt people to linger, stay, inhabit; space only fit for cars or passing traffic. How can empty space be turned into public space? How can pedestrian flow be encouraged? What programmatic elements can provide a reference point for a shared urban life?

AIGLE (CH) — 116
KØBENHAVN (DK) — 120
NYNÄSHAMN (SE) — 124
RØDOVRE (DK) — 128
SELB (DE) — 132

USES
FROM FALLOW LANDS
TO CITY LIFE

ALMERE
(NL)

78

ALMERE - DUIN
POPULATION: APPROX. 190,000 INHAB.
STRATEGIC AREA: +/- 15 HA
PROJECT AREA: 450 M2
SITE PROPOSED BY: MUNICIPALITY OF ALMERE AND AMVEST (DEVELOPER AND INVESTOR)
SITE OWNER: MUNICIPALITY OF ALMERE AND AMVEST (DEVELOPER AND INVESTOR)

Transformation of a forest into ecological density resident
Almere is a New Town, founded to accommodate a substantial proportion of the growing population of Amsterdam and its environs. It is situated in the Flevopolder, some metres below sea level. With the development of the DUIN plan, Almere is present on the IJmeer waterfront, on a strategic, highly visible, and easily accessible location. The remit is to design an unusual and unique building that can first serve as an eye-catching information centre or cultural pavilion and can subsequently be "reused" as a detached house in the woods. The timber should as far as possible be sourced locally. The study brief is a landscape design for the existing woods with additional focus on the construction of a new water system and, in particular, on ways to develop the "woodlands" here.

OLAF JANSON (NL)
JOOST MAATKAMP (NL)
ARCHITECTS
KOEN LOOMAN (NL)
BUILDING ENGINEER
RENS WIJNAKKER (NL)
LANDSCAPE ARCHITECT

RUNNER-UP

EUROPAN RESULTS
FROM FALLOW LANDS TO CITY LIFE

ALMERE (NL)

Envisioning Baucis, Observatory for an Artificial Wilderness

Team point of view A residential area is envisioned where people live in contact with the roughness of nature. Respectful to the earth, the neighbourhood will only lightly touch the soil. The human world will be raised on a system of piles. This superimposed structure makes the area accessible while preserving the wilderness. It functions as an in-between space for people to live in nature.
The pavilion is an iconic building that first serves as an information centre and afterwards, in another location, as a house. The archetypical house is adapted, creating a strong image which symbolizes free architecture in this area. Shifting the basement creates a large outdoor space in the heart of the building, producing good exposure to the surroundings and the sun.

Jury point of view Envisioning Baucis is a well-balanced, well-considered and practicable design. Because of its distinct form, it provides a strong icon. The fact that this form was achieved by "adapting" the archetypal house is rather obvious, but in this case also effective. As a pavilion this building can fulfil several functions… The grid of the urban development plan shows respect for the landscape…

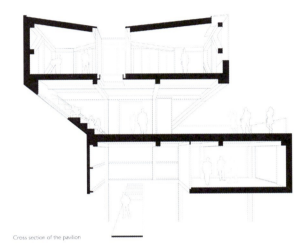

Cross section of the pavilion

EUROPAN RESULTS
FROM FALLOW LANDS TO CITY LIFE

ALMERE (NL)

★ WINNER

TIMUR SHABAEV (RU)
ARCHITECT

MARIA KRASNOVA (RU)
ARTIST

Frame

Team point of view The brief was to design a building which would serve first as an eye-catching cultural pavilion and info-box in the centre of a future housing district in Almere, and then later be sold as a private villa and moved to the woods. The building's design resolves the contradiction between these two seemingly incompatible uses.

The building is a steel frame, which carries a box that can be placed vertically (cultural pavilion) or horizontally (villa). The box's different positions produce different spatial scenarios: as a cultural pavilion, the building is a billboard, a giant pixel screen with a void in the middle, serving as a stage for public concerts and festivals; moved to the woods, it becomes a patio-house, surrounded by trees, someone's Home Sweet Home.

Jury point of view Of all the entries for Almere, Frame presents the most successful combination of a strong concept and a convincing design. The pavilion is an iconic image that effectively marks the spot in a manner fitting for Almere. It can at a later date be dismantled and "tilted", and subsequently serve as a home. For both functions the makers have succeeded in giving expression to their professional skills as designers in a clear and uncomplicated way…

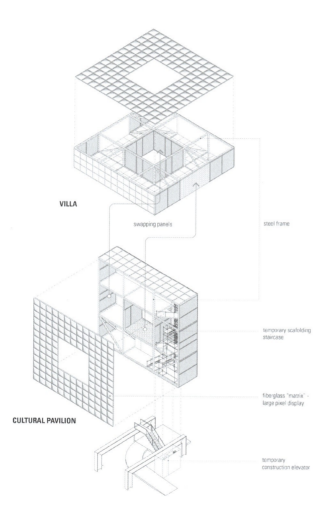

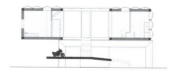

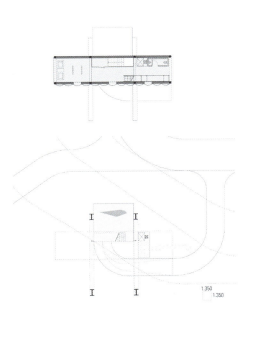
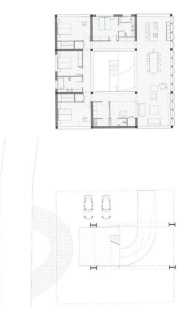

USES
FROM FALLOW LANDS
TO CITY LIFE

INGOLSTADT
(DE)

82

INGOLSTADT - BAYERNOIL AREA
POPULATION: 125,000 INHAB.
STRATEGIC AREA: 106 HA
PROJECT AREA: 75 HA
SITE PROPOSED BY: INGOLSTADT
TOWN COUNCIL / BAYERNOIL
SITE OWNER: BAYERNOIL REFINERY
COMPANY

Transformation of a former refinery

The redevelopment area in the eastern part of Ingolstadt offers a unique opportunity to determine and define new uses for an industrial wasteland, which reflect the specific identities of the locality and provide a combination of urban and natural structures appropriate to the scale of the site. The objective is to develop an urbanistic and programmatic concept that expands the range of uses in Ingolstadt, enhances the city's significance as a residential and business location on an interregional level and includes climate control. Qualitative standards are to be developed in order to reconcile natural with built structures.

LYDIA RAMAKERS (DE)
NORA WILDERMANN (DE)
ARCHITECTS
KATRIN RHEINGANS (DE)
ARCHITECT, URBAN DESIGNER

RUNNER-UP

EUROPAN RESULTS
FROM FALLOW LANDS TO CITY LIFE

INGOLSTADT (DE)

83

Dreaming/Awaking

Team point of view The refinery plot can be seen as a heterotopia between excellent infrastructural connection, spatial singularity and programmatic isolation. An inclusive process of reinterpretation through a festive reclamation of the existing structure will generate new meaning and make this forgotten non-place visible. The resulting vibrancy will be a seed for future development.

In the process, a practical target plan is replaced by a visual declaration of intent and scenic structures, whose meaning can be shifted by further building interventions. These layers of void-structures, shaped by the decontamination works, create freedom from somewhat authoritarian systems and thus offer the possibility of linking multiple perspectives and approaches without subjecting them to a rigid structure.

Jury point of view … The authors developed a strategy that enables the vibrancy of the location to be used as part of a transformation process from its current state as an industrial landscape to complexly grown urban structures. The idea is to create a binding framework by visualising some ideas, by creating a basic structure out of the existing roads, basins and free spaces that functions as a largely unregulated landscape, but in the process maintains the existing urban qualities of the site…

Linked with the article *Rhythms and timeframes*, p. 269

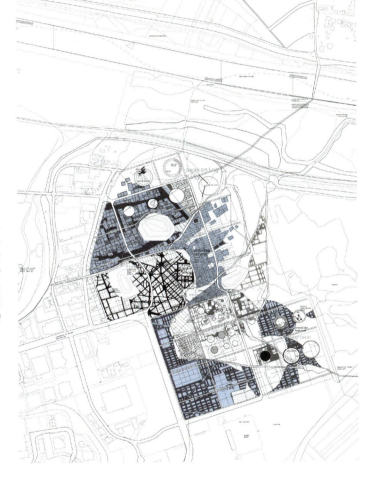

EUROPAN RESULTS
FROM FALLOW LANDS TO CITY LIFE

INGOLSTADT (DE)

★ WINNER

SEBASTIAN BALLAUF (DE)
FRANCESCA FORNASIER (IT)
MAXIMILIAN OTT (DE)
ARCHITECTS

84

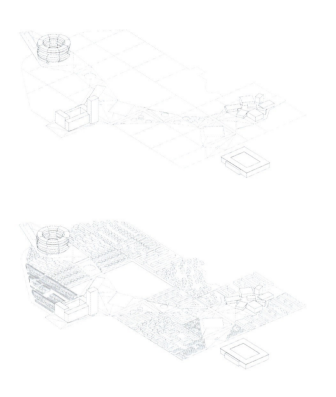

Ammerang

Team point of view The project's aim is to create a specific island within the structure of the city by embedding it into the state and the region. Filling the planes of the gridded area with different landscape structures turn the site into a patchwork of rasterised landscape. A polygonal strip of folded landscape with public uses extends beyond the whole project site to its very far borders, connecting spaces of significance to Ingolstadt. On its edges are located 3 mixed-use buildings. Because of their large scale, the objects give character to the area and provide visual orientation. The object's functions produce new public meaning for the site, the state and the region. Because of the huge size of the project site, the redevelopment of the area needs different planning scenarios, in phased steps, through definition of spatial rules for an unpredictable future. In this way, the site may eventually become a meaningful part of the city within the growing agglomeration of Ingolstadt.

Jury point of view This submission tries to establish a relation between strategic, tactical and operational planning levels. The big challenge is to overcome psychological barriers in the redevelopment of a former refinery, on a site located "behind" a business zone but with good environmental conditions such as the Donau riverbanks and Kalberschutt forest… The submission's phasing proposal seems realistic, as does the economic balance, with flexibility towards Ingolstadt's main structure, encompassing space, programme and city-scale implementation.

Linked with the article *Linking with uses*, p 249

85

USES
FROM FALLOW LANDS
TO CITY LIFE

MONTHEY
(CH)

86

MONTHEY – CLOS-DONROUX
POPULATION: 16,350 INHAB.
STRATEGIC AREA: 37 HA
PROJECT AREA: 10.1 HA
SITE PROPOSED BY: CITY OF MONTHEY
SITE OWNER: CITY OF MONTHEY, PRIVATE OWNERS

New district: new landscape?
The Clos-Donroux industrial area is straddling the Monthey and Collombey-Muraz limits. Until 2003 the area was used by the Giovanola Company whose buildings are still standing. Become property of the City of Monthey, the buildings are leased to various companies and associations. Formerly located at the urban periphery, the Clos-Donroux site is now part of a fast-expanding district. The city intends to regain control over the development of the area and use it as a symbol of urban revival. The project must provide a quality environment accessible to people from Monthey and the region. Professional activities, high density housing, public infrastructure and public space, must be combined to create an internal cohesion as well as an external consistency with the periphery of the project.

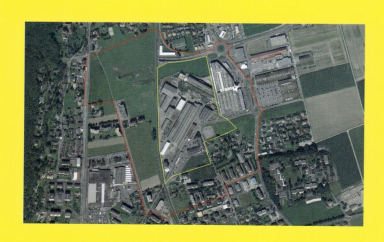

JOSÉ MARÍA SÁNCHEZ GARCÍA
(ES) ARCHITECT

MARTA CABEZÓN LÓPEZ (ES)
RAFAEL FERNÁNDEZ CAPARRÓS (ES)
LAURA ROJO VALDIVIELSO (ES)
MARILÓ SÁNCHEZ GARCIA (ES)
ARCHITECTS
ENRIQUE GARCÍA-MARGALLO SOLO
DE ZALDIVAR (ES)
ENGINEER-ARCHITECT
JAIME GARCIA DE OTEYZA (ES)
ELENA GONZÁLEZ MENES (ES)
ANA RIVERO ESTEBAN (ES)
STUDENTS IN ARCHITECTURE

RUNNER-UP

EUROPAN RESULTS
**FROM FALLOW LANDS
TO CITY LIFE**

MONTHEY (CH)

Line Code

Team point of view The proposal is born of an interpretation of the place as the footprint of the industries prior to urbanization. Existing traces define our schedule.

The conceptual idea is based on the density distribution of the programme throughout the site, focusing on programme bands that alternate density, variable green outdoor spaces and covered spaces where the construction programme focuses.

Starting from a general schedule, concentrated programme densities are situated, with greater density at the edges, setting towers that overlook the mountains and respond to the boundaries of the site.

Pre-existing structures are revised and reinterpreted to define directions and hierarchies in the public social space; we retain the main industrial structures, we release them from their enclosures and integrate them into the wider space.

Jury point of view The project with mention creates a genuine urban space with an industrial character, a landscape feel (with the creation of towers) and in keeping with the density of a valley. Thanks to its morphological resonance, it uses very elevated components in such a way as to free up space on the ground, and it carries the promise of profound urban change on the Rhône plain...

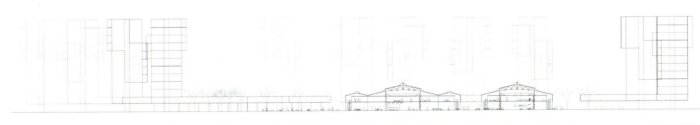

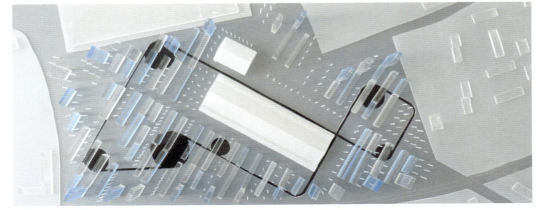

EUROPAN RESULTS
FROM FALLOW LANDS TO CITY LIFE

MONTHEY (CH)

★ WINNER

MEHDI AOUABED (FR)
ALBERTO FIGUCCIO (IT)
ARCHITECTS

Three gates Three mobilities

Team point of view The site of project is localized in the peripheral zone between two cities, that it will have to be developed in the longitudinal sense of the valley.

This will have the role of splice of the cities for an only future linear city. The new zone benefits of the existing infrastructures of the industrial zone. This zone will have the ability to receive the activities and the infrastructures that the historical centres will not be able to assume seen their morphologies. In the configuration of the future city, the new zones of activities assume the role of connecting between the centres. In order to define a new identity of the place, the project identifies three gates characterized by three mobility and three public buildings. Those three gates are connected by a linear, vegetalised and pedestrian space public, where are concentrated the trade and of activities. Moreover the urban strategy proposed allows a demolition for phases of the existing industrial activity.

Jury point of view The project provides the surrounding area under consideration with an efficient and progressive town planning resource, as well as fundamental structures. The very title is symbolic of the importance of access ... The project skilfully places the area firmly in the movement of the great Rhodanian linear city in the process of becoming.

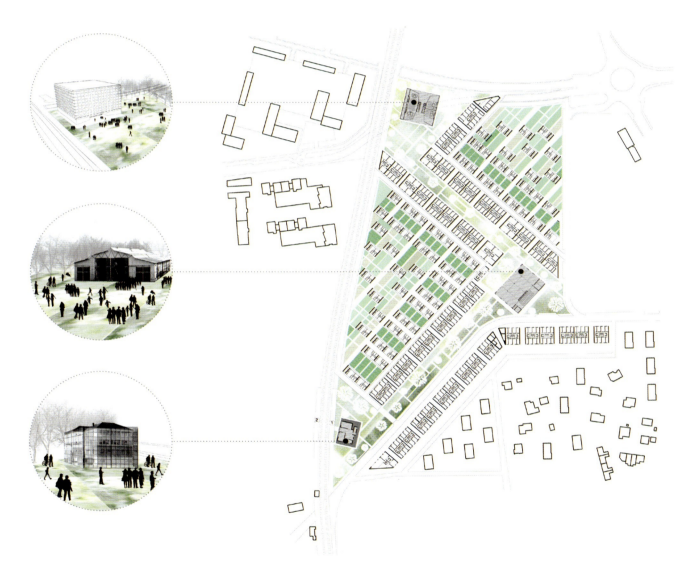

1st PHASE

2nd PHASE

USES
FROM FALLOW LANDS
TO CITY LIFE

SAMBREVILLE
(BE)

90

SAMBREVILLE
POPULATION: 26,981 INHAB. FOR 34.2KM2 OR 794 INHAB./KM2
STRATEGIC AREA: +/- 18 HA
PROJECT AREA: +/- 5 HA
SITE PROPOSED BY: MUNICIPALITY
SITE OWNER: COMMUNAL PROPERTY

Left bank

The site is part of the recomposed Sambreville municipality and is located on the territory of one of its main entities, Auvelais. It is sandwiched between the Sambre River and a railway. There is no building currently located on the site. The opposite bank, just in front of the site, features an important building dedicated to the municipal administration and to the offices of political authorities, as well as a set of middle-level housing and the church of Auvelais.

The goal is to build on the site (left bank) a mixed pole comprising habitat, tertiary industry activity, local business, as well as social facilities for the population. The site should open up towards the other bank (city centre) and towards directly neighbouring territories.

BENOIT COULONDRES (FR)
FLORENCE GAUDIN (FR)
ARCHITECTS

RUNNER-UP

EUROPAN RESULTS
**FROM FALLOW LANDS
TO CITY LIFE**

SAMBREVILLE (BE)

QCM

Team point of view Sambreville is genetically apart, because it emerges from the union of several localities. The site consists of an old town centre and a urban sprawl along an express road. Literally, the project links those two parts of disconnected territory.
For this purpose, the site is irrigated by a compact and legible grid pattern, this increases its porosity and links its identity to the old centre's one and over-all to the compact town identity. This ambition leads to the choice of a strong built density. The project also links the site to its history by the reintroduction of Water as a technical and social resource, structuring element of the landscape. The water of Sambre is the shared area, the fundamental reliance element: It is the echo between a closed and lived landscape and a cultural and territorial one.

Jury point of view … Proposal of a strategy open and scalable. Water is one of the core elements of the project by combining the Sambre and the creation of ponds for various uses: collecting rain water, phytopurification, landscaping that conserve in every location a link to water and biodiversity. The flexible layout of paths perpendicular to the bank creates a framework characterized by a mix of buildings promoting social diversity and by a freedom of layout allowing for the evolution of the project…

Linked with the article *Common resources and mutation*, p 263

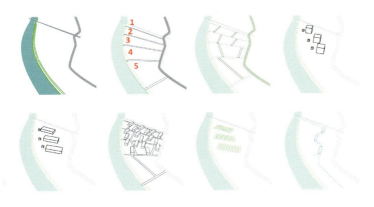

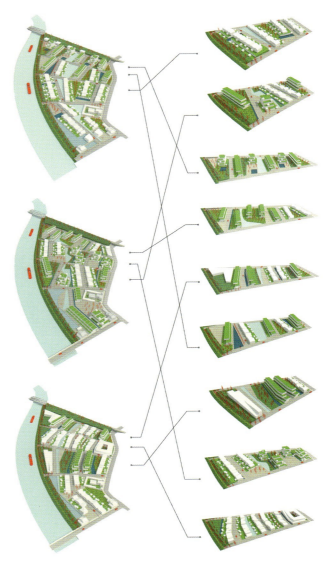

EUROPAN RESULTS
FROM FALLOW LANDS TO CITY LIFE

SAMBREVILLE (BE)

RUNNER-UP

GIOVANNI AURINO (IT)
DANILO CAPASSO (IT)
LAURA FALCONE (IT)
ANNA SIRICA (IT)
BRUNA VENDEMMIA (IT)
ARCHITECTS

CARMINE CIUCCIO (IT)
STUDENT IN ARCHITECTURE

Ville+Sambre+ville

Team point of view The project site is located on the left bank of the river Sambre, which is today considered the *rear side* of the city, while the right bank is characterized by a more structured city form. The project title is *ville+Sambre+ville*: its core is the creation of a public riverside park, beginning at the site and extending northwestward, in the study areas and beyond; the park will be a major attractor, that will improve the riverside and give equal urban status to both banks. The connection between the two parts of the city is then made by the river itself and by its renewed pedestrian-cycle bridge. The project proposes the construction of a residential eco-neighbourhood on the site: living in Sambreville could be an opportunity for proximity with nature without moving too far from major urban centres.

Jury point of view ... The project builds on the Sambre, which becomes a structural part of the project. Well-defined hierarchy of pedestrians pathways, bike alleys and roads for cars. Attractiveness of housing clusters around shared common spaces. Integration of housing and nature by progressive interpenetration under the form of two combs. Coherent, fitting and realistic at all levels, which appears to be a real sustainable neighbourhood...

Linked with the article *Reshaping shared spaces*, p 242

SZEGED
(HU)

USES
FROM FALLOW
LANDS TO CITY LIFE

93

Diversity recharged

In recent decades, the functions of the well-structured and renewed inner city has started to develop to the west with new commercial functions appearing mainly around the outer ring. The city intends to develop a new mixed-use urban hub in the strategic area with a wide range of functions and with increased density, which, as well as serving retail needs in the immediate vicinity can create a city-scale centre with a strong architectural identity and with administrative, commercial and residential functions. The former electricity production plant ceased operations in 2009. The site needs to be integrated into the urban fabric, with the implementation of a completely new spatial and functional system emphasising new public spaces and a diversity of office, leisure, recreational, residential, retail and cultural functions.

SZEGED
POPULATION: 167,000 INHAB.
STRATEGIC AREA: 60 HA
PROJECT AREA: 2.6 HA
SITE PROPOSED BY: MUNICIPALITY OF SZEGED
SITE OWNER: EDF DEMASZ ELECTRICITY SUPPLIER COMPAGNY

EUROPAN RESULTS
**FROM FALLOW
LANDS TO CITY LIFE**

SZEGED (HU)

★ WINNER

GERGELY ALMOS (HU)
TAMAS KUN (HU)
TAMAS MEZEY (HU)
ARCHITECTS

94

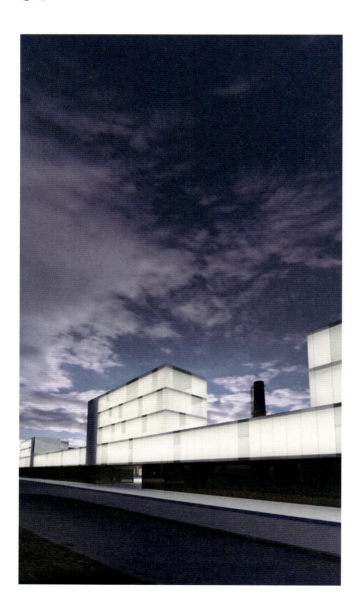

The red balloon

Team point of view Attaching new functional buildings to their immediate environment essentially determines the new character of the place. Because of their industrial origin, there is no connection between these types of constructions and the differing character of their environment.
At present, the block of the abandoned gasworks stands out as an "island" in a mostly residential texture. The emblematic chimney, the octogonal torso-like concrete columns of a cooling tower, the monumental hall spaces of halls, attractive but scattered details – all with their different externals, materials and scales – make us feel that we've arrived in a totally different world... in a "fable".
We suggest a kind of framing building line – a "wall" – that can manage all the mutual reactions between the mainly residential environment and the refurbished industrial – new "city centre" – block.

Jury point of view The winning project emphasizes the landscape and green quality of the site that arises from the size of the plot and from the extraordinary qualities inside the project area, but creates a strong image of built environment and social space as well. The project itself has to be understood rather as a statement, which creates a new quality of landscape and public spaces inside the area.

Linked with the article *Reshaping shared spaces*, p 242

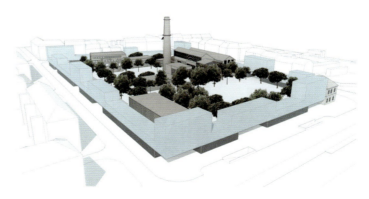

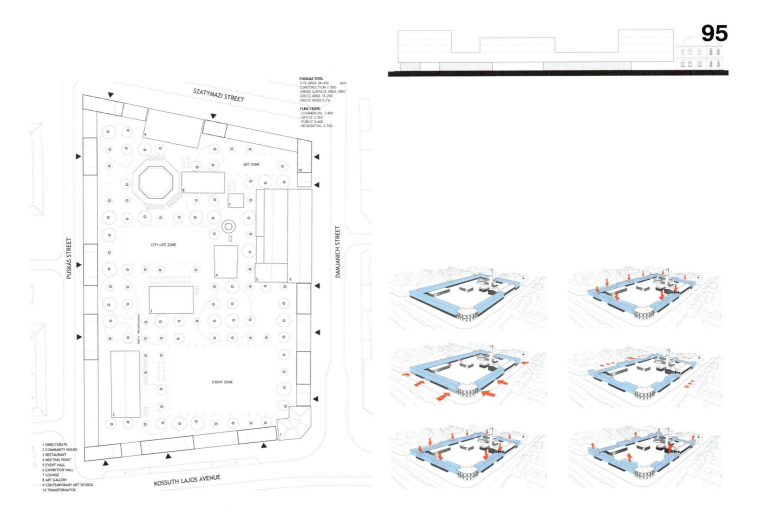

USES
FROM FALLOW LANDS
TO CITY LIFE

WARSZAWA
(PL)

96

WARSAW - PODSKARBIFISKA STREET
POPULATION: 1,714,446 INHAB.
STRATEGIC AREA: 175.20 HA
PROJECT AREA: 24 HA
SITE PROPOSED BY: WARSAW MUNICIPAL GOVERNMENT OFFICE
SITE OWNER: STATE TREASURY AND WARSAW MUNICIPALITY

Benefit of friendly radiation
In the last decade, Warsaw's development has accelerated rapidly. A growing population and territorial development have produced urban sprawl. The organisation of EURO 2012 and the construction of the city's largest concert hall, Sinfonia Varsovia, highlighted the need for a transformation of the areas on the east bank of the Vistula River, included the district of Praga. The project should take into account the social and cultural specificities of the district and prevent social exclusion of local residents. An optimal ratio of housing, sports and recreation areas, modern industry and employment should facilitate the further harmonious and sustainable development of the district. A clear structure of connections with the city needs to be created. The project should solve the problem of existing communication barriers, namely the railways and their specific isolation.

MATEUSZ HERBST (PL)
ARCHITECT

RUNNER-UP

EUROPAN RESULTS
**FROM FALLOW
LANDS TO CITY LIFE**

WARSZAWA (PL)

Taking from within

Team point of view This project is all about transforming local conditions into a positive force for change, so there are a number of ways to read it as a "reconnection".
Spatially, it incorporates the rules of surrounding housing blocks into a "project site" area to make the new addition feel like continuation rather than a separate "island".
Socially, it supports certain activities and services that will generate an inflow of inhabitants and suggests a strategy for their participation in the site's development process so they perceive it as "theirs".
Environmentally, it stresses the sustainable water and energy management features, emphatically present in public space, designed to form – together with deliberately preserved characteristics of the industrial past – its new identity.

Jury point of view The "Taking from Within" project was developed on the basis of a sound social and functional analysis of the site. Both the zoning of the interior competition area and its incorporation and profiling in an interplay with the adjacent neighbourhoods and bordering city districts directly refer to the needs of the population on site. The submission takes up the social and historic identity of the location, creating a new coherent urban building block…

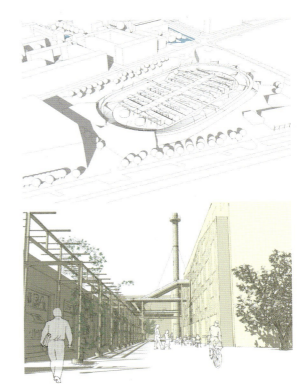

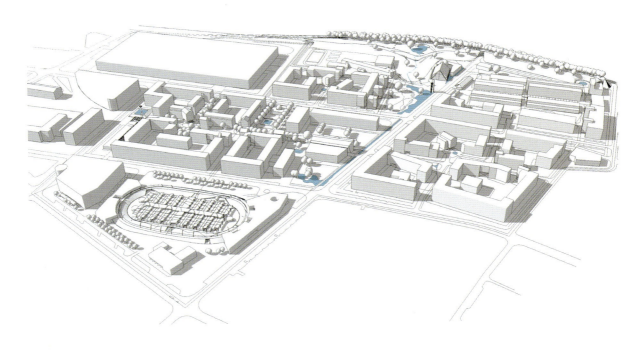

EUROPAN RESULTS
FROM FALLOW LANDS TO CITY LIFE

WARSZAWA (PL)

★ WINNER

BARBARA SKRZYPCZYK (PL)
MARCIN SKRZYPCZYK (PL)
ARCHITECTS

KATARZYNA CHABANNE (PL)
ENVIRONMENTALIST

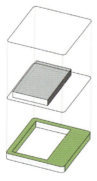

L-M-S Urban Scale

Team point of view The concept implies developing an innovative method for the formation of design space. The project proposes a sustainable strategy that embraces public dialogue and reintroduction of the local unemployed into the job market. The development of the project site is presented at three scales. Large depicts the spatial organisation of the project site with a 13-block grid referring to the orthogonal division of the district. At the medium scale, each new block comprises a green periphery of public character as well as built structures within. At the small scale, the site regains its positive image by the restoration and modernisation of existing post-industrial and sports complexes. The design also aims to turn Podskarbinska Street into a key communication line connecting the site with other parts of the district.

Jury point of view … The Jury appreciated the innovative potential of the project, which actually only becomes apparent at the second glance, but is even more sustainable. The submission provides convincing proposals for the development of the site on different levels. The proposal is very well thought out and constitutes all together a valuable contribution to contemporary urban discourses in the context of post-industrial landscapes.

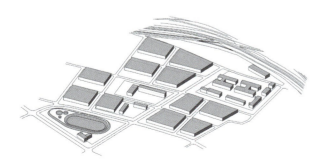

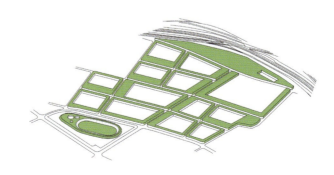

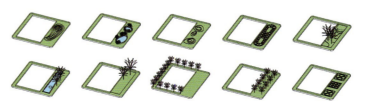

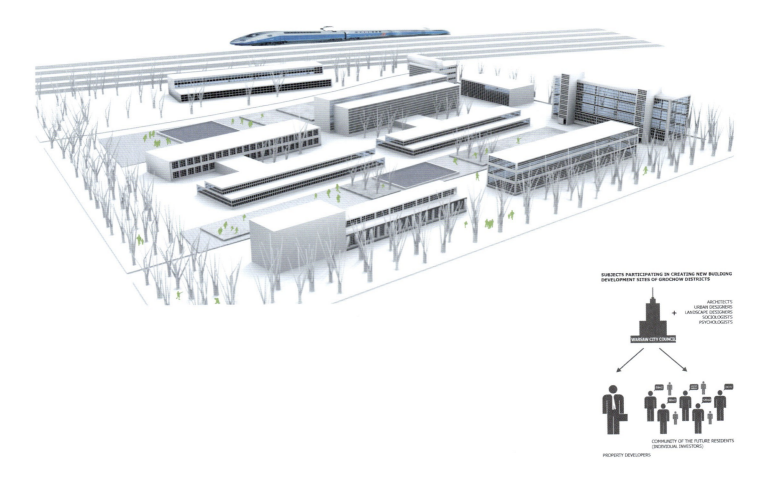

PROCESS OF REVITALISATION AND REGENERATION

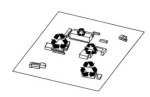
FREEING UP LAND
FOR DEVELOPMENT

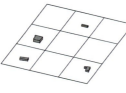
CREATION OF NEW BLOCKS

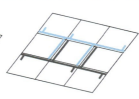
DEVELOPMENT OF LOCAL
INFRASTRUCTURE: BRINGING
IN SERVICES FOR

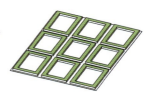
GREEN

BUILT-UP

USES
FROM ISOLATION
TO SOCIAL INTEGRATION

MALMÖ
(SE)

100

MALMÖ - HOLMA
POPULATION: 298,000 INHAB.
STRATEGIC AREA: 34 HA
PROJECT AREA: 9 HA
SITE PROPOSED BY: MKB
FASTIGHETS AB AND RIKSBYGGEN,
HOUSING COMPANIES
SITE OWNER: MKB FASTIGHETS
AB AND RIKSBYGGEN, HOUSING
COMPANIES

The social city
The Holma area is a large-scale development built in the mid-1970s on former agricultural land. It is an area typical of its time, with prefabricated concrete blocks placed in an orthogonal grid, separated motor and pedestrian traffic and a lack of certain public facilities.
The main task is to design a building strategy for the eastern parts of Holma, at present mostly dedicated to parking, including residential buildings as well as a mix of other functions. The brief also seeks proposals on how to develop the area as a whole and improve the social spaces and networks. The development should also help to sew the heterogeneous surrounding areas into a single urban fabric.

JOHAN AHLQUIST (SE)
CARLOS MARTINEZ (US)
URBAN SKOGMAR (SE)
ARCHITECTS

RUNNER-UP

EUROPEAN RESULTS
FROM ISOLATION
TO SOCIAL INTEGRATION

MALMÖ (SE)

101

Greenish village

Team point of view Greenish Village emphasizes the importance of sustainability, mixed use, the creation of meeting places and attractiveness in the future planning of Holma. The first target is the street Holmavångsvägen. This will be a lively, dense mixed-use street with retail, offices and residences. The second target is the elevated green areas. These areas will feature a variety of outdoor activities ranging from sports, agriculture, leisure and relaxation. The third target is the green promenade. This will be equipped with public amenities, cycling and pedestrian lanes. The continuous promenade that extends the length of the area will provide the residents with easy access to outdoor activities and environmental qualities. The fourth target is the public ground. A diversity of public spaces will be implemented in the development of the site. The fifth target is the connection of Holma to the city's green belt. The area's link to the city's green belt will allow people from the city of Malmö and other parts to visit.

Jury point of view … Architecturally, the project suggested an intriguing and attractive atmosphere in the green courtyards it proposed, even if the overall plan seemed somewhat monotonous. The jury felt that these grouped towers had the potential to solve the tricky problem of scale on such a site. The project dealt with various scales of inhabitation in a single architectural expression…

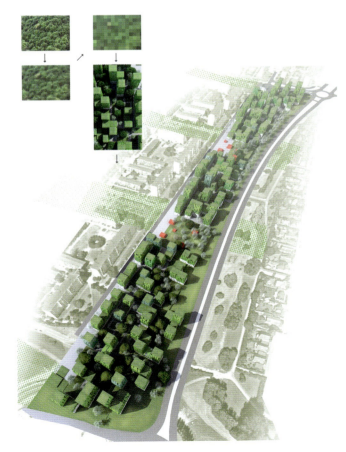

EUROPEAN RESULTS
FROM ISOLATION TO SOCIAL INTEGRATION

MALMÖ (SE)

RUNNER-UP

MALIN DAHLHIELM (SE)
ANNA EDBLOM (SE)
ARCHITECTS, URBAN PLANNERS
KARIN KJELLSON (SE)
ARCHITECT

102

Green grid

Team point of view Green Grid aims to strengthen urban connections and interfaces, and to define and intensify public spaces. It shows the spatial potential of Holma, and allows for gradual development without boundaries or gaps between existing and new structures. In order to incorporate rather than separate areas, surrounding roads are transformed to function both as regional connections as well as local streets with space for pedestrians and cyclists. New buildings and streets tie into the urban fabric and create attractive interfaces with opportunities for commerce and local city life. A park boardwalk, new community gardens, a fruit park and a local square stimulate interactivity and recreation. The future Holma is part of a seamless city where people meet and strangers coexist.

Jury point of view Green Grid was chosen for its apparent desire not to distinguish between the existing modernist suburb of Holma, and what might be added to it in the future. The authors had clearly considered Holma as a whole, trying to integrate and solve all the edges of the place, and resisting the creation of new boundaries between old and new…

Linked with the article *Reshaping shared spaces*, p. 242

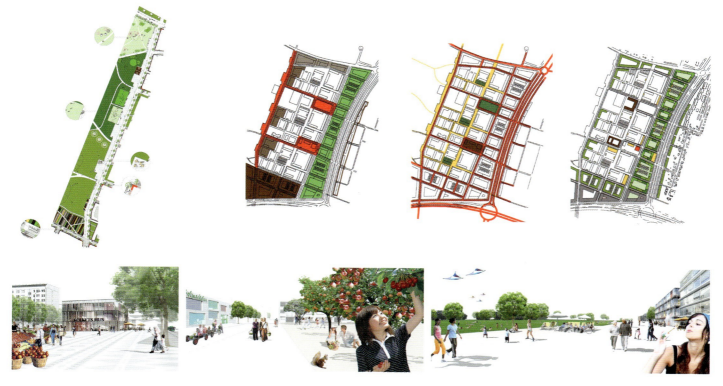

CAPELLE AAN DEN IJSSEL
(NL)

USES
FROM ISOLATION
TO SOCIAL INTEGRATION

103

Reconstruction of a housing area
The municipality of Capelle aan den IJssel is keen to develop areas in consultation with the (future) residents. The designs are based on lifestyles rather than financial categories. The goal, in consultation with the partners, is to develop housing and other areas as sustainably as possible, through the use of ground-level access housing. The adjacent buildings are designed with ample and practical public space and with sufficiently green and spacious zones to give residents the sense of living in a pleasant, safe and functional environment. There should be a clear distinction between public and private areas.

CAPELLE AAN DEN IJSSEL - DE HOVEN 2IN
POPULATION: 65,000 INHAB.
STRATEGIC AREA: 53.5 HA
PROJECT AREA: 1.6 HA
SITE PROPOSED BY:
WONINGSTICHTING COM.WONEN
AND THE MUNICIPALITY OF CAPELLE AAN DEN IJSSEL
SITE OWNER: WONINGSTICHTING COM.WONEN (REAL ESTATE)
AND THE MUNICIPALITY OF CAPELLE AAN DEN IJSSEL (PUBLIC AREA)

USES
FROM ISOLATION
TO SOCIAL INTEGRATION

WÜRZBURG (DE)

106

WÜRZBURG - HUBLAND (FORMER LEIGHTON BARRACKS)
POPULATION: 134,000 INHAB.
STRATEGIC AREA: 9 HA
PROJECT AREA: 1 HA
SITE PROPOSED BY: CITY OF WÜRZBURG, STADTBAU GMBH
SITE OWNER: CURRENTLY BIMA (BUNDESANSTALT FÜR IMMOBILIENAUFGABEN)

Transforming a former military area into a new quarter
The departure of the military offers an opportunity to establish a completely new residential, working and leisure district that consolidates Würzburg's status as a residential and scientific centre and contributes to climate protection. In contrast with the densely built city centre, an urban landscape is to be developed in which cells of differing building densities and uses are embedded in an intensive landscape. The resulting facilities of the State Horticultural Show in 2018 are to be retained as long-term assets for the new urban district. During the Show, future-orientated urban housing projects are to be developed along the airfield that demonstrate the dialogue between city and landscape.

CAPELLE AAN DEN IJSSEL
(NL)

USES
FROM ISOLATION
TO SOCIAL INTEGRATION

103

Reconstruction of a housing area
The municipality of Capelle aan den IJssel is keen to develop areas in consultation with the (future) residents. The designs are based on lifestyles rather than financial categories. The goal, in consultation with the partners, is to develop housing and other areas as sustainably as possible, through the use of ground-level access housing. The adjacent buildings are designed with ample and practical public space and with sufficiently green and spacious zones to give residents the sense of living in a pleasant, safe and functional environment. There should be a clear distinction between public and private areas.

CAPELLE AAN DEN IJSSEL - DE HOVEN 2IN
POPULATION: 65,000 INHAB.
STRATEGIC AREA: 53.5 HA
PROJECT AREA: 1.6 HA
SITE PROPOSED BY:
WONINGSTICHTING COM.WONEN
AND THE MUNICIPALITY OF CAPELLE AAN DEN IJSSEL
SITE OWNER: WONINGSTICHTING COM.WONEN (REAL ESTATE)
AND THE MUNICIPALITY OF CAPELLE AAN DEN IJSSEL (PUBLIC AREA)

EUROPAN RESULTS
**FROM ISOLATION
TO SOCIAL INTEGRATION**

CAPELLE-AAN-DEN-IJSSEL (NL)

★ WINNER

ELENA CHEVTCHENKO (UA / NL)
ANDREW KITCHING (GB)
KEN THOMPSON (GB)
ARCHITECTS

DAVE MORISON (AU)
ARCHITECT

104

Polder Salad

Team point of view The historical landscape of the area, the polder, provides a model for environmentally sustainable water management. The tabula-rasa development of the 1960's ignored this characteristic landscape and established an environment of monotypological, socially and ecologically unsustainable development.
Polder Salad reinstates the polder structure, bringing water into a network of intimate streets defining human-scale urban blocks which accommodate a variety of adaptable dwelling typologies.

Jury point of view Polder Salad proposes a simple structure based on the proposed watercourses that form a continuation of the former ditches in the polder landscape. Within this, a marked differentiation is possible ... The scale proportions are correct, there is sufficient flexibility and the concept offers space for phased development… Good quality of the public space round the block of flats on the corner.

Linked with the article Cultural interferences, p 256

105

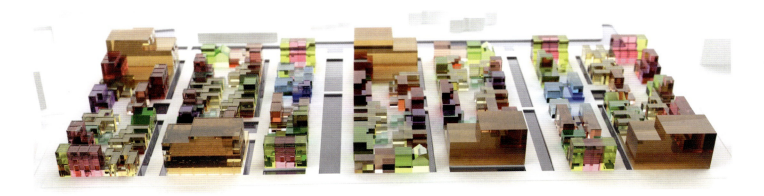

Polder model

1900

+ Environmental sustainability
+ Polder structure: sustainable water management
+ Respect for water visible in linear structuring of space

60's model

1960

− Unsustainable water management
− Monotypological
− Public realm: technical green, technical roads

Polder salad

2015

+ Environmental & social sustainability through diversity
+ Sustainable water management and integrated public realm
+ Array of adaptable typologies to suit changing lifestyles

Dwelling typologies - 1:500

Number of units
Study area total: **285 units**
Apartments: 112 units (40%)
Ground level entry: 173 units (60%)

Intervention area total: **118 units**
Apartments: 45 units (40%)
Ground level entry: 73 units (60%)

● 4.5m row house
3 bed, 117m² / 4 bed, 140m²
39 units

● 6m row house
3/4 bed, 148m²
35 units

● 7.5m row house
4 bed, 140m²
17 units

● 9m courtyard house
4 bed, 127 m²
14 units

● 12m courtyard house
3 bed, 100m² / 4 bed, 130m²
28 units

● 7.5m courtyard house
3 bed, 147m²
17 units

● 4.5m deck house
4 bed, 146m²
5 units

● 6m deck house
4 bed, 148m²
3 units

● Apartment buildings
3/4 room apartments, 73m² - 98m²
112 units

USES
FROM ISOLATION
TO SOCIAL INTEGRATION

WÜRZBURG (DE)

106

WÜRZBURG - HUBLAND (FORMER LEIGHTON BARRACKS)
POPULATION: 134,000 INHAB.
STRATEGIC AREA: 9 HA
PROJECT AREA: 1 HA
SITE PROPOSED BY: CITY OF WÜRZBURG, STADTBAU GMBH
SITE OWNER: CURRENTLY BIMA (BUNDESANSTALT FÜR IMMOBILIENAUFGABEN)

Transforming a former military area into a new quarter
The departure of the military offers an opportunity to establish a completely new residential, working and leisure district that consolidates Würzburg's status as a residential and scientific centre and contributes to climate protection. In contrast with the densely built city centre, an urban landscape is to be developed in which cells of differing building densities and uses are embedded in an intensive landscape. The resulting facilities of the State Horticultural Show in 2018 are to be retained as long-term assets for the new urban district. During the Show, future-orientated urban housing projects are to be developed along the airfield that demonstrate the dialogue between city and landscape.

DOMINGO MELENDO ARANCÓN (ES)
FRANCISCO PARRÓN ORTIZ (ES)
ARCHITECTS

FERNANDO LÓPEZ BARRIENTOS (ES)
MIGUEL ANGEL SUÁREZ MORENO (ES)
ARCHITECTS

RUNNER-UP

EUROPEAN RESULTS
FROM ISOLATION TO SOCIAL INTEGRATION
WÜRZBURG (DE)

107

Helianthus

Team point of view (Smell the flowers while you can. We're one, but we're not the same)
Talking about extensions, trajectories, sets… Thinking of architecture as landscape spaces. Don't create species but ecosystems, communities of living beings whose vital processes are interrelated, sets of individuals that coexist, help, oppose; being in constant change and interaction… like an edible landscape. The city is rebuilt individually by the fragments that each of us use. Inhabiting the enchanted house.
…It loses rigidity, acquires flexibility, separates and sails in gentle rhythm. Like a branch, it sways from side to side, looking for the fastest stream or the quietest shore… HELIANTHUS.
"… In architecture, the opposite is (may be) also true". (Fernando Távora)

Jury point of view The design and detailing of the submission are plausible and well thought out. The proposal develops a radical alternative to the requirements of the master plan and implements this alternative consistently, including layout plans. The housing typologies and the idea of inserted maisonette flats are surprising and show that the author fully considered how this large-scale format can offer individual homes…

Linked with the article *Reshaping shared spaces*, p 242

EUROPEAN RESULTS
**FROM ISOLATION
TO SOCIAL INTEGRATION**

WÜRZBURG (DE)

RUNNER-UP

ANDREAS KROMPASS (DE)
VANESSA PHILIPP (DE)
PHILIPP REICHELT (DE)
WERNER SCHÜHRER (DE)
HEIKE UNGER (DE)
ANDY WESTNER (DE)
CHRISTIAN ZÖHRER (DE)
ARCHITECTS

108

Le Nouveau Trianon

Team point of view English Landscape Park meets Baroque French Garden. "Le Nouveau Trianon" connects the landscape shaped area in the north with the geometrically designed Leighton-Garden in the south.
The small-scale banded structure reflects the natural environment of 'Lehnleiten' and leads it to the formal gardens at the university.
Multi-storey buildings form the link between housing development and the campus. They are an architectural statement towards the axis of the former runway. The base-storey interlinks the streetscape of the neighbourhood with the open space of the gardens.
Each of the three buildings combines community spaces at ground floor with residential space on the upper floors. The two opposing landscape views are united by ambitious plans to create a variety of housing types.

Jury point of view The bold and self-assured new interpretation of the former runway as a Baroque axis is initially baffling. On closer view it is, however, convincing. Referring to "Le Petit Trianon" in Versailles the draft proposal calls for a stronger combination of the Lehnleiten's natural landscape qualities and the planned geometrical park, and of the urban structures between the future large-scale university extensions and the small-scale residential development in these the master plan…

 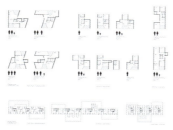

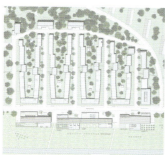

CLERMONT-FERRAND
(FR)

USES
FROM ISOLATION
TO SOCIAL INTEGRATION

Between-cities space
Historically, the site was a peripheral area and a sink space for a number of the city's less salubrious services. Today, it is at the centre of the urban scheme associated in particular with the arrival of the new Estaing Hospital and the future Paris Orléans Clermont Lyon high-speed railway line. The transformation is continuing with the removal of the municipal abattoirs and the demolition - reconstruction of the existing social housing and the planned regeneration of the whole business zone and the upgrade to the station hub.

The objective of the project is to change the role of the site from Sink zone to destination area as a significant desirable urban Nucleus. There will be around 1000 dwellings articulated with a structuring public space served by a tram line, shops and services. As the entry point to the expanded city centre, it will need to reflect the living patterns of the users of the radiating amenities and activities around it.

109

CLERMONT-FERRAND - SAINT-JEAN
POPULATION: 143,000 INHAB. (CITY); 290,000 INHAB. (CONURBATION)
STRATEGIC AREA: 39 HA
PROJECT AREA: 10.7 HA
SITE PROPOSED BY: CITY OF CLERMONT-FERRAND
SITE OWNER: CITY OF CLERMONT-FERRAND, LOGIDÔME AND PRIVATE

EUROPAN RESULTS
**FROM ISOLATION
TO SOCIAL INTEGRATION**

CLERMONT-FERRAND (FR)

★ WINNER

PIERRE BAILLY (FR)
GÉRAUD SAFFRAY (FR)
ARCHITECTS URBAN PLANNERS
CHARLES DAUBAS (FR)
URBAN PLANNER

YANN EOUZAN (FR)
ESTELLE PETIT (FR)
GRAPHIC DESIGNERS
THOMAS SÉRIÈS (US)
DIGITAL PERSPECTIVES

110

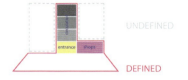

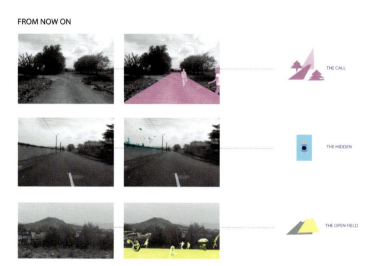

Nudge City

Team point of view Prescriptions, obligations and behavioural norms do not make a sustainable city: a normative or technical approach can only create a desert city in the long run. There can be no sustainability without versatility and space's ability to arouse desire in the long run.
In this project, we placed uses at the centre of a true tactic reflection. The mere question for us was: "How can the project build on desires and incentives to have the actors, places and practices evolve altogether?" We can't decide for change, especially in a context where public action is weakened by budget cuts and administrative division. But maybe then the project can rely on individual and collective reactions to produce global change in a positive way. Desire generates uses, uses bring value, value opens way to qualitative change.

Jury point of view … The fact that this project was unanimously approved by the jury is undoubtedly because it introduces a new approach to the urban project, where it is no longer form that dominates but the process of transformation. The relevance of its vision of the sustainable city and the intelligence of its approach make it an exemplary project.

Linked with the article *Linking with uses*, p. 249

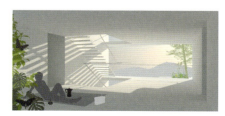

USES CREATE VALUE / VALUE CALLS FOR MUTATION

WHEN INDIVIDUAL LONGINGS CREATE COLLECTIVE VALUE

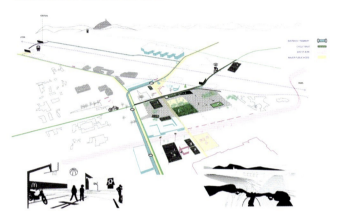

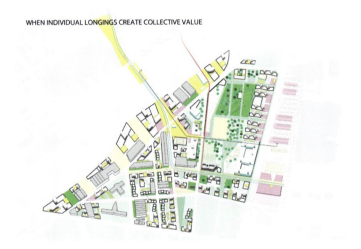

USES
FROM ISOLATION
TO SOCIAL INTEGRATION

LINZ
(AT)

112

LINZ - CITY
POPULATION: 190,000 INHAB.
STRATEGIC AREA: 5.4 HA
PROJECT AREA: 3.84 HA
SITE PROPOSED BY: CITY OF LINZ
SITE OWNER: CITY OF LINZ

Opening up a modernist landmark
Built as Europe's largest tobacco factory, planned by famous architects (Peter Behrens and Alexander Popp) this jewel of international modernism was abandoned in 2009. Recognizing its strategic potential for the future growth of Linz, the city bought the site in order to be able to direct its overall development. The city aims to strengthen its profile as an innovative town in the productive and cultural sectors. The conversion of large scale areas as well as the implementation of large infrastructure projects will contribute to the dynamism of a town which provides a significant level of employment.

JULIO DE LA FUENTE (ES)
NATALIA GUTIÉRREZ (ES)
ARCHITECTS

PAUL-ROUVEN DENZ (DE)
STUDENT IN ARCHITECTURE

RUNNER-UP

EUROPEAN RESULTS
**FROM ISOLATION
TO SOCIAL INTEGRATION**

LINZ (AT)

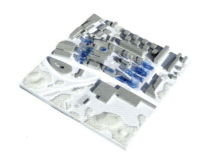

Linzertus: linzer insertus

Team point of view *Insertus* (Latin): fragment of live flesh which is implanted in any part of the human body to repair an injury.
Linzertus (Europan 11): urban regeneration therapy composed of several programmatic grafts to activate the Tabakfabrik buildings, creating a new life cycle in the neighbourhood (updating Tabakfabrik). This precision healing therapy will be done over time, through a step-by-step implementation. A link between the Tabakfabrik and the city is created using the local colour "Linzer Blue". A variety of blue grafts operate in several phases over time to reactivate the complex, with a high degree of visibility and a positive impact on the surrounding neighbourhoods. A strategy of potentials and opportunities resolves the current situation: from island to permeable location.

Jury point of view The project takes high risks concerning the issue of building-preservation: the authors open the protected facades in the ground floor in order to create strong connections with the surrounding areas ... On the other hand the projects suggests a convincing strategy of a series of precise interventions in different areas, which could give to the city a valuable catalogue of transformation…

Linked with the article *Linking with uses*, p 249

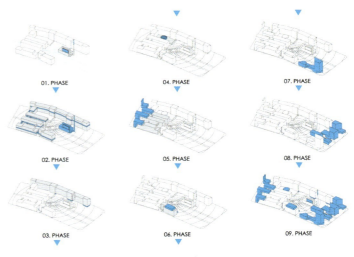

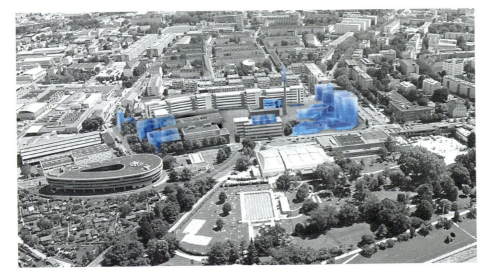

EUROPEAN RESULTS
**FROM ISOLATION
TO SOCIAL INTEGRATION**

LINZ (AT)

RUNNER-UP

SANDRA GNIGLER (AT)
GUNAR WILHELM (AT)
ARCHITECTS
LORENZ POTOCNIK (AT)
URBAN PLANNER

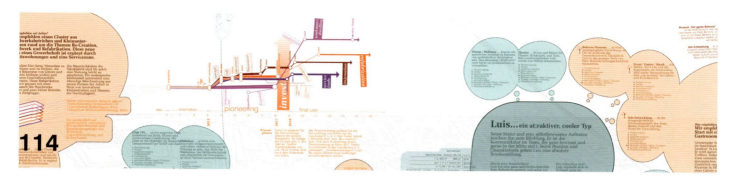

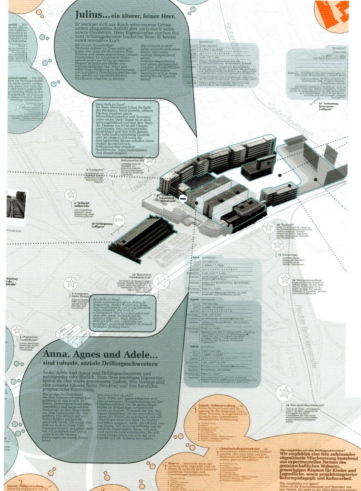

Portrait of an Ensemble

Team point of view The portrayal of the Tabakfabrik ensemble provides a descriptive narrative of a highly complex constellation of building properties, internal and external interaction, and hidden potential. The creation of characters with names, team roles, and recommendations for use results in easily comprehensible and memorable possibilities for the future of the structures. This portrait then serves as a basis for all further considerations. A conceptual layer underpins the portrait and its subsequent suggestions for use. This consists of three main development topics, which are not directly connected to the individual personalities of the "team". These three central issues have the common aim of transforming the Tabakfabrik into an island of socio-economic innovation. As a consequence, the ensemble dedicates itself to change, nonconformist thinking, and breaking the rules and routines of the conventional world.

Jury point of view The project cleverly propagates the potential of the whole area by forming its individual buildings into a narrative, a "group" that reflects on their collective future. The project looks carefully at different contextual scales, combining existing potentials with prospective scenarios… The project offers the city a manual for the development of a strategy: the necessity of defining where they want to be in 20 years.

Linked with the article *Rhythms and timeframes*, p. 269

FRANCESCO FUSARO (IT)
MARCELLO GALIOTTO (IT)
MARCO MONTAGNINI (IT)
NICOLA MONTINI (IT)
ALESSANDRA RAMPAZZO (IT)
GIAN LUCA ZOLI (IT)
ARCHITECTS

ALESSIA BARBIERO (IT)
FRANCESCO DELLA MOTTA (IT)
ENRICO NASCIMBEN (IT)
LUDOVICO PEVERE (IT)
PAOLA SCALVINI (IT)
STUDENTS IN ARCHITECTURE

RUNNER-UP

EUROPEAN RESULTS
**FROM ISOLATION
TO SOCIAL INTEGRATION**

LINZ (AT)

Urban Monolith

Team point of view The value of the Tobacco Factory in the density of Linz needs to be upgraded through the integration of existing and new buildings, old and new functions. Dedicating this complex to people's lives means that they will be able to take possession of a piece of city's history. The big complex will focus on youth creativity, on contemporary art exhibitions viewed via walkways weaving within the monolith. The compact block design, raised above the water base, completes the plot at the western boundary, and at the same time encourages a controlled permeability, achieved by preferential views inwards. People will be able to stay in the Old Cigarette Factory, used as a hotel and as housing space, where greenhouses stimulate meditation and intuition.

Jury point of view The project shows how to make the site a powerful locus. It creates a strong marker at the corner, achieving a convincing balance between new and existing buildings, opening up to the Danube, creating good quality in the inner spaces…

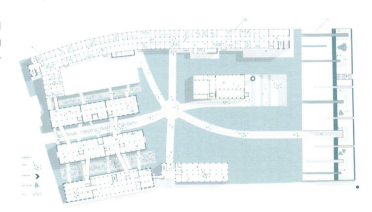

URBAN CONCEPT | Axonometric 3D views
Relations to the context and new opening of tobacco factory to the city

Exsisting buildings without the recent accretions | The water blade / Buildings reflected double their majesty shining through water | The monolith and the hole / part 1 / The lifting protects the tobacco factory from the crowded road, but at the same time aids the entrance to the entire complex, through the underground tram stop | The monolith and the hole / part 2 / Vertical cuts make the monolith see-through and enlightened inside, encouraging best views

USES
FROM IN-BETWEEN PLACES
TO SHARED SPACES

AIGLE
(CH)

116

AIGLE
POPULATION: 8,757 INHAB.
STRATEGIC AREA: 15 HA
PROJECT AREA: 3 HA
SITE PROPOSED BY: CITY OF AIGLE
SITE OWNER: PRIVATE OWNERS

At the heart of the city

Located at the heart of the city and extending from the Place de la Gare to the Place de l'Hotel de Ville, the site consists of listed buildings, which are the remnants of a time when going through Aigle was the only way to reach Italy. Buildings inherited from the industrial past - such as the large mills - stand in the middle of the site. To control the urban sprawl the City wants to increase the density in the downtown area and to boost it to be more attractive. The site could become the articulation point between several adjacent areas currently undergoing redevelopment.

FAÏÇAL OUDOR (FR) **PAUL ROLLAND** (FR) ARCHITECTS	CYRILLE BEIRNAERT (FR) STUDENT IN ARCHITECTURE	RUNNER-UP	EUROPEAN RESULTS **FROM IN-BETWEEN PLACES TO SHARED SPACES** AIGLE (CH)

Stage and squares

Team point of view The project clarifies the urban shape by creating a huge ground treatment and two complementary squares, which unify the whole centre of the city and harmonize the spaces. New spots to discover are offered to strollers and improve the urban pattern.

As the historical centre became a big pedestrian area, it can be filled with programmatical interventions, which are surgically distributed. Two major topics increase Aigle's attractivity: the Wine Research and Learning Centre and the Fontaines festival. As the urban intervention unifies, the historical centre becomes a real stage where cultural events can take place. The Aigle space and identity is offered to the stalker. The cultural patrimony and local identity act as a reliable support of the city blossom.

Jury point of view A platform, with a uniform design, linking the centre of the city to two additional little squares, is used as the basis of the design for "the staging" of the public spaces of the project … Two or even three major programs enhance the town's attractiveness… And partial projects create new intertwined spatial compositions over the transversal public platform…

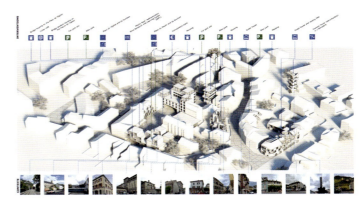

EUROPEAN RESULTS
**FROM IN-BETWEEN PLACES
TO SHARED SPACES**

AIGLE (CH)

★ WINNER

FRÉDÉRIC MARTINET (FR)
VINCENT TRARIEUX (FR)
ARCHITECTS

JULIEN BARGUE (FR)
ARNAUD FAUCHER (FR)
HYDROLOGY AND ENVIRONMENTAL
ENGINEERS
SIMON PORTELAS (FR)
STUDENT IN ARCHITECTURE

118

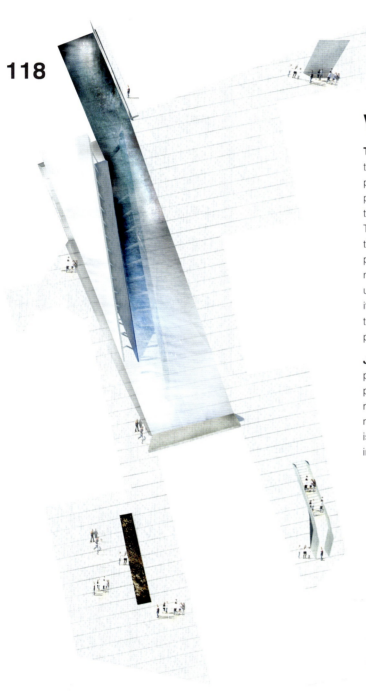

White

Team point of view The *disconnectedness* of Aigle is invisible. It is immaterial in nature, arising from the gradual and cumulative isolation of housing, public amenities, shops and offices, like a series of autonomous and hyper-programmed entities. These entities fragment the use of space, and with it the practice of day-to-day life.

The *reconnection* proposed by our project is rooted in the strangeness of the place, in its *white* materiality. It makes it a spectacular and luxurious place, but one in which the luxury and spectacle are invisible. The project is no claim to being a work of art or an architectural object. It operates as an urban project, with a precise and open programme. Five shapes demarcate its outlines, offering an infinity of uses. Their installation is climatic; it maintains a differential relationship with the city fragments that surround it. The project is designed to age.

Jury point of view The project has designed a structure whose purpose is to provide diversified public space with different potential appropriations… The structure will lie at the heart of the city, and work as a regeneration catalyst. The new possibilities so created must precede a more classical renovation project, reconstituting the urban form and the islands. The planned project will create an increased visibility, in keeping with the scale of the agglomeration…

Mimes — Cinema plein air — Fête des vendanges — Fête d'automne — Mardi soir — Romeo & Juliette

Performance artistique — Jeudi matin — Patinoire — Fête de printemps — Cour de gym — Aigle Plage

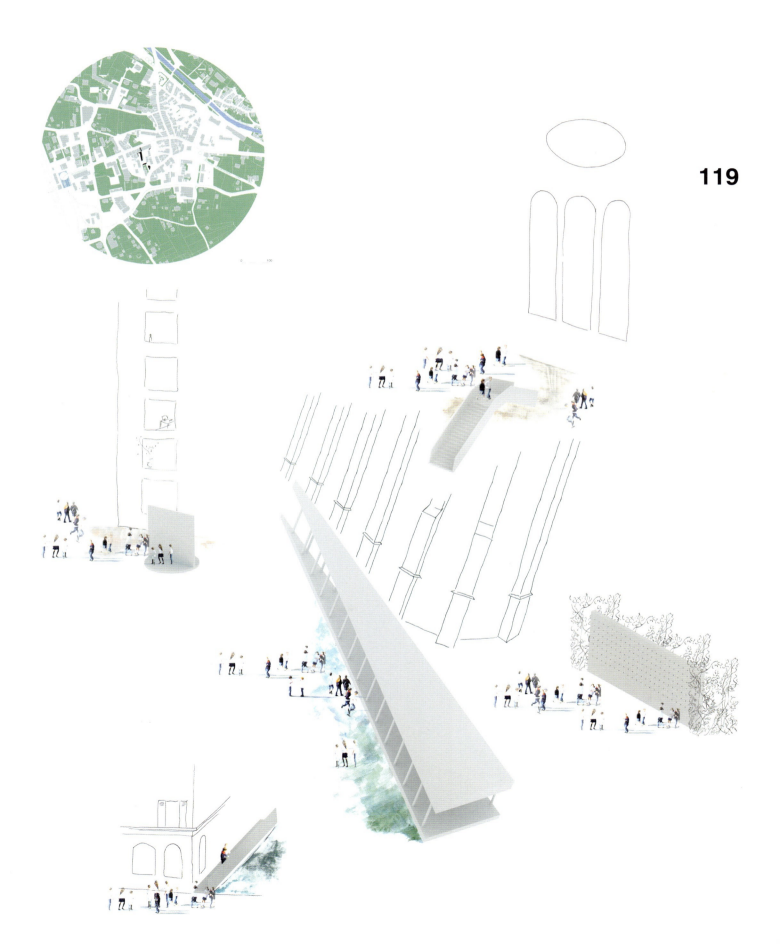

119

USES
FROM IN-BETWEEN PLACES
TO SHARED SPACES

KØBENHAVN
(DK)

120

COPENHAGEN – ØSTERBRO,
SANKT KJELDS PLADS AND
RADIAL STREETS
POPULATION: APPROX. 530,000 INHAB.
STRATEGIC AREA: APPROX. 100 HA
PROJECT AREA: APPROX. 0.5/8 HA
SITE PROPOSED BY: CITY OF COPENHAGEN
SITE OWNER: CITY OF COPENHAGEN AND PRIVATE LANDOWNERS

A city district in motion

The project site is in the northern part of the City of Copenhagen, in an area called Sankt Kjelds Kvarter, which is being renewed over the course of the next five years. The investment in the site should support the efforts to create better housing and urban spaces and thus more growth and a higher quality of life in Copenhagen. There is a special focus on making it easier and more enjoyable to walk or cycle within the district and on creating better links between Sankt Kjelds Plads and the two S-train stations and two future Metro stations on either side of the project site.

RUNE BUNDGAARD JØRGENSEN
(DK)
BJØRN MOGENSEN (DK)
MADELEINE SEMBRING (SE)
LAURA WEDDERKIND BANK (DK)
ARCHITECTS

RUNNER-UP

EUROPEAN RESULTS
**FROM IN-BETWEEN PLACES
TO SHARED SPACES**

KØBENHAVN (DK)

The urban space and the spacious urbanity

Team point of view We have created a set of values inspired by the everyday to produce the noble in the general and the ability to create something unique through recognizable means. We have added extra layers to the existing urban fabric and peeled others away, to dignify and highlight the qualities that have been present all along.
We have divided the rejuvenation of Sct. Kjelds neighbourhood into three programmatic elements that can be implemented gradually.
Traffic and urban space are differentiated by creating an obvious hierarchy through the paving strategy.
Creating elevated pocket parks on the existing islands of asphalt.
Giving Sct. Kjelds Plads a more dense urban neighbourhood core, by constructing three new buildings. A new chausse paving unifies the square and generates a shared space separated by granite bollards. We hope this will be the landmark that Sct. Kjelds Plads never had.

Jury point of view The jury appreciates the entry's low-key and poetic approach to the site. Taking its point of departure in the use of red bricks in the architecture of the area, it demonstrates a fine sensibility to the design of public space. Hence, it raises the pertinent discussion of how much intervention is actually needed in urban planning, proposing only minor changes such as the planting of trees, changing the paving and reusing existing outdoor lighting fixtures in imaginative new ways…

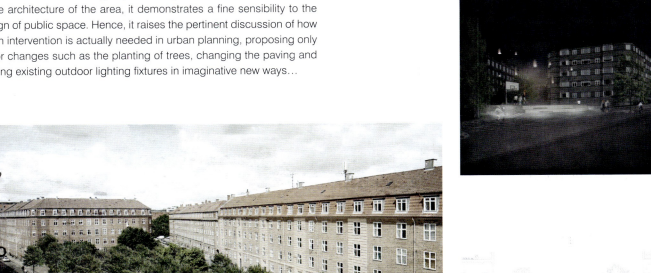

EUROPEAN RESULTS
FROM IN-BETWEEN PLACES TO SHARED SPACES

KØBENHAVN (DK)

★ WINNER

FLEMMING RAFN THOMSEN (DK)
ARCHITECT URBAN PLANNER
OLE SCHRØDER (DK)
ARCHITECT

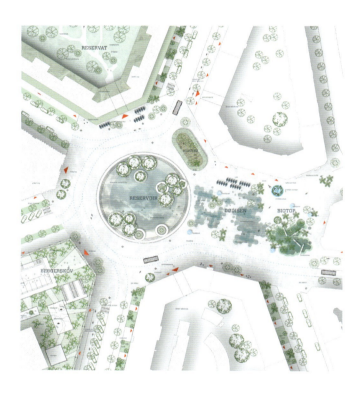

The last city quarter

Team point of view Based on Camillo Sittes' sympathetic understanding of humanistic urban planning, the aim of this entry is to create a neighbourhood that is self-reliant. From past urban planning, where the primary focus was property speculation, capital and commercial potential, we want to plan an artificially natural neighbourhood, with the ability to develop into a self-regulating district, with a minimum of top-down intervention, external resources and municipal interference. Urban spaces coupled with process-oriented development practices must finally reject static models in favour of a renewable, local and natural strategy. In short, a city in balance, where the regulated and the unregulated may clash, where unknown stories will be told and teach us new things, and where sensible new opportunities arise in the city.

Jury point of view The jury is impressed by the convincing urban landscape approach, which confronts the problems of the site by planting trees and creating biotopes with green spaces and ponds. The project balances in a sensitive manner a visionary intervention with a pragmatic approach by building upon the existing structures and systems of the site whilst adding new identity to the area by creating biotopes with various permeable surfaces and green spaces…

Linked with the article *Common resources and mutation*, p 263

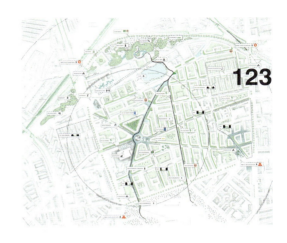

Idag heterogene bebyggelser — Imorgen en homogen bebyggelse — Med et inkluderende gårdrum

Eksisterende befæstede veje — Nye grønne rum i gaderne — 18,5% færre befæstede arealer — Fra transitrum... — til samlende byrum!

USES
FROM IN-BETWEEN PLACES
TO SHARED SPACES

NYNÄSHAMN
(SE)

124

NYNÄSHAMN - ESTÖ
POPULATION: 26,000 INHAB.
STRATEGIC AREA: 17 HA
PROJECT AREA: 6 HA
SITE PROPOSED BY: MUNICIPALITY OF NYNÄSHAMN
SITE OWNER: MUNICIPALITY OF NYNÄSHAMN

Central park

In the middle of the last century, the site was a vibrant part of Nynäshamn, serving the community with well frequented sports fields. Over the last two decades it has lost significance and most of the major sports activities have been relocated to the north of the town. A rift in the urban fabric has occurred, causing a perceived distance between the central town and the southern district of Estö.

The main task is to develop a scheme that transforms the area into an attractive public space, which has the capacity to tie the town and its parts together. This urban goal is to be achieved primarily through landscape means. The programme may contain mixed functions, possibly with an emphasis on leisure activity and nature features. As the open field land is close to sea level, it is not possible to erect larger, permanent buildings, although this may be considered for the surrounding heights.

GAÉTAN BRUNET (FR)
ANTOINE ESPINASSEAU (FR)
CHLOÉ VALADIÉ (FR)
ARCHITECTS, URBAN PLANNERS

RUNNER-UP

EUROPEAN RESULTS
FROM IN-BETWEEN PLACES TO SHARED SPACES

NYNÄSHAMN (SE)

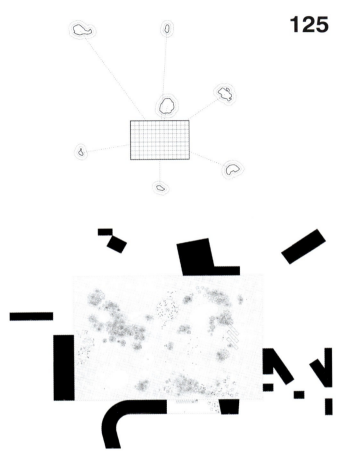

Too big square

Team point of view The *too big square* is an ambiguous place. Between clearing (subtraction) and oasis (singularity) it stands as an attitude before the dichotomy of the mass and the void (fullness and emptiness). Its generous dimensions allow it to assimilate into one single space-landscape the hills that surround it and the fragmented fabric they foster. By its tangibility, the too big square gathers different urban conditions and scattered architectures; by its proportions, it maintains a type of gentleness and insignificance between the worlds that it consents. Both a space of connection and amplitude, the *too big square* is an area of negotiation. Smoothing distances, it does not deny the lieu its fragility and its low suburban intensity, but leaves room for the unpredictable. A chosen urbanity emerges from this new common space, stimulated by the simple generosity of the place.

Jury point of view This provocative proposal took a unique approach to this place that seemed to offer valuable insights into the contemporary city… The Too Big Square redefined the site as the location of a huge piazza that operated at the scale of the city region, connecting the scattered parts of the expanded, zoned urban form of Nynäshamn…

Linked with the article *Cultural interferences*, p 256

EUROPEAN RESULTS
FROM IN-BETWEEN PLACES TO SHARED SPACES

NYNÄSHAMN (SE)

★ WINNER

JAN DERVEAUX (BE)
ARCHITECT
RITA LEAL (PT)
FRANZ RESCHKE (DE)
ANNA VOGELS (DE)
LANDSCAPE ARCHITECTS

FREDERIK SPRINGER (DE)
STUDENT IN LANDSCAPE ARCHITECTURE

Skärscape

Team point of view The landscape surrounding the Stockholm Skärgård, with its some 25,000 islands, was created and formed by different processes (Shifting, Elevating, Scratching, Eroding) and is today multifunctional. The programmatic emptiness and the scenic expanse within the city of Nynäshamn provides space for a hybridisation of the regional landscape and open local structures.

The formation and usage principles of the Skärgård were interpreted for the local site:

"Distortions" and "Scars" in the ground surface create a subtle yet strong park network. Through densification of the existing landscape qualities and qualification for different possible uses and multiple connections to the surrounding structures, Skärscape becomes the central link in the wider city and the open environment.

Jury point of view The jury rewarded the restrained and unprogrammed nature of this proposal, beautifully represented in a way that suggested a characterful landscape, but that did not prescribe too much about what might happen there. The result was a proposal that is a stylised meditation on the Swedish landscape, that resists imposing arbitrary, "friendly" landscape features. It also appears very realisable in terms of scale and form…

Linked with the article *Common resources and mutation*, p. 263

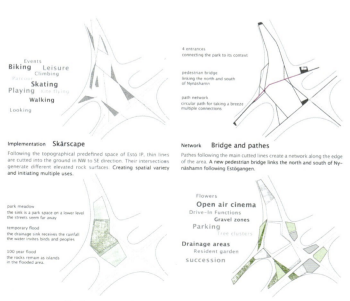

USES
FROM IN-BETWEEN PLACES
TO SHARED SPACES

RØDOVRE
(DK)

128

RØDOVRE - ISLEV DISTRICT
POPULATION: 36,000 INHAB. (RØDOVRE) / 5,500 INHAB. (ISLEV)
STRATEGIC AREA: 191 HA
PROJECT AREA: 17 HA
SITE PROPOSED BY: MUNICIPALITY OF RØDOVRE
SITE OWNER: MUNICIPALITY OF RØDOVRE AND OTHER OWNERS

Do you see the potential of the suburb?
Islev flourished thanks to the dream of the good life outside the crowded city. Some 50 years have passed since then, and as society has changed, new agendas are taking over. The goal is to breathe new life into Islev, by clarifying what dreams can still be achieved and updated to life in the future, and what new dreams can be added.
The municipality's vision is for the project site to become the natural heart of Islev with a strong local profile that provides the entire district with a functional, identity boosting lift. Islev needs to be strengthened as a local community with rich day-to-day experience, where people live close to all the basic amenities of daily life as well as cultural and leisure facilities.

CÉDRIC CHAUSSE (FR)
CHARLOTTE PORTIER (FR)
ARCHITECTS, URBAN PLANNERS

OLIVIER MARQUET (FR)
ARCHITECT, URBAN PLANNER
LUDOVIC POYET (FR) ARCHITECT

RUNNER-UP

EUROPEAN RESULTS
**FROM IN-BETWEEN PLACES
TO SHARED SPACES**

RØDOVRE (DK)

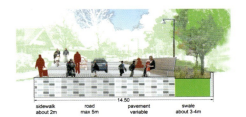

Scenes from the suburbs

Team point of view With the saturation of their city centres many big cities are turning to the question of the regeneration of their outer suburbs. These suburbs are becoming the focus of new development as the limits of inner city growth are reached. These suburbs should not just be considered as simply residential areas but should also possess their own attractiveness and dynamics, not least because they are becoming more readily accessible. They must find their place in a complex network that involves local, regional or national initiatives. Our response is to propose a consolidation at the local level in developing the notion of the "Home area", or the "microvillage" of the 21st century, with places for intergenerational exchange, socialising, work and shopping, and so forth: to create new scenes for/from the suburbs.

Jury point of view This proposal is rewarded for its detailed analysis and comprehensive approach. The main challenges of Islev are addressed in a consistent manner throughout with the idea of generating a new identity using five key elements: A renewal of Ungdomsbyen; a new image of Slotsherrensvej; a shared space on Islevbrovej; and an extension of Islev Torv. The jury finds that this provides a solid basis for further development…

Linked with the article *Linking with uses*, p 249

EUROPEAN RESULTS
**FROM IN-BETWEEN PLACES
TO SHARED SPACES**

RØDOVRE (DK)

★ WINNER

SØREN LETH (DK)
ARCHITECT, URBAN PLANNER
RASMUS THERKILDSEN (DK)
ARCHITECT

SYLWIA BOGDAN (PL)
ARCHITECT, URBAN PLANNER
JEPPE BONNE OLSEN (DK)
INGRID EIDE (NO)
ANDRIUS ROPOLAS (LT)
STUDENTS IN ARCHITECTURE

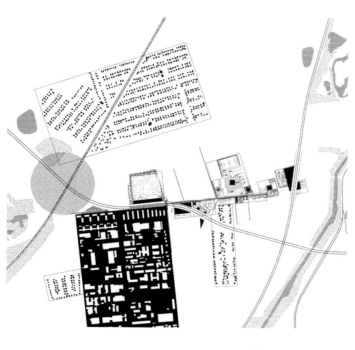

Islev ID

Team point of view Rødovre is situated right on the edge of the uninterrupted urban fabric of Copenhagen in the ring of dense suburbs surrounding the city.
Instead of creating a new centre we propose to connect the concentrations of activities at local level. The strategy focuses on reinforcing urban life in the heart of the activities whilst qualifying the connections between them. To achieve this goal, the concentration of destinations need to be strengthened by adding a new program to the existing activities. It is a typology for urban life that could be implemented in other locations.
Islev Id is a new dynamic and identity, creating a hub for Islev and at the same time a social focal point for the whole area. The Islevbrovej Street and Line create new possibilities for usage and a spread of activities.

Jury point of view The proposal offers an elegant solution to the immediate remit and establishes a long-term legacy for the transformation of the region's intrinsic qualities whilst simultaneously creating an original, beautiful and charismatic urban space from few resources. "Islev Identity" has the potential to create a recognisable and unique space from the light rail development and along Ring 3. A new centre will develop the district's enclaves with communal areas that will enrich public life through activities, education and recreation, rather than excessive commercial activity…

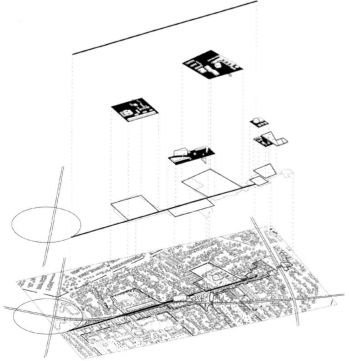

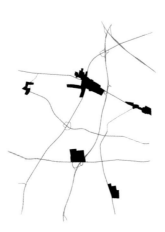

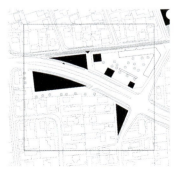

USES
FROM IN-BETWEEN PLACES
TO SHARED SPACES

SELB
(DE)

132

SELB - WESTERN PART OF
THE TOWN CENTRE
POPULATION: 16,000 INHAB.
STRATEGIC AREA: 21 HA
PROJECT AREA: 3.2 HA
SITE PROPOSED BY: SELB TOWN
COUNCIL
SITE OWNER: SELB TOWN COUNCIL,
VARIOUS PRIVATE PROPERTY
OWNERS

Activating the inner city
With an integrated urban development concept, Selb Town Council has formulated a set of goals to promote sustainable urban development within existing demographic and economic constraints. The weakened western part of the town centre of Selb is to be upgraded. Many of the vacant shop units, buildings and fallow land show serious urban planning deficits. The urban planning goals include improving mobility, barrier-free paths and the reactivation of vacant residential and commercial houses. The questions raised are: how can unattractive residual spaces be brought into the public sphere and what uses will enhance urban life?

ALEXA BODAMMER (DE)
URBAN PLANNER, ARCHITECT
CHRISTOPH RICHTER (DE)
JAN TRUTZ (DE)
ROLAND ZÜGER (CH)
ARCHITECTS

RUNNER-UP

EUROPEAN RESULTS
**FROM IN-BETWEEN PLACES
TO SHARED SPACES**

SELB (DE)

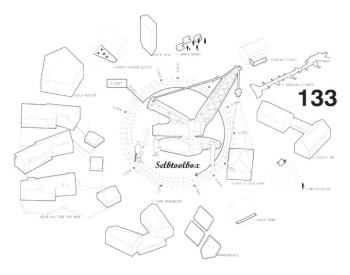

Selbland

Team point of view SELBLAND comes alive through architectural and landscape marquetry for Marienstraße and Marienplatz. To realize the new built spaces, the SELBOPTIONS are explored and processed by an active public, planning experts and an architectural team. The SELBTOOLBOX provides custom-made interventions guiding the process. The remnants of Selb's porcelain industry are connected to the heart of the city by the WHITE–BOND: a white pavement and a lighting design; the SELBMUSEUM as well as the SELBVIEW form towering landmarks. A GREEN–GANTRY, the programmed renaturing of the Selb creek articulates the urban edge and sets it in relation to the factory-outlet and the new buildings. The ALL TO-GETHER NOW housing typologies and refurbishments like YARD NEIGH-BOURS establish a vivid mix of residents and visitors. The SELBLAND project is a processual design-concept, based on diverse and binding public interaction within the urban realm.

Jury point of view This carefully structured urban concept for Selbland strengthens main public spaces and places interesting new emphasis for the city. The authors propose a modern repair of the city with precisely set architectonic implants and economically interesting motivation for the residents, i.e. the impetus to develop something "themselves and together". The idea is to define Selb spatially with smart approaches and playful-humorous explanatory motifs, to rearrange it and to open up vital new opportunities in the existing structure…

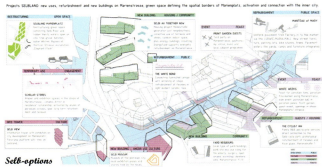

EUROPEAN RESULTS
FFROM IN-BETWEEN PLACES TO SHARED SPACES

SELB (DE)

★ WINNER

ANDREAS BAUMER (DE)
THOMAS BERNHARDT (DE)
GILLES-BENOIT TREVETIN (FR)
ARCHITECTS

TXELL BLANCO-DIAZ (ES)
EGLE SUMINSKAITE (LT)
STUDENTS IN ARCHITECTURE
JOPPE KNEPPERS (NL)
ARCHITECT

Dornröschen - Reinitializing Selb or 'Kissing awake the sleeping beauty'

Team point of view Through a range of strategies and interventions the porcelain-city of Selb will be elevated to a regional centre for art, trade, tourism, and culture. The route connecting the transformed porcelain factory and the historic city centre will become the main artery of Selb. Sustainable refurbishment and carefully selected new construction will form a string of pearls along the so-called "porcelain route" to stimulate development in their vicinity.
Embracing the industrial tradition of Selb will form the basis for a long-term revitalization of the city. Simultaneously the city will be able to sharpen its profile by offering attractive new life/work concepts and room for individual development within established structures. Through this process Porcelain will continue to play a key role!

Jury point of view … Overall, the submission shows an interesting and innovative path between positioning the city of Selb strategically as a porcelain location and architectural implants… Conclusions are drawn for the city's core area based on superordinate structural measures for traffic routing, the development of a multipurpose park around the porcelain factory and a city park alongside the renatured Selb River…

Linked with the article *Linking with uses*, ⊃ 249

134

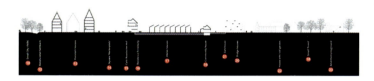

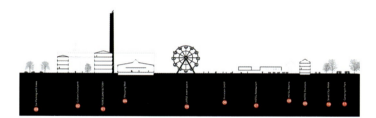

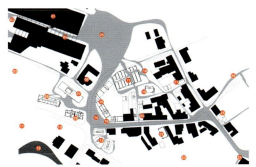
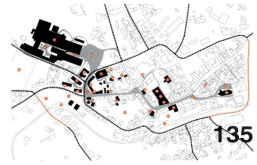

135

EUROPAN 11
WINNING PROJECTS

THEME 3

Connectivity

In the context of sustainable development, the theme of "connectivity" relates to methods of linking the global and the local, scales of space and time, as well as natural environments and social environments. What exists is examined from a dynamic perspective regarding the relationship between mobilities, urban practices and public spaces.

From border to seam 138

How do you affect the shift from a boundary that creates separation (infrastructure, topography, etc.) to a seam that establishes links? The boundary (between town and country, suburban and urban, between districts, etc.) can be extrapolated in numerous ways to develop new urban connectivity.

ALCALÁ DE LA SELVA (ES) 138
MARCHE-EN-FAMENNE (BE) 143
ALLERØD (DK) 146
SAN BARTOLOMÉ (ES) 150
TOULOUSE (FR) 154
TURKU (FI) 158

From void to link 162

Sites are characterized as leftovers from infrastructure or green pockets in urbanized areas. They offer an opportunity to build new housing and to create a new space that not only connects different urban patterns within the city, but also connects different groups of people. Empty spaces have an inherent potential for the development of high-quality public space, in terms of ambition, ecology, social value and culture, to create spaces that are shared successfully by different social groups.

HAUGESUND (NO) 162
CERDANYOLA DEL VALLÈS (ES) 165
GETARIA (ES) 169
NORRKÖPING (SE) 173

From place to territory 177

Contemporary urban environments are the product of various processes introducing territorial dynamics within local environments and enlarging local micro activities into a territorial scale. New connections are created, or reinforced, within the main metropolitan space. Some communities join forces into larger territorial groupings to encourage such connectivities. When territorial dynamics dominate local environments there is a need to respond to their impact. How can such a place take advantage of this dominance of the territorial to establish connectivities without being overwhelmed by the impact of the incomer?

SAVENAY (FR) 177
ALCORCÓN (ES) 182
GUIMARÃES (PT) 186
PORVOO (FI) 190
ROMAINMÔTIER (CH) 194
SKIEN-PORSGRUNN (NO) 198
STAINS (FR) 200

CONNECTIVITY
FROM BORDER TO SEAM

ALCALÁ DE LA SELVA
(ES)

138

ALCALÁ DE LA SELVA
POPULATION: 513 INHAB.
STRATEGIC AREA: 22 HA
PROJECT AREA: 22 HA
SITE PROPOSED BY: DIRECTORATE GENERAL OF URBAN PLANNING (GOVERNMENT OF ARAGON) AND ALCALÁ DE LA SELVA MUNICIPAL COUNCIL
SITE OWNER: MUNICIPAL AND PRIVATE

Sustainable tourism and landscape
This site is linked with a ski resort in Teruel Province and therefore has a population influx in winter and summer. The main population centre is Alcalá de la Selva, but other townships and housing estates, all built in the 1980s and 1990s, are scattered around the vicinity, forming a complex urban system with an obvious lack of facilities. The Municipality wants to create the necessary links between these districts. The proposal focuses on the connection between the consolidated historic town and the first "district", Virgen de la Vega, which will be used as a model for future action.

JAVIER ACEDO ANDRÉS (ES)
PAULA ANASAGASTI GUTIÉRREZ (ES)
LUCÍA MARTÍN LÓPEZ (ES)
ARCHITECTS

RUNNER-UP

EUROPEAN RESULTS
FROM BORDER TO SEAM

ALCALÁ DE LA SELVA (ES)

Traveller, there is no road, you make your path as you walk

Team point of view The necessity of readaptation of the Alcalá de la Selva area is result of a high population difference through seasons, and its associated urban development.

The proposal "Caminante, no hay camino, se hace camino al andar" intends to reactivate the territory by way of a social and economic reconnection of the urban and natural fabric. An open strategy of resource management throughout time is proposed, along with a series of guidelines that influence different fields, affecting productive systems and landscape. This strategy is determined by the valley basin, the river and the A228 road. Through these hub lines, new focal points and cores are proposed to regenerate the social and productive system. Even different spacial strategies are suggested for landscape reorganization.

Jury point of view This proposal provides a detailed analysis of the existing territorial system and then develops a brilliant, thoroughly illustrated strategy capable of tackling the development of the initially required zone and, if necessary, the entire surrounding area as well. It may even be able to go beyond the purely municipal level and tackle larger-scale challenges...

Linked with the article *Rhythms and timeframes*, p 269

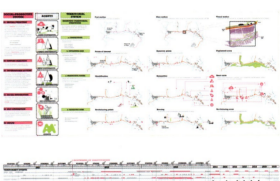

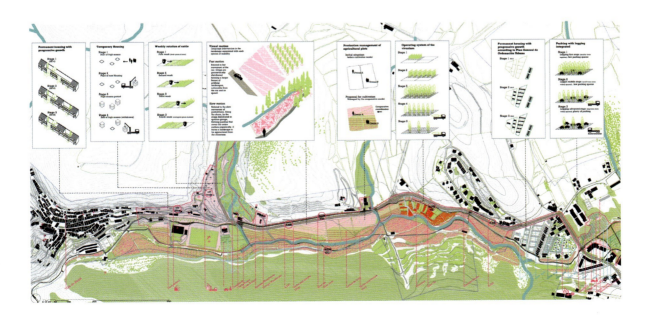

EUROPEAN RESULTS
FROM BORDER TO SEAM

ALCALÁ DE LA SELVA (ES)

★ WINNER

POL VILADOMS CLAVEROL (ES)
ARNAU SASTRE CUADRI (ES)
CECILIA RODRÍGUEZ VIELBA (ES)
ARCHITECTS

Productive landscape

Team point of view The project operates as a reconnection in many different ways.
Firstly, it creates a route through a linear park between the villages of Alcalá de la Selva and Virgen de la Vega. Through this operation, the agricultural heritage of the place is reclaimed. People play a major role in the development of the project. Despite its outstanding natural and architectural environment, the place is unable to attract more residents and tourists. The project seeks to create a link between people and place through reconnection with the territory. Agricultural production is the main key to this objective.
Ultimately, it is essential to create a link between the image of the proposed landscape and production. This is possible thanks to the vineyard landscape, which offers the potential pleasure of picking the grapes, as well as making wine and living on one's own land.

Jury point of view The project diagnoses, proposes and delivers an architectural solution with remarkable quality for a precise, stimulating territory: the urban and rural areas that coexist in Alcalá de la Selva. The proposal is based on profound, comprehensible principles; principles that use the physical, formal and cultural heritage to shape and develop the memory of the place, while at the same time facilitating processes that focus on the immediate future, both near and far, with an eye for productive landscapes.

Linked with the article *Common resources and mutation*, p 263

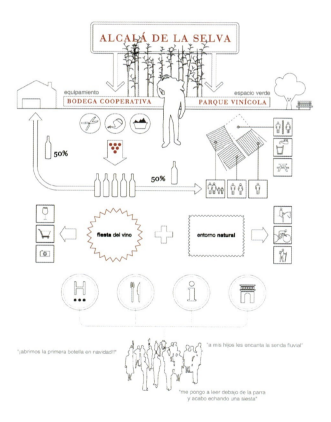

142

MARCHE-EN-FAMENNE
(BE)

CONNECTIVITY
FROM BORDER TO SEAM

143

The link
The transformation of this area is both a must and a challenge. A must because the parcel extends along the future main boulevard of the city, currently under complete renovation; A challenge because of its topographic, relational and functional aspects. On one hand the project will have to tackle the parking issue for residents and future occupants of new buildings. On the other hand, the level difference between the front and back of the area while respecting the neighbouring buildings. Finally, the commercial function called upon by Boulevard at this location should be mixed with the demand for new housing from the Municipality. The site proposes thus a complex urban site located at the frontier between through traffic and the old city centre.

MARCHE-EN-FAMENNE
POPULATION: 17,238 INHAB. FOR 122KM2 OR 141 INHAB./KM2
STRATEGIC AREA: +/- 0.2 HA
PROJECT AREA: +/- 0.1 HA
SITE PROPOSED BY: MUNICIPALITY
SITE OWNER: COMMUNAL PROPERTY, WITH RIGHTS TEMPORALLY ASSIGNED TO A PRIVATE PARTY INTERESTED TO DEVELOP THE SITE

EUROPEAN RESULTS
FROM BORDER TO SEAM

MARCHE-EN-FAMENNE (BE)

★ WINNER

ANCA DIANA POPESCU (RO)
SORIN VLADIMIR POPESCU (RO)
ARCHITECTS

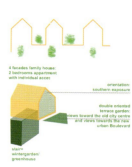

144

The space of encounters

Team point of view In the beginning there were some old houses and a church surrounded by forests and plains, then those houses grew into a town, then the town became a walled town, then after a long time it became a town tired of its own walls, then the town tore down its walls, then the dismantled wall became a street, then new houses began to grow on the other side of the remains of the wall, then the town grew even larger, then the old houses and the old church became a little lonely and separated. Then beside the ancient church, facing the new houses and the old houses on the boundary, a void formed. The Old Town disliked voids in its ancient fabric, the New Town thought it knew better. A reconnection had to be found between the Old and the New, between the memory of the dismantled wall, and the life around it, between the ancient and the modern.

Jury point of view … The project draws maximum advantage of a plot with a narrow geometry, difficult to work with.
It creates a dynamism by aligning four houses on the boulevard and withdrawing the last two houses to be aligned with the street. The scale of the six houses is in perfect harmony with existing buildings. Judicious work on space (full and empty), on the geometry of the houses and of the interstitial spaces. The original layout of housing frees up green privatized terraces…

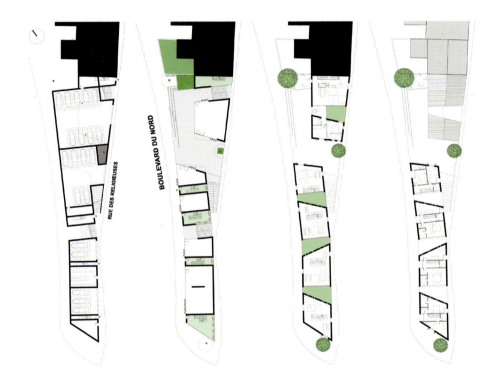

CONNECTIVITY
FROM BORDER TO SEAM

ALLERØD
(DK)

146

ALLERØD, LILLERØD-BLOVSTRØD DISTRICT
POPULATION: ALLERØD (24,000 INHAB.), BLOVSTRØD (2,700 INHAB.), LILLERØD (16,200 INHAB.)
STRATEGIC AREA: 300 HA
PROJECT AREA: 50 HA
SITE PROPOSED BY: MUNICIPALITY OF ALLERØD
SITE OWNER: MUNICIPALITY OF ALLERØD, PRIVATE OWNERS

New surroundings for suburban life
Like many other suburban municipalities in Denmark, Allerød experienced explosive urban growth in the 1960s and 1970s, when districts of detached houses took a firm hold on the open landscapes around the capital city. Allerød is now looking for a visionary master plan for a contemporary residential district in the suburb, where living sustainably is a natural part of everyday life. Plans for the dense suburb should not impair the qualities of the villa district and should integrate sports, existing companies, nature and landscape in the experience of the district. The challenge lies in creating links to and cohesion with existing districts (Lillerød town centre and Blovstrød), structures and functions and the surrounding natural environment.

JENNIFER GOMES (PT)
RAQUEL VIULA (PT)
ARCHITECTS

JORGE GIL (PT)
LEE HWA-SEOP (KR)
LAIA MULET (ES)
SEBASTIEN MULLER (PT)
SUSANA OLIVEIRA (PT)
ARCHITECTS

RUNNER-UP

EUROPEAN RESULTS
FROM BORDER TO SEAM

ALLERØD (DK)

Nest

Team point of view The Nest is a place for nature and nurture. It creates a green, diverse and accessible environment for the future inhabitants of Ny Blovstrød. It extends Blovstrød by linking directly to the existing street system and provides connections to the surrounding forests. The scenic ring connects to the local landscape while the fast ring offers an alternative route for regional connections. The green belt brings existing woodland into the site, providing shelter and biomass for heating. Its open space is devoted to sports activities, private and communal allotments and meeting places. Building siting and massing follow the need for daylight and solar access, and the housing typologies for each population group are distributed to cater for everyday needs within walking distance.

Jury point of view The jury appreciates the well presented diagrams showing the overall strategies for the site. This network of strategies offers a thorough set of answers to the requirement of the brief for ways of connecting the new settlement of the site with existing settlements. This entry's intertwined structures based on functionality and programme make a convincing bid for the creation of a lively public and semi-public space in which paths, squares, greens and other meeting places can complement and enhance one another…

Linked with the article *Rhythms and timeframes*, p. 269

EUROPEAN RESULTS
FROM BORDER TO SEAM

ALLERØD (DK)

★ WINNER

EYRÚN MARGRET STEFANSDOTTIR (IS)
METTE BLANKENBERG (DK)
ARCHITECTS

148

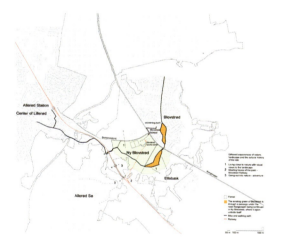

section A-A

When Nature Interferes with Everyday Life

Team point of view The new development is a link between two existing suburban areas in Allerød. It creates an urban band that binds the city together.
In complement with the existing topography, 600 new dwellings are constructed so that settlement and landscape are woven together. The landscape seeps between housing and public squares, and close attention is paid to nature, through sustainable and structuring elements such as rainwater collection basins, solar cell farms, shared gardens, orchards and waste sorting stations. Collective practices create interactivity between people and offer a glimpse of future ways of living. Ny Blovstrød differs from Blovstrød's existing structure of detached houses with private gardens, adding a greater social mix with different lifestyle aspirations.

Jury point of view The jury has singled out this proposal as the best suited for further development. The integration of new dwellings with a public landscape, driven by sustainable collective practices provides a strong vision for the development of Ny Blovstrød while at the same time improving the connections between Blovstrød and Lillerød. In particular, the use of rainwater management seems a convincing strategy for utilising the existing landscape and stimulating sustainable lifestyles…

Linked with the article *Common resources and mutation*, p 263

CONNECTIVITY
FROM BORDER TO SEAM

SAN BARTOLOMÉ
(ES)

150

SAN BARTOLOMÉ (LANZAROTE ISLAND)
POPULATION: 18,517 INHAB.
STRATEGIC AREA: 50.17 HA
PROJECT AREA: 9.45 HA
SITE PROPOSED BY: CITY OF SAN BARTOLOMÉ AND CANARY ISLAND REGIONAL GOVERNMENT
SITE OWNER: CITY COUNCIL 77.15%; THE REST, PRIVATE

From city to landscape

The goal is to develop quality public housing in a rural setting declared as a UNESCO Biosphere Reserve. Once Sector Nº 2 is urbanized, public initiative social housing and public amenities will be built alongside the green zone structure. This initiative will bring major improvements to San Bartolomé. Special attention should be paid to the treatment of the transition between the urban and the natural environments, between public, private and communal spaces, in which the design of the green zone is regarded as the main focus of the proposals. Also important are the number of housing units proposed and the design of the areas between housing, inside the plots and relative to the surrounding green public areas.

RUBÉN RAMOS JIMÉNEZ (ES)
HÉCTOR SALCEDO GARCÍA (ES)
ARCHITECTS

JOSÉ JAVIER RODRÍGUEZ BARBUDO (ES)
ARCHITECT

RUNNER-UP

EUROPEAN RESULTS
FROM BORDER TO SEAM

SAN BARTOLOMÉ (ES)

Topographic activity

Team point of view Proposed intervention strategies are developed in an integrated manner as a set of linked scenarios, creating an urban tapestry of resources connected by four specific circuits that ensure efficient access from the town of San Bartolomé to the new development north of town.
In this system we distinguish four main elements:
1. Nodes, as common scenarios of shared resources
2. Drifts, as specific connection circuits
3. Core, consisting of new sports facilities
4. Doors, hooked small-scale urban spaces connecting with the town centre
It operates as a stimulus to new activities, and as a link with the surrounding landscape, integrating needed residential and amenity uses in a topographic solution, which creates an ecosystem midway between urban park and agricultural tradition.

Jury point of view *Activated Topography* was appreciated by the Jury because of the suggestive strategy to colonize the land on the basis of the relationship between the topography and the surrounding natural ecosystem, the urban programmes and the new flows of citizens. The trigger for this operation is an interesting public park that spreads across the whole area containing the urban programmes in special conditions…

EUROPEAN RESULTS
FROM BORDER TO SEAM

★ WINNER

SAN BARTOLOMÉ (ES)

PALOMA BAQUERO MASATS (ES)
JAVIER CASTELLANO PULIDO (ES)
TOMÁS GARCÍA PÍRIZ (ES)
LUIS MIGUEL RUIZ AVILÉS (ES)
JUAN ANTONIO SERRANO GARCÍA (ES)
ARCHITECTS

JUAN BACHS RUBIO (ES)
ALEJANDRO CARLOS GALINDO DURÁN (ES)
CRISTÓBAL ADRIÁN GARCÍA ALMEIDA (ES)
JOSÉ ENRIQUE INIESTA MOLINA (ES)
MARÍA DE LARA RUIZ (ES)
ALEJANDRO PEDRO LÓPEZ FERNÁNDEZ (ES)
ELENA MARÍA LUCENA GUERRERO (ES)
ARCHITECTS

"Rurban" geology

Team point of view On the island of Lanzarote two forms of volcanic landscape transformation converge: the rhythm of the earth and the rhythm of human life. We can talk about the coexistence and overlap of changing processes that belong to different scales: the geological and the urban. Agriculture has turned people into powerful agents of the 'displacement of material', as powerful as the wind from which they protect themselves.
The project takes the idea of accumulating and overlapping layers in the landscape construction. We use a geological section from a site adjacent to our sector has a reference for the development of the proposal, planning a 'perforated basement' and an architecture that has the ability to recognise the strata in which it is inserted.
Several elements that structure the territory were found in the area: "low walls" that protect from the wind, sand barriers, cisterns for storing rainwater for irrigation, tanks for homes, etc. We consider these pre-existing elements valuable for the landscape development.

Jury point of view This interesting proposal relates the new architecture to the island's geological history and its agriculture-based land structure. The jury particularly appreciated the project's well-chosen solution for the new urban growth and its interface with the walls and the voids in the existing town centre. The proposed design is in continuity with San Bartolomé's urban fabric and identities...

Linked with the article *Cultural interferences*, p 256

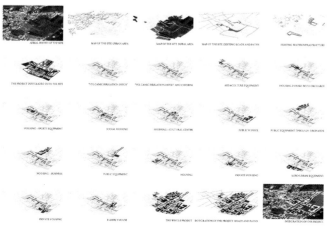

153

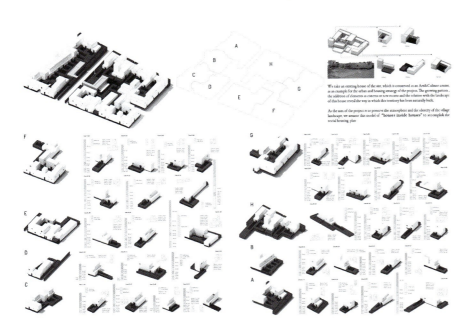

We take an existing house of the site, which is conserved as an Art&Culture center, as an example for the urban and housing strategy of the project. The growing pattern, the addition of elements as cisterns or new rooms and the relation with the landscape of this house reveal the way in which this territory has been naturally built.

As the aim of the project is to preserve the atmosphere and the identity of the village landscape, we assume this model of **"houses inside houses"** to accomplish the social housing plan

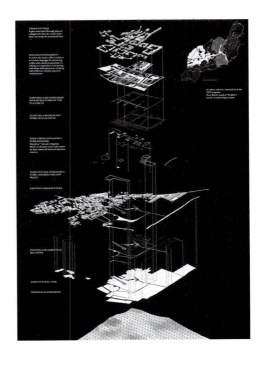

CONNECTIVITY
FROM BORDER TO SEAM

TOULOUSE
(FR)

154

TOULOUSE – LE RAISIN
POPULATION: 440,000 INHAB. (CITY);
703,000 INHAB. (CONURBATION)
STRATEGIC AREA: 26.5 HA
PROJECT AREA: 3.3 HA
SITE PROPOSED BY: CITY OF
TOULOUSE AND GREATER
TOULOUSE URBAN COMMUNITY
SITE OWNER: CITY OF TOULOUSE

Urban step between city and suburbs

Located at the heart of a disparate urban fabric, the Raisin Technical Centre, a site employed for the maintenance of vehicles and equipment used by the City the Greater Toulouse Urban Community, is going to be relocated. This is an opportunity to re-establish links between this area and the rest of the city, as part of a larger urban master plan including the nearby construction of a new urban hub associated with the arrival in 2020 of a high-speed railway line (LGV) at Toulouse – Matabiau. In the long run, there are 20 ha of land for potential development, offering the possibility of a profound change in the district's urban structure.

The goal, therefore, is to create a new urban nucleus beyond the canal du Midi and continuous with the suburbs, to coincide with the extension of Toulouse city centre.

LOIC BRENTERC'H (FR)
ARCHITECT URBAN PLANNER
ERWAN MARIN (FR)
ARCHITECT URBAN PLANNER,
LANDSCAPE ARCHITECT

NELLY BUSSAC (FR)
ARCHITECT URBAN PLANNER
GWENAËL MASSOT (FR)
ARCHITECT
THIBAUT STEPHAN (FR)
STUDENT IN GEOGRAPHY

RUNNER-UP

EUROPEAN RESULTS
FROM BORDER TO SEAM

TOULOUSE (FR)

The Meta-Block: a model from Toulouse

Team point of view The purpose of the meta-block is to extend and redefine the historical city way of life. The inhabitant's habits and living visions have changed but they still need to feel the cultural vibes from Toulouse. The meta-block can be defined as a contemporary mutation of the traditional block from Toulouse. The architectural composition is taking its source from the existing urban context. We have searched for an architecture from Toulouse that is responding to our actual living values. Our approach is to be able to qualify it, name it, and give it a justified belonging. At the garden side, the meta-block is allowing an abundant natural light to come in every flat; it also offers large terraces, a double orientation, and private/shared gardens. The green and built networks are overlapping each other to become one.

Jury point of view This project cleverly revisits the typologies of housing in Toulouse, proposing a new typology simultaneously capable of following a street line, providing building flexibility within blocks and allowing a great diversity of architectural styles… It opens up the site by a network of walking and cycling routes, by overhead bridges and by a series of connections to the surrounding urban fabric…

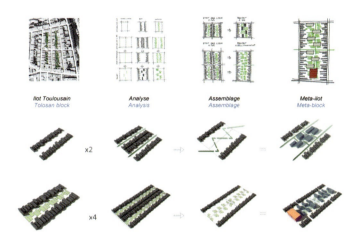

EUROPEAN RESULTS
FROM BORDER TO SEAM
TOULOUSE (FR)

★ WINNER

ESTELLE BOURREAU (FR)
JEAN-BAPTISTE COLTIER (FR)
AURÉLIE FABRE (FR)
ARCHITECTS

156

Poetry of the random

Team point of view The site is enclosed between the canal and the railway lines. Our project reconnects it to the city by means of structuring elements that organise the space and make it attractive: the Mall, the Platform, the Hall, the Concourse, the Meadow, the Neighbourhood. The project is to be understood as a new urban landscape inspired by the elements that give old Toulouse its identity. Starting with a rigourous framework, we organise the district rationally, then we introduce a fragmentation that generates a variety of urban events. Each block obeys the same principles, resulting in the formation of a considered and felt randomness. The deformation emerges from within, opening up spaces in which activities can take place. Linearity is maintained on the block's exterior, to make the site more permeable. Our aim is to promote the unexpected, create a poetry of place and pleasure in moving through the city.

Jury point of view This project has the capacity to connect the existing infrastructures together with great clarity. The introduction of a multi-programme building along the tracks has the effect of integrating the footprint of the railway into the urban landscape, rather than resisting it. The decision to use empty space to structure the different scales present on the site leads to the creation of a metropolitan scale public space that opens up the site through walking and cycling routes…

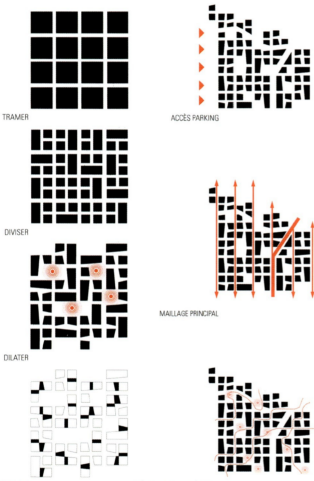

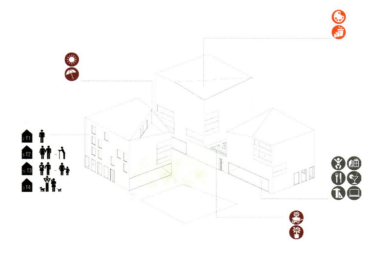

CONNECTIVITY
FROM BORDER TO SEAM

TURKU
(FI)

158

TURKU - HARITTU
POPULATION: 177,000 INHAB.
STRATEGIC AREA: 32.5 HA
PROJECT AREA: 9.5 HA
SITE PROPOSED BY: CITY OF TURKU
SITE OWNER: CITY OF TURKU, TURKU AND KAARINA PARISH UNION

Sustainable family housing area on the edge of the city

The site is located on the city boundary of Turku (around 4 kilometres from the centre) and it is the first uniform area when approaching the city from the east. The empty wasteland is situated adjacent to the old Helsinki–Turku highway. On the other side of the highway a new city district, called Skanssi, is currently being built. As a part of that construction, a new roundabout will be placed next to the competition site.

The aim is to build a dense, lowrise residential area with a distinct human scale. The new area should be safe, pleasant, and suitable for young families. Part of the site will function as a shared outdoor living area for people of all ages. The plan should support a sense of community, between both neighbours and all residents in the area. The area should be given a distinctive look and character.

MARK BALZAR (AT) **PETER STEC** (SK) ARCHITECTS	ANNA CSÉFALVAYOVÁ (SK) MARIANNA MACZOVÁ (SK) DOMINIKA BELANSKÁ (SK) DANICA PIŠTEKOVÁ (SK) STUDENTS IN ARCHITECTURE	RUNNER-UP	EUROPEAN RESULTS **FROM BORDER TO SEAM** TURKU (FI)

Orchard Avenues

Team point of view The landscape boundary is evolving. The shift from the hard compact wall of fortified cities to the infinite blurred contour of sprawl reflects centuries of social change. After the mostly unattainable vision of Garden Cities, we follow the emergence of a more specific goal: living on the edge between complex built areas and rich ecosystems. In geometrical terms: a dense and limited urban area, with an infinite boundary to landscape.

For Turku, we envision such a boundary by proposing to pull both the surrounding landscape and the urban pockets into the site. These areas never intersect. But we carefully extend and design their interface, creating a blurred transition from one to the other. On one side are the continuously branching corridors of vegetation: the Orchard Avenues. In a reversal, the other side becomes access: the Urban Courts. In between, a gradient of house types creates a visually permeable membrane.

Jury point of view As an idea the proposal is fun and unique. The logic of the suburb has been turned on its head: what looks like the street is in fact a garden. The plantings and small gardens form green corridors between the blocks of detached houses and cars are placed in the rear yards of the spaciously designed blocks. The proposal also raises questions about how the maintenance of the green strips would work in practice…

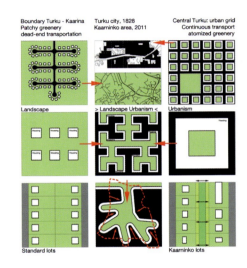

EUROPEAN RESULTS	★ WINNER	SAMI VIKSTRÖM (FI)
FROM BORDER TO SEAM		ARCHITECT
TURKU (FI)		

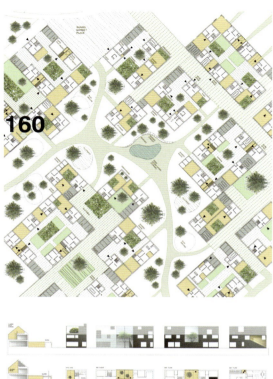

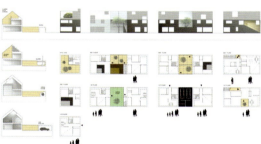

Garden state

Team point of view The aim was to create a stronger sense of community than that of the existing town structure. It proved necessary to take a look back to the old Finnish tradition of organizing small houses around a courtyard. Shared multifunctional outdoor spaces create a sense of attachment to a context that is larger than the house itself. The spatial solution is arranged as a fractal structure that forms a gradual transition from public to private. The concept of reconnection is thus approached by multilayered states of privacy that enable people of different backgrounds to interact in richer and more unexpected ways than usually possible. The result is a housing area that is both rural and urban: urban in its density and clear spatial hierarchy, rural in its immediate relation to the surrounding nature.

Jury point of view The proposal is, despite an apparent ordinariness, exceptionally interesting. It establishes a good starting point to study further how social and economic sustainability could be incorporated as part of the residential environment of the future. Garden State is the contemporised version of the Garden City, which opens up completely new dimensions for the suburb and dense and low-rise building…

Linked with the article *Cultural interferences*, p 256

161

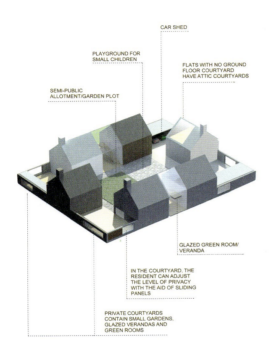

- SEMI-PUBLIC ALLOTMENT/GARDEN PLOT
- PLAYGROUND FOR SMALL CHILDREN
- CAR SHED
- FLATS WITH NO GROUND FLOOR COURTYARD HAVE ATTIC COURTYARDS
- GLAZED GREEN ROOM/VERANDA
- IN THE COURTYARD, THE RESIDENT CAN ADJUST THE LEVEL OF PRIVACY WITH THE AID OF SLIDING PANELS
- PRIVATE COURTYARDS CONTAIN SMALL GARDENS, GLAZED VERANDAS AND GREEN ROOMS

CONNECTIVITY
FROM VOID TO LINK

HAUGESUND
(NO)

162

HAUGESUND - FLOTMYR
POPULATION: 34,500 INHAB. 150,000 (HAUGALAND REGION)
STRATEGIC AREA: 99.2 HA
PROJECT AREA: 8.4 HA
SITE PROPOSED BY: MUNICIPALITY OF HAUGESUND
SITE OWNER: MUNICIPALITY OF HAUGESUND

From urban void to gateway

Flotmyr, as a void, provides a field of possibilities to strengthen Haugesund's position as the regional centre, as well as its future contribution to the development of Haugesund's Historic Centre. Maintaining flexibility to accommodate various future urban developments at Flotmyr is a crucial part of the planning. Five areas of investigation are outlined in the programme: public spaces, high density, innovative transportation, diversity and an integrated city. The brief is to design a robust urban structure from which the new Flotmyr can develop.

GONZALO COELLO DE PORTUGAL (ES)
MARTA GRANDA NISTAL (ES)
ARCHITECTS

ANA MORIYON (ES)
STUDENT IN ARCHITECTURE

RUNNER-UP

EUROPEAN RESULTS
FROM VOID TO LINK

HAUGESUND (NO)

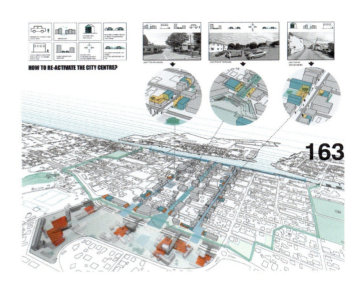

Hip-hubs

Team point of view Hip-Hubs proposes connection through reactivation through the following staged strategies from 2012 until 2030:
- Reinforcement of connective East-West routes: new commons of activity will reconnect Flotmyr with the seafront, with a network of public spaces bridging a high-speed Flotmyr traffic by-pass that will restore the Street as a place for play and social interactions
- Zip-ring around the city-centre: the network of different derelict sites will become a coherent public space where green events will unfold along 3.5km
- Consolidation of the urban fabric, the Hip-Hub strategy: a Hip-Hub is a spatial connection device, a unit that combines a building with a sheltered space around it. It generates different growth and organises various uses around itself.

Jury point of view The Jury appreciates the way this proposal addresses not only new development within the bounded site of Flotmyr, but also the relationship of the site to the city centre as a key aspect in its revitalization. The scheme proposes weaving existing leftover urban spaces into a green ring supporting expanded formats of mobility within the city. Also appreciated is the way the project considers the factor of time as a key aspect of the development…

Linked with the article *Linking with uses*, p. 249

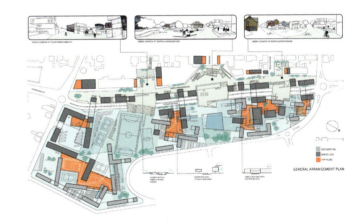

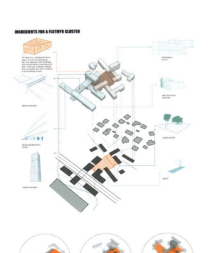

EUROPEAN RESULTS
FROM VOID TO LINK

HAUGESUND (NO)

RUNNER-UP

KATJA ENGEL ZEPERNICK (DK)
ANETT GRØNNERN OLSEN (NO)
URBAN PLANNERS
MERETE KINNERUP ANDERSEN (DK)
JONAS ROAR HANSEN (DK)
ARCHITECTS

Flotmyr is back on the postcard

Team point of view Flotmyr currently has the character of a "non-place" in terms of the use of the area and its effect as a barrier. Conversely, Flotmyr has great potential for redevelopment because of its attractive location between the historic downtown, the residential area and the Stadium. Flotmyr can therefore change from a neglected "non-place" to a place that attracts people.
The project relinks the city in a new way with physical connections and attractive functions, at the same time as harmonising it with its surroundings with a variation of typology and scale.
Flotmyr will be a place where people can live with easy access to green areas, physical and cultural activities and in close proximity to the city centre. For people outside, it will be a place they look forward to visiting as an experience of a lively city. Flotmyr will function as a modern hub where connections are clear and accessibility is high.

Jury point of view The design offers a sensitive mediation between the denser urban grid of the historical centre and the lower density residential fabric to the east and south of the site. The scale and typological diversity of the project is appropriate and integrated with the surrounding context while at the same time potentially structuring an urban experience…

Linked with the article *Reshaping shared spaces*, p. 242

CERDANYOLA DEL VALLÈS
(ES)

CONNECTIVITY
FROM VOID TO LINK

165

Residential technology park

The study zone is in the north eastern corner of a 340 ha urban area called "Parc de l'Alba", wich is just a few kilometres from Barcelona city, in the Cerdanyola del Vallès municipality. The envisaged transformation in this sector covers four major areas: a science, technology and business park, including the Alba synchrotron, a sustainable residential district with 3,500 new homes, a 140 ha green corridor that is more than 1km wide, and a transport interchange. The purpose is to develop a new residential sector in response to –and in congruence with- the housing needs generated by the technological development underway in "Parc de l'Alba" and the Autonomous University of Barcelona (UAB).

CERDANYOLA DEL VALLÈS - PARC DE L'ALBA
POPULATION: 58,747 INHAB.
STRATEGIC AREA: 29.7 HA
PROJECT AREA: 3.3 HA
SITE PROPOSED BY: CATALONIA REGIONAL GOVERNMENT
SITE OWNER: PUBLIC CONSORTIUM

EUROPEAN RESULTS
FROM VOID TO LINK
★ WINNER

CERDANYOLA DEL VALLÈS (ES)

JOSEP FERRANDO (ES)
MARC NADAL (ES)
DAVID RECIO (ES)
ARCHITECTS

ANNE-LISE ROUSSAT (FR)
JORDI PÉREZ (ES)
BORJA RODRÍGUEZ (ES)
STUDENTS IN ARCHITECTURE

166

Blat

Team point of view The proposal seeks to leave the smallest footprint possible in its context, so that the memory of golden tones moving with the breeze is maintained as a foreground to the views to the village.

The proposal aims to colonise the place through its geometry, becoming a footprint that mirrors the heterogeneity of the features that imbue the place. The plan blurs the boundaries of the property with the aim of building a village that rises like a "Kasbah". This aggregation system allows great flexibility. The system, where a bed or a table can be placed interchangeably in different cells, helps us recognize the capacity of the space prior to specialization.

The proposal works on the hierarchy of spaces, promoting the spaces intermediary to the dialogue between public and private. The emphasis on the ratio of full to empty seeks to enhance the continuity of the natural landscape and make the proposal part of this, with the aim of finding a balance between living, socializing and working.

Jury point of view This project proposes the installation of the same large construction in different positions to generate the city, building low-cost public spaces that leave a minimal footprint in the context and a recollection of its previous aspect. The volume organisation around courtyards that are linked to the outside via large fissures produces an extremely efficient aggregation system… Proposal of a rich variety of communal areas and room types…

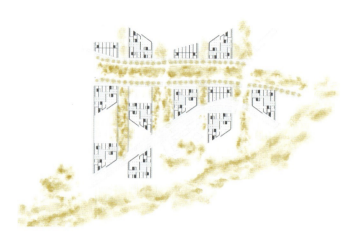

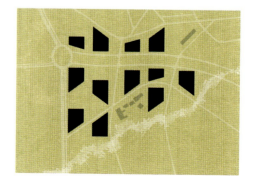

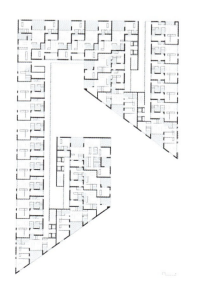

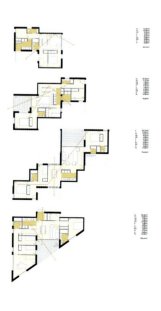

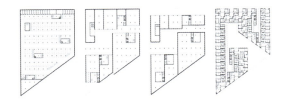

167

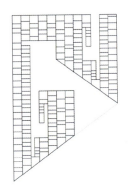  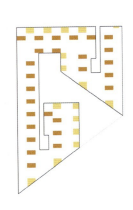 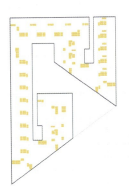

EUROPEAN RESULTS
FROM VOID TO LINK

RUNNER-UP

JAVIER FERNÁNDEZ CONTRERAS (ES)
DINGTING CHEN (CN)
ARCHITECTS

CERDANYOLA DEL VALLÈS (ES)

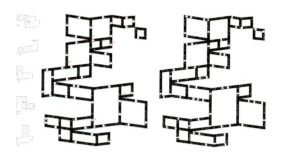

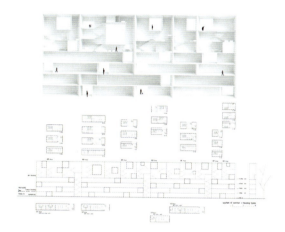

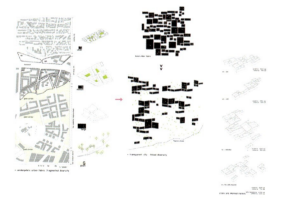

The transparent city

Team point of view The idea of Reconnection in architecture undoubtedly has to do with generating the optimum conditions for different identities to coexist and find their own place in the contemporary city.
Our proposal is simple: different blocks of different sizes give shape to different scales of public space, as to sue people's differing preferences. The multi-scalarity so generated will be simultaneously perceptible from any side of the project, so that intimacy and human interaction will coexist at the same place.
We propose to make the blocks simultaneously dense and transparent, and to do so, we have reduced the bay to 5m, so that the blocks can literally be seen as *inhabited walls*. We have grouped them in clusters that maximize the number of individual houses and creates successive layers of urban landscape. We have perforated the blocks with a profuse kaleidoscope of voids, which provide cross-views and light.
The resulting blocks have been compacted and skewed in a movement that creates cosy patios and generous open spaces. The heterogeneous voids will allow successive layers of buildings, open spaces and nature to be seen at a glance.

Jury point of view A proposal for an estate midway between a closed and a linear block design generates an urban fabric with a wealth of interconnected public spaces, both outside the building and in the courtyards, drawing a highly evocative overlapped outline and enriching the town plan's proposed street grid. By this means, the void configures the architecture, which takes the form of a narrow corridor that bends and creates courtyards of different sizes, resulting in a single large-scale building...

Linked with the article *Reshaping shared spaces*, p. 242

GETARIA
(ES)

169

Looking at the mouse

The strategic area, Potzuaga-gaina, is an allotment south of the urban area of Getaria, set on a hillside that drops towards the town centre and the sea. It is now an independent urban sector that has been zoned entirely as residential land. The aim is to respond to the municipality's housing demand by proposing a new type of residential development overlooking the sea, in continuity with the consolidated urban area.

Proposals should tackle the issue of integrating the new buildings into the landscape, especially in the area near the cemetery. They should also provide an appropriate solution for the connection to the town, and resolve the transition into the countryside, without restricting the possibility of future developments on the hillside.

GETARIA - A.U XVIII_POTZUAGA-GAINA
POPULATION: 2,628 INHAB.
STRATEGIC AREA: 28 HA
PROJECT AREA: 2.85 HA
SITE PROPOSED BY: BASQUE GOVERNMENT, GETARIA MUNICIPAL COUNCIL
SITE OWNER: DIFFERENT OWNERS

CONNECTIVITY
FROM VOID TO LINK

EUROPEAN RESULTS
FROM VOID TO LINK

GETARIA (ES)

★ WINNER

JOSE MANUEL CALVO DEL OLMO (ES)
GUILLERMO GOSALBO GUENOT (ES)
JOSÉ LÓPEZ PARRA (ES)
ARCHITECTS

ESTHER MUÑOZ MARTÍNEZ (ES)
PHOTOGRAPHER
ANA PAGÁN APARICIO (ES)
GRAPHIC DESIGNER

170

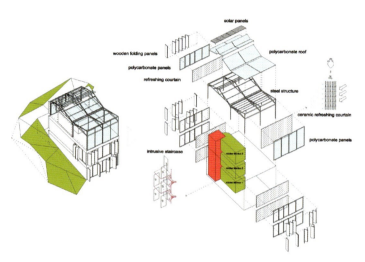

The intrusive stairs

Team point of view We began by saying: "Getaria is a place that has urbanized its landscape by proposing a cross-connectivity full of sidewalks and cars, because of its topography. What happens if the transversality makes use of the territory?"
Tourism is an important aspect too. What can we do? We can work through two identities: Getaria's territory and its economy.

Jury point of view This proposal achieves a difficult balance providing answers for the questions raised in the competition and also for the issues self-generated by the project itself… The land use strategy… proposes an "urban" scenario in which the very existence as well as the qualities of the public realm, emerging from the dialogue between the blocks, guarantees the most valuable aspect of the urban phenomenon, while allowing a larger scale grouping of buildings to be inserted successfully into the local environment…

Linked with the article *Common resources and mutation*, p. 263

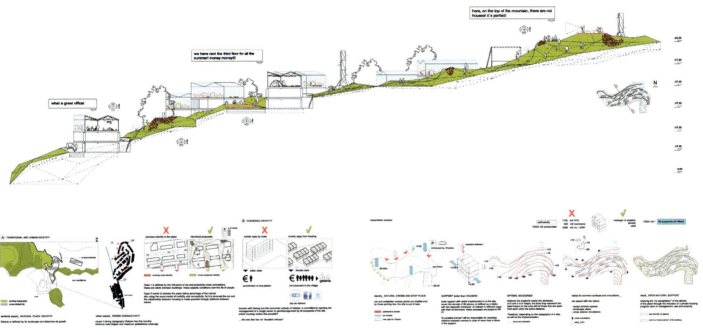

EUROPEAN RESULTS
FROM VOID TO LINK

GETARIA (ES)

RUNNER-UP

MARC BAJET MENA (ES)
ENGINEER
PAU BAJET MENA (ES)
OSCAR LINARES DE LA TORRE
(ES)
ARCHITECTS

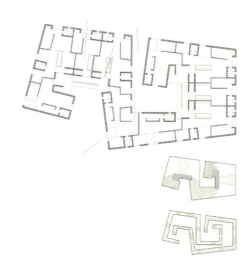

For Getaria and *of* Getaria

Team point of view A project in getaria and for getaria. The decisions taken for the formal solution of this project were characterized by constantly remembering the landscape, culture and architectural specifications of this remarkable enclave, Getaria. The project didn't spring suddenly from a sketch on paper, but from the detection of the needs of the situation and the programme, that generated certain inputs. This input, taken as a self-imposed law, has been the real driving force behind the project. In this way we have avoided making any planning decisions that would lead to an architecture that is out of context with the place, its people and its time. We have designed a project in Getaria, *for* Getaria and *of* Getaria.

Jury point of view This proposal opts for clustering and density, a solution that has yielded good results in the course of Europe's history, as part of its intention to preserve the local environment… The set of public spaces provided by this project is attractive and has great social potential, although the buildings are its least rich aspect.

NORRKÖPING
(SE)

CONNECTIVITY
FROM VOID TO LINK

NORRKÖPING - NORRA VRINNEVI
POPULATION: 130,000 INHAB.
STRATEGIC AREA: 140 HA
PROJECT AREA: 16 HA
SITE PROPOSED BY: MUNICIPALITY OF NORRKÖPING
SITE OWNER: MUNICIPALITY OF NORRKÖPING

Integrating the suburban landscape

Vilbergen in the northwest of the site is a neighbourhood developed in the mid-1970s. It is a ring shaped area with a park and community centre in the middle, providing the local inhabitants with recreation, service and shopping possibilities. The area is inward facing and slightly disconnected from the city. The oversized road Gamla Övägen, east of Vilbergen, cuts through the site and creates a strong barrier to the Vrinneviskogen nature reserve. To the south, at the edge of the city, the hospital is an isolated compound, a safe distance from its surroundings.

The main task is to redevelop the amorphous area around the Gamla Övägen road and create a new built landscape with mainly residential buildings, which creates connections and enhances continuity on different scales, both linking with the inner city and binding the isolated fragments.

EUROPEAN RESULTS
FROM VOID TO LINK

NORRKÖPING (SE)

★ WINNER

PELLE BACKMAN (SE)
EBBA HALLIN (SE)
ARCHITECTS

174

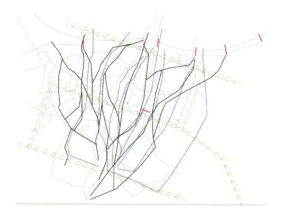

Delta-X

Team point of view SLY *is a Swedish word. It means young trees without economic value.* SLY *is whatever grows when you're not looking, the first stage of a forest.* SLY *is slow-moving and ever-altering.*

Any path may lead from a to b, but within a city this may be its least important role. The delta principle is about spreading all flows.

Three SLY axes penetrate the area. Existing streets and paths and new connections form a mesh of mixed traffic. Everything else is divided into hundreds of new lots for sale, lease or rent. Unused property will be overgrown with SLY – the rest with constructions and activities.

The plan questions the value of aiming for a finished state and encourages people to make a mark on the city. It is engineered to germinate the unexpected. The main product is active participation.

Jury point of view This project is provocative and sophisticated… raising political, ethical and architectural questions while offering a plausible planning strategy and suggestions of real talent in landscape design… It questioned the consolidation of large city periphery sites into single ownership, and its critique had real power, suggesting a flexible, even anarchic, method of dividing the area into plots, and encouraging a participatory process…

Linked with the article *Rhythms and timeframes*, p. 269

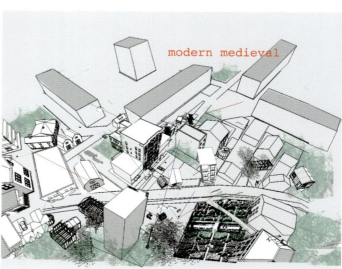

175

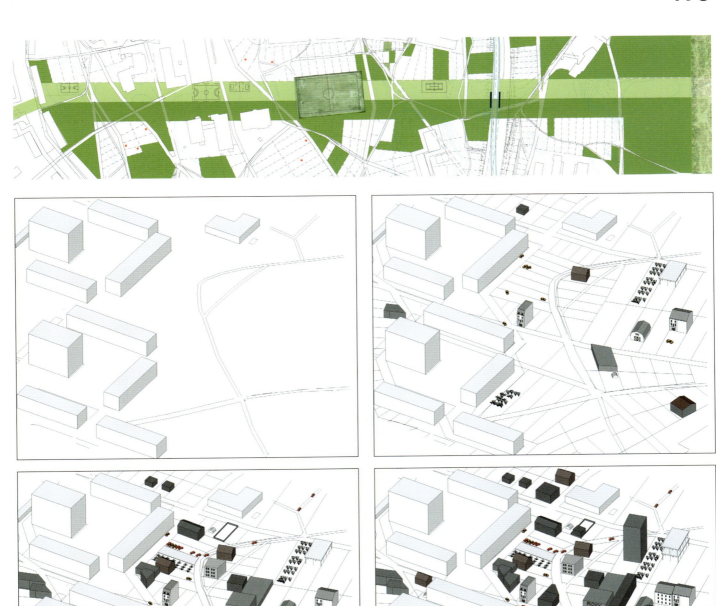

EUROPEAN RESULTS
FROM VOID TO LINK

NORRKÖPING (SE)

RUNNER-UP

MICHAL BERNART (CZ)
GILLES BERRINO (IT)
GIORGIA DE CASTRO (IT)
RENÉ DLESK (SK)
DEBORA MAGRI (IT)
VITO MARCO MARINACCIO (IT)
FRANCESCA MAZZIOTTI (IT)
MICHELE MORRONE (IT)
ROY EMILIANO NASH (IT)
MATTEO PARINI (IT)
PAOLO FILIPPO PELANDA (IT)
CESARE VENTURA (IT)
ARCHITECTS

VALENTINA CHIAPPA NUNEZ (IT)
MARTA PARINI (IT)
MARCELLO SCARAVELLA (IT)
LUCA DE STASIO (IT)
BARBARA VALENTINI (IT)
STUDENTS IN ARCHITECTURE

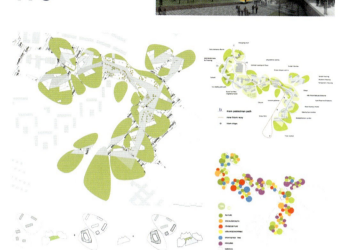

Synapcity

Team point of view The design in a low-density area, divided by the physical and mental barrier formed by the main road, tries to create a generative method of transformation.
The new "cellular urban development" based on factors such as proximity, sustainability and connection aims to produce a certain degree of connectivity starting from the cell, basic unit of the regeneration process. The "space in between" cells generates a continuous deformation and mutation of the master plan, due to programmatic, morphological and topographical factors, in order to achieve flexibility in 'change of use' within short and long time periods. A thick new multifunctional ground associated with a generic and flexible network are the new urban "glue", that allows the flexible use of space and gives the opportunity to adapt different typologies of buildings.

Jury point of view This project had many elements that the jury found intriguing and fruitful to discuss, suggesting new housing typologies that question orthodox development models for suburban contexts, while trying to be in tune with the scale and character of the natural landscape nearby...

Linked with the article *Reshaping shared spaces*, p 242

SAVENAY
(FR)

CONNECTIVITY
FROM PLACE TO TERRITORY

177

"Station-town", secondary eco-city nucleus

Savenay is recognised as the structural centre of the Nantes/Saint Nazaire eco-metropolis. This makes the town a prime location for housing, shops and services. With the advantage of the station, the Acacias business zone, which backs onto the south side of the railway lines and is of poor urban quality and hard put to develop, can become a genuine urban district. With a total area of 40 ha, it will eventually accommodate 1000 dwellings, i.e. 2500 people, shops, services, offices and crafts.
The primary objective of the project is to devise new urban forms for a "station district village"

SAVENAY - LA GARE
POPULATION: 7,000 INHAB. (CITY);
21,000 INHAB. (CONURBATION);
800,000 INHAB. (METROPOLIS)
STRATEGIC AREA: 59 HA
PROJECT AREA: 3.3 HA
SITE PROPOSED BY: SCOT DE LA MÉTROPOLE NANTES SAINT NAZAIRE, COMMUNAUTÉ DE COMMUNES LOIRE ET SILLON, CITY OF SAVENAY
SITE OWNER: COMMUNAUTÉ DE COMMUNES LOIRE ET SILLON

EUROPEAN RESULTS
FROM PLACE TO TERRITORY
SAVENAY (FR)

RUNNER-UP

LIONEL ROULLET (FR)
MATTHIEU THUILLIER (FR)
ARCHITECTS

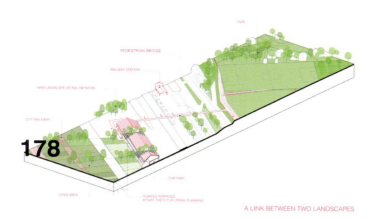

A LINK BETWEEN TWO LANDSCAPES

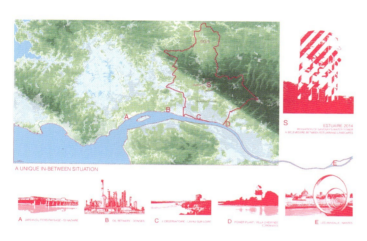

A UNIQUE IN-BETWEEN SITUATION

SB \ SH

Team point of view Away from the site, the purpose of the refurbishment of the water tower as a viewpoint is to integrate Savenay within the cultural landscape of the Nantes-St Nazaire eco-city, and to highlight the exceptional interstitial location the town enjoys.

The bridge creates a physical link, a connection between hills and plain, between the Sillon de Bretagne and the estuary marshlands. It spans the re-natured rail network, which becomes an inaccessible park, an empty space that structures and closes the loop of large infrastructures around the town. At one end, extending from a former railway hall, a long multipurpose building, interspersed with terraces, begins the formation of the future neighbourhood. It is structured to promote links between the station and the pastures to the south, and new buildings consonant with the scale of the town.

Jury point of view The Jury recognises the relevance of this project from a strategic and territorial perspective. Although this approach initially seems localised, it develops a certain effectiveness in its linear extension through an optimisation of uses around the station. With its proposal to base the development of the new district on the refurbishment of an existing building in the station hub, it ensures the integration of the new district into the surrounding fabric. Another strength of the proposal is that it casts a certain poetic light on the railway cluster…

URBANIZATION SCENARIOS

MAGNIFY EMPTYNESS
The rail network, a new structurating empty space

XIANG WANG (FR)
WENMU TIAN (CN)
ARCHITECTS

RAN SHE (CN)
CHENGMEI ZONG (CN)
ARCHITECTS

RUNNER-UP

EUROPEAN RESULTS
FROM PLACE TO TERRITORY

SAVENAY (FR)

Dock life

Team point of view The route from the city of Nantes to its outer harbour St. Nazaire passes through a landscape that has coherence and strong identity: wetlands close to the estuary, enlivened by moving trains.
Connecting a new district to this network first requires us to maintain this coherence of landscape at the metropolitan scale. The parallelism of the project embodies the movements and the long green strip sets off the "rural and urban waters". On a more local scale, reconnection takes the form of spatial continuity and the visual relationship with the existing city. The urban morphology is designed to reflect a humid environment. Just as the docks reach out to the sea, the platforms stretch out towards nature. Its aesthetic is simple and unique to the place: everything is designed with an eye to coexistence with the water.

Jury point of view The Jury was interested to see the establishment of a 'porous boundary' in the southern part of the site. This strip acts as an interface between the new district and the woodland, whilst bringing the inhabitants of Savenay a new set of uses… The jury also recognised the advantage of this proposal in terms of mobility and integration with the existing fabric. In addition, the project takes a subtle approach to the hydrological nature of the site…

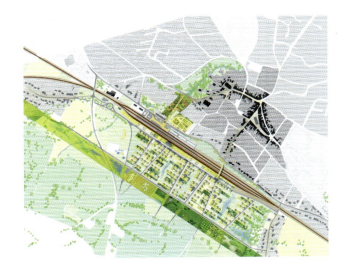

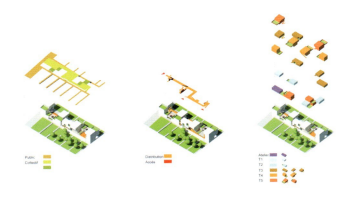

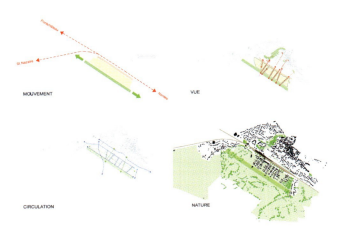

EUROPEAN RESULTS
FROM PLACE TO TERRITORY

SAVENAY (FR)

★ WINNER

THIBAULT BARBIER (FR)
LANDSCAPE ENGINEER
LAETITIA LAFONT (FR)
ARCHITECT

THE URBAN SCALE : THE TRAIN STATION QUARTER

Mesures ligériennes

Team point of view The "Mesures ligériennes" are introduced as "reconnection" tools witch are, mainly articulating the initial boundary with a territorial strategy. They are expressed as a "physical reconnection", a pedestrian bridge operating "cultural reconnection" between the north and south bank of the railway: built form, architecture, uses and programs in progress are inspired from the context and interact to write a common story, the story of Savenay and the ecocity. They propose new alliances and cohabitations with the plain's natural milieu, a hybrid landscape reinterpreting the hedge farmland's grid and the estuary's hydraulic system. They operate and link the economical procedures and the local constructive resources in order to create "reconnections" for a specific way of development, "ligérienne".

Jury point of view The project is remarkable for its mixed strategy of sparing interventions and economy of resources… which reflect the wish to develop Savenay from several connection points and not only from the new district… The Jury was interested to see the in-depth work encompassing all the problems of the site, notably with interventions in the old centre,… around the station and coinciding with the pedestrian crossing… and an interpretation of the plot structure and existing woodland that gives the project a landscape dimension…

Linked with the article *Common resources and mutation*, p. 263

THE TERRITORIAL SCALE : THE GEOLOGICAL LINE OF BRITTANNY

CONNECTIVITY
FROM PLACE TO TERRITORY

ALCORCÓN
(ES)

182

ALCORCÓN - MADRID
POPULATION: 180,000 INHAB.
STRATEGIC AREA: 70 HA
PROJECT AREA: 28 HA
SITE PROPOSED BY: ALCORCÓN CITY COUNCIL
SITE OWNER: DIFFERENT OWNERS

Recycling a connection space in Alcorcón
Alcorcón is a municipality in Madrid's first metropolitan ring, 14 km from the city centre. Current proposals envisage large-scale development for the northern zone of the municipality, which will be characterized by the recovery of the city's fractal geometry. This currently unplanned industrial zone acts as a hinge between the existing city of Alcorcón and the new district.
The aim of the project is to plan this zone so that it can be used as an interface between "the past and the future", enhancing the sense of connectivity between the two realities.

CRISTINA GOBERNA (ES)
URTZI GRAU (ES)
ARCHITECTS

RUNNER-UP

EUROPEAN RESULTS
FROM PLACE TO TERRITORY

ALCORCÓN (ES)

Roundabout Profilactics

Team point of view Europan 11's brief for the site *Alcorcón*, Spain entitled "Recycling a Connection Space in Alcorcón" identifies the wrong "deliance". The mix of industrial areas, agricultural terrain and empty lots surrounding *Cañada de Pozuelo* is a fantastic example of *terrain vague*. There is no need to reintegrate the site into the city. It is already part of it. Rather, location and existing conditions call for preservation – intensification even. Still, our proposal operates a "reconnection", a different one indeed. We leave the *terrain vague* almost untouched to highlight the link between *Alcorcón* and an overlooked public space often not identified as such. The preservation of the peripheral landscape entails the valorization of the informal leisure it hosts. Motocross, car 4x4, BMX, fireworks, paragliding, kite flying, paint-ball, bird watching, car-sex define types of socialization proper of big cities which paradoxically require vast non-urbanized contexts. We structure our proposal accordingly, moving from strategies of preservation of the *terrain vague* to the types of domesticity it entails, to a possible relation with the city that won't destroy its fragile qualities.

Jury point of view The project proposes a twofold strategy. Firstly, in the likely event that North Alcorcón is not developed, the project limits housing construction to the level of the existing industrial warehouse roofs, maintaining the landscape's potential intact. Secondly, in the unlikely scenario of North Alcorcón's development, the project will erect a barrier to growth in the manner of a prophylactic, protecting the site from the encroaching brick tide…

Linked with the article *Cultural interferences*, p. 256

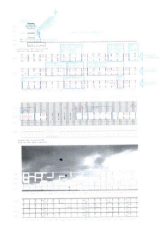

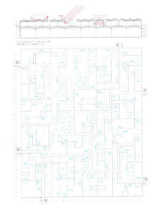

EUROPEAN RESULTS
FROM PLACE TO TERRITORY

ALCORCÓN (ES)

★ WINNER

DIEGO JIMÉNEZ LÓPEZ (ES)
JUANA SÁNCHEZ GÓMEZ (ES)
ARCHITECTS

GONZALO ROLDÁN ÁLVAREZ (ES)
ANTONIO JESÚS TORRES SÁNCHEZ (ES)
ARCHITECTS

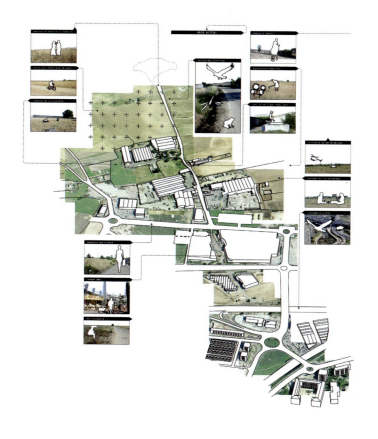

Arbolópolis

Team point of view Arbolópolis arises from a single strategy: the planting of a grove with multiple species as a tool to articulate urban, productive, environmental and recreational interests with a new landscape adjacent to the existing fabric.
We use the tree as an element (intuitively) linked to the predominant features of the landscape. The tree acts as a link with the future landscape and guarantees an urbanization process that maintains an ecological balance. Today the agricultural fabric is mixed with small industry or with urban symbols, such as the mall, or even with exotic elements like a small deer park. Looking ahead, management can create an irreversible urban planning process that would bring dramatic change and confront this unique eclecticism. The trees draw together and reconcile present and future because they are valid in both scenarios, whether North Alcorcón is kept as it is or developed.
Through its morphology, with different webs of density, the project recognizes the existing built elements and activity slows and makes its mark, giving it a heritage value. The temporality of the species used allows for the intrusion of future planning and their diversity reflects environmental conditions.

Jury point of view This project presents a unique tree planting strategy that has an open-ended timeframe and is valid in two alternative scenarios: whether the site is maintained as it is, or if North Alcorcón is developed. Besides being critical of the municipality's construction-focused intentions, this biological strategy works in a holistic way, given that it is able to articulate the interests of business, development and recreation…

Linked with the article *Rhythms and timeframes*, p 269

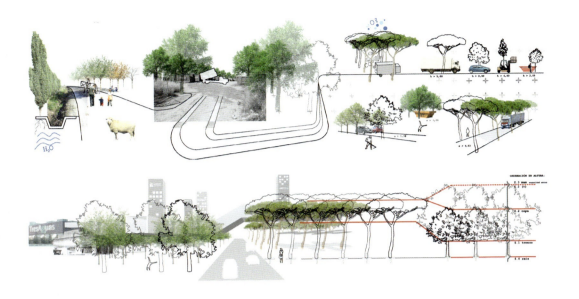

CONNECTIVITY
FROM PLACE TO TERRITORY

GUIMARÃES
(PT)

GUIMARÃES - SILVARES
POPULATION: 161,876 INHAB. (CITY),
1,016 INHAB. (CONURBATION)
STRATEGIC AREA: 154.30 HA
PROJECT AREA: 32.52 HA
SITE PROPOSED BY: GUIMARÃES MUNICIPALITY
SITE OWNER: PRIVATE OWNERS/ PUBLIC DOMAIN

Regenerating the qualities: a new centre

Given the city's growth towards its western boundaries in the direction of the River Ave, the municipality's urban development strategy is to create a large park in Veiga de Creixomil, to regenerate the main road infrastructures and to establish dedicated areas for economic activities that attract and help to retain people and assets. The brief is to regenerate the public space in the centre of the parish, strengthening community spirit and improving the centre's role as a social hub; to restructure the road network in the area, increasing discipline in the traffic entering and leaving the city and expanding traffic flow capacity; and to create an area strongly characterised by tertiary and commercial activities that complement those existing in the city centre. A green corridor is to be proposed, which will enhance the area and link it to the valley.

DANIEL DUARTE PEREIRA (PT)
FERNANDO FERREIRA (PT)
ARCHITECTS

GABRIELA SILVA (PT)
ARCHITECT
SARA FERREIRA (PT)
DANIEL MACEDO (PT)
STUDENTS IN ARCHITECTURE

RUNNER-UP

EUROPEAN RESULTS
FROM PLACE TO TERRITORY

GUIMARÃES (PT)

In between place's time

Team point of view We analyse the transformation over time of an infra-structured territory in Silvares, identifying distinct landscapes. We defined this area as a landscape of ruptures: in-between places.

The strategy of reconnection was developed by recognizing these ruptures as permanent to the site and elements of engagement over time. To this end, the project was structured in two closely connected time phases. In the first phase, a seeding structure is created that functions as a free-space with an uncertain programme.

The second stage tests the insertion of the required program over the seeding structure through flexible occupation, giving its owners the freedom to change to suit their needs.

To sum up, the project constitutes an open and flexible mechanism of transformation over time.

Jury point of view The suitability to the area characteristics is underlined (ownership structure, topography).

However, the proposal's positive aspects on a time-phased management are not translated into an overall strategic vision. The proposal is mostly based on separate projects (procedural flexibility)...

Pre-existing

1st STAGE
Seeding Structure

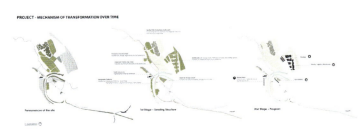
2nd STAGE
Program_Silvares Forum

EUROPEAN RESULTS
FROM PLACE TO TERRITORY

GUIMARÃES (PT)

★ WINNER

CÉDRIC-CLAUDE BOUTEILLER (FR)
FLORENT CHIAPPERO (FR)
MARIA JOÃO PITA (PT)
OLIVIER MÉNARD (FR)
PHILIPPE-SERGE SEPULVEDA (FR)
ARCHITECTS

188

270° Landscape, regeneration of an urban sequence

Team point of view The study area forms an urban sequence located at the articulation of networks and architectural typologies that belong to a wide range of scales. It is a highly contrasted zone, with an ambition to develop its industrial and commercial park while maintaining its local identity. In this area, different component of the landscape can be spotted, each with its own identity, but they do not interact today.
Our project aims to develop the dialogue between all the entities while affirming their singular character. We propose for each an appropriate tool. These tools are independent but can only operate in a system of relations. Together they form a complete project on which we based our proposal.

Jury point of view A well done analysis, understandable and useful for discussion and further development.
Approaches the question of centrality with both an attractive image and uses. The project gives meaning to the road structure and shows clear intentions, for example regarding central "boulevard" concerns, admitting flexible use by means of phased implementation.

Linked with the article *Linking with uses*, p.249

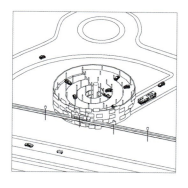
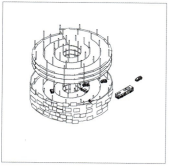
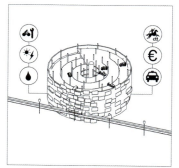
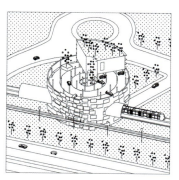
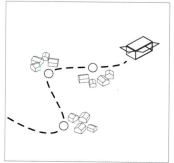
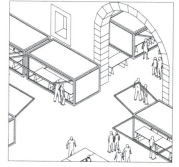

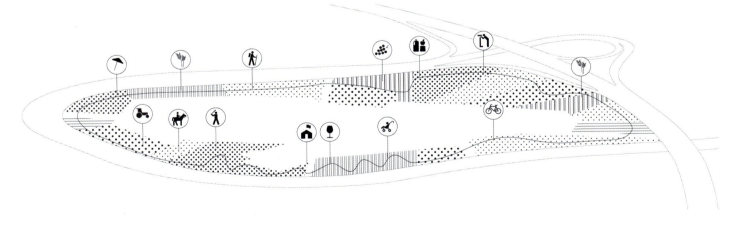

PARKING LOT | LEISURE ZONE | RING | CIVIC CENTRE | CEMETERY | FREGUESIA | NEW ACTIVITY ZONE | NEW RN206 | CURRENT ACTIVITY ZONE | CIRCULAR PARK | TOLL | FUTURE DEVELOPMENT ZONE

CONNECTIVITY
FROM PLACE TO TERRITORY

PORVOO
(FI)

190

PORVOO - HATTULA
POPULATION: 48,750 INHAB.
STRATEGIC AREA: 160 HA
PROJECT AREA: 82 HA
SITE PROPOSED BY: CITY OF PORVOO
SITE OWNER: CITY OF PORVOO AND A COUPLE OF PRIVATE

Developing an old industrial area into an attractive new city district
The site, previously an industrial area, is located northwest of the centre of Porvoo. The site is bounded by the Porvoonjoki river, Highway 7 and the surrounding neighbourhoods of detached houses. The site is part of the historic river landscape. On the opposite side of the river is the medieval centre of Porvoo. The project site is also connected to the national urban park. The aim is to develop the old industrial area into an attractive new neighbourhood that fits the surroundings and the unique tradition of the city. Special attention should be paid to the following three aspects: the scale of Porvoo, the industrial tradition of the area and the relation to the nature. The new functions in the area of the old railway station (protected) should maintain and develop the cultural history of the place.

LAURA HIETAKORPI (FI)
SAANA KARALA (FI)
JENNI POUTANEN (FI)
ARCHITECTS

RUNNER-UP

EUROPEAN RESULTS
FROM PLACE TO TERRITORY

PORVOO (FI)

Diamonds

Team point of view "Diamonds" creates new island-like urban structure within the natural elements. The urban qualities of Old Porvoo and the existing structure of the site are starting points for the new design.

Diamond shaped sub-areas offer waterfront-like living inland without actual canals. It also allows contact and views to the river and historical sites. The built areas are dense in order to establish urban structure within them and and a clearly defined contrast with the natural environment.

The diamonds have mixed functions, creating reconnection between people. There is a public functions building in every diamond for some shared functions. Within courtyards there are some smaller scale shared functions, which are an easy and low-key way to get to know the neighbourhood. Private and public space mix effortlessly.

Jury point of view Building has been concentrated in efficient block clusters – diamonds linked by a somewhat clumsily aligned street. Building has been divided up into appropriately sized areas that are perhaps slightly too similar in shape. Building becomes increasingly denser towards the city and the connection with the railway station milieu is natural…

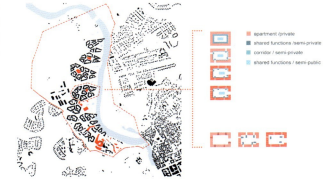

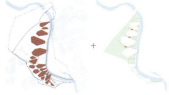

EUROPEAN RESULTS
FROM PLACE TO TERRITORY

PORVOO (FI)

★ WINNER

JOUNI HEINÄNEN (FI)
LANDSCAPE ARCHITECT
VALTTERI HEINONEN (FI)
PIA SJÖROOS (FI)
ARCHITECTS

Embroidery

Team point of view The project links the city structure west of the Porvoo River to the wider landscape and to the old city centre. The meandering composition maximises adhesion to the river and creates a series of varied riverside park spaces. The single main street is framed by solid and lively urban structure. Semi-open blocks on the riverside offer views to the river. The sensitive design approach, use of a dense and urban scale and the creation of a walkable environment links the project to the historic centre of Porvoo. The southernmost hotel and tourist area combined with the workplace area around the old railway station is the main connection to the old city centre and also to the history of the planning area. Perpendicular park axes and pedestrian bridges link the area with its surroundings.

Jury point of view ... The approach of Embroidery is strong and balanced and has focused on the central issues in regard to the design premise. The work is rich in ideas and well researched on many levels. The traffic solution it proposes functions well, and the relations between building and the landscape and the surrounding city are uncontrived ... The principles presented in the proposal are clear and flexible, providing a good premise for the further development of a unique and recognisable area.

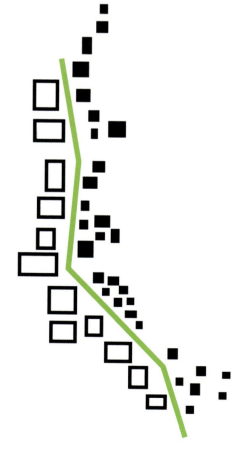

193

- ACTIVE PARK
- MEADOW PARK
- MAIN OPEN PARK SPACES
- LANDSCAPE FIELD
- ARABLE LAND
- OPEN PEDESTRIAN ENVIRONMENT AND THE SERIES OF SQAURES
- GREEN CONNECTIONS
- POTENTIAL GREEN CONNECTIONS

CONNECTIVITY
FROM PLACE TO TERRITORY

ROMAINMÔTIER
(CH)

194

ROMAINMÔTIER AND CROY –
LE VALLON DU NOZON
POPULATION: ROMAINMÔTIER 455
INHAB., CROY 318 INHAB.
STRATEGIC AREA: 500 HA (VALLON)
PROJECT AREA: 40 HA (CROY), 35 HA
(ENVY " SUR LE SIGNAL ")
SITE PROPOSED BY: MUNICIPALITIES
OF ROMAINMÔTIER AND CROY
SITE OWNER: MUNICIPALITIES,
PRIVATE OWNERS

Nozon Valley

Romainmôtier and Croy are located in a unique environment at the heart of the beautiful natural scenery of the "Vallon de Nozon" at the foot of the Jura. The two villages are easily accessible from the major urban centres of the Swiss Plateau. Romainmôtier is a protected medieval village known mainly for his Abbey. However, the attract on of Romainmôtier's heritage lasts only a few months in summer.

Croy stands at the interface of the public transport networks serving the "Vallon": the railway station and the regional bus lines. The municipal authorities of Croy and Romainmôtier want to boost the attractiveness of their villages and of the "Vallon de Nozon" with a sustainable and controlled urban development.

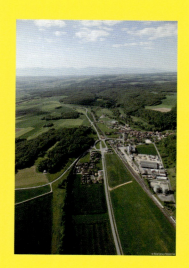

MOISÉS ROYO MÁRQUEZ (ES)
ARCHITECT

MARCOS GARCÍA BRAVO (ES)
JOAQUÍN RODRÍGUEZ PEÑA (ES)
ARCHITECTS
ANA JIMÉNEZ ROMERO (ES)
JAVIER ROMERO LOZANO (ES)
STUDENTS IN ARCHITECTURE

RUNNER-UP

EUROPEAN RESULTS
FROM PLACE TO TERRITORY

ROMAINMÔTIER (CH)

Terracement – Play Mobile

Team point of view The proposal generates new relations to the landscape, considered the most relevant element in the surroundings, instead of creating predictable links to the existing urban development. This will preserve the identity of the town, besides adding a layer of new ways of living and working around consolidated areas that will attract new residents. Both urban patterns will establish a fresh dialogue by juxtaposition.

The structure resolves three different categories: VERSALITY (the organization of cores established a new morphology of expressive space); the capacity to bring about ALTERATION of surroundings (re-ordering; re-solutions; re-use); and ADAPTATION to all type of users through the development of furnishing modules.

Depending on the needs of users and climatology, the terraced structure makes the interior part of the exterior and controls how the area grows through time.

Jury point of view … To the question – how could the area be developed so as to attract a large number of new dwellers? – the project answers with an experimental approach. It puts forward an unusual way of living and working – from temporary stays to permanent residence – and to this end, offers a terraced mega-structure, made up of very slim ready-to-combine modules, that relate to the great landscape in a detached, unromantic way…

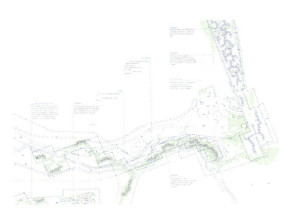

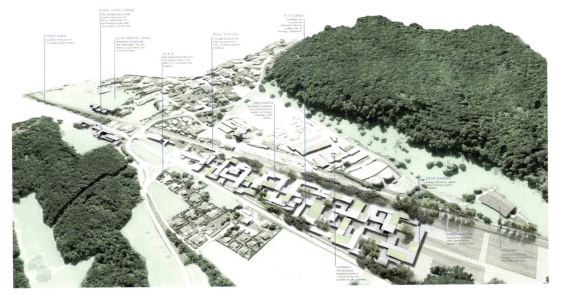

EUROPEAN RESULTS
FROM PLACE TO TERRITORY

ROMAINMÔTIER (CH)

★ WINNER

VINCENT ARNÉ (FR)
AUDE MERMIER (FR)
ARCHITECTS

196

Adapted Geometry: forest, farms, buildings, form follows necessity

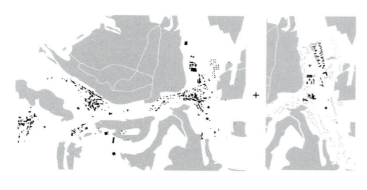

PARADOXICAL SCALES / FRACTAL STRUCTURES : villages /forest , settlements / clearings

Built edges / Garden-metropolis

Team point of view *Sharing:* Living in Croy and in Romainmôtier means living in a wide landscape between the Jura and the Alps, a couple of steps from Lausanne but also from Paris and Zurich. Tourists, residents, old and new, are sharing a setting, a landscape and a heritage.
Settings: Two villages, one dedicated to tourism, the other agricultural; one hidden in the valley, the other on the plains (in the fields), connected to the regional towns via a railway system. Contrasting situations: forest clearings, meadows, dispersed or clustered lifestyles, around a courtyard or a vegetable garden; from the small cottage to the large farmhouse, from the Abbey to the grain silo. *Proposals:* A constellation of emblematic, collective features; appearances in the landscape: hotel, train station, supermarkets; or a sequence of discrete, domestic elements merging within the texture of houses and existing activities. Establishing the forthcoming area within the previous structure is to create a dialogue, to cultivate coexistence and to energise without separating.

Jury point of view The project proposes an urbanisation strategy based on a carefully thought-out analysis of the area's real estate potential. The layout forms a complex program which cannot simply be resumed in terms of residences, even though great importance is placed on the latter: it adds services such as a crèche, a school, a post office, and a cultural centre...

Linked with the article *Common resources and mutation*, p. 263

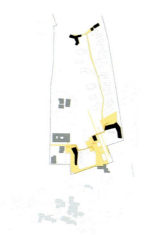

espaces publics: centralité, maillage

usages: centralité, diversité, diffusion

liaisons douces (piétons et vélos)

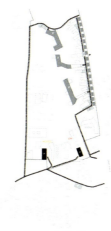

stationnement public et privatif
variable: 1 à 1,5 place de parc/logement

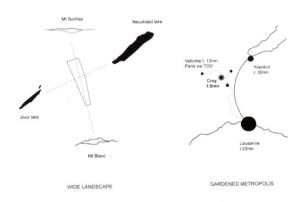

WIDE LANDSCAPE   GARDENED METROPOLIS

milieu habité, clairière nord-sud

immeubles en lisière de bois
120 logements, 3 à 5 niveaux

maisons et lanières à l'est
100 logements, 2 à 3 niveaux

maillage et desserte des logements

CONNECTIVITY
FROM PLACE TO TERRITORY

SKIEN-PORSGRUNN
(NO)

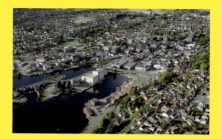

198

SKIEN - PORSGRUNN
POPULATION: SKIEN 51,670 INHAB.,
PORSGRUNN 34,540 INHAB.,
GRENLAND AREA 117,273 INHAB.
STRATEGIC AREA: 88,300 HA
PROJECT AREA: SKIEN 140 HA,
MENSTAD 296 HA, PORSGRUNN
146 HA, HERØYA 149 HA
SITE PROPOSED BY: SKIEN
MUNICIPALITY, PORSGRUNN
MUNICIPALITY, TELEMARK COUNTY
SITE OWNER: VARIOUS PUBLIC
AND PRIVATE OWNERS

Connecting cities

Skien and Porsgrunn are two bordering towns in Telemark County that for many years have had intertwined histories. The cities also interact physically: extensive urban sprawl over recent decades has converted the two cities into one continuous urban field of over 100,000 inhabitants. This has provided generous access to space and quality living, but the sprawl has led to an unfortunate infrastructural situation. A mere 5% of travellers use public transportation. Skien Municipality, Porsgrunn Municipality and Telemark County want to instigate a discussion on the sustainable development of the twin city area. The competition calls for an exploration of the potential in the twin city collaboration and is looking for a development that will strengthen the area's position in the region. The municipalities and the county want to use infrastructure as the driving force for change.

PIERLUIGI D'ACUNTO (IT)
ARCHITECT, ENGINEER
NORMAN HACK (DE)
ARCHITECT

RUNNER-UP

EUROPEAN RESULTS
FROM PLACE TO TERRITORY

SKIEN-PORSGRUNN (NO)

Link+

199

Team point of view LINK + offers an answer to the question of how a light rail track can act as a seed for further development of the proposed sites in and in between Porsgrunn and Skien.

First, an evaluation system was developed to quantify the potential and constraints of the proposed light rail track. Alternative routes were produced, compared and optimized against multiple parameters. Second, potentials for injecting strategic programmes along the light trail track were investigated. The programmes were matched to the sites, their characters and their intended development goals. The infrastructural need to link both sites of the river to the light rail, the idea of activation through programmes and the uniqueness of the Telemark canal as the most valuable asset of the region, converge in the concept of placing the programmes on the bridges.

Jury point of view The jury appreciated the simplicity and coherence of this proposal. The presentation communicates an optimal choice for a light rail route and its infrastructural nodes between the cities, resulting from a traffic analysis that compares a set of alternative rail lines. The scheme concentrates on the development of each node as a potential attractor, or place of encounter, for the larger region through a series of bridges across the river…

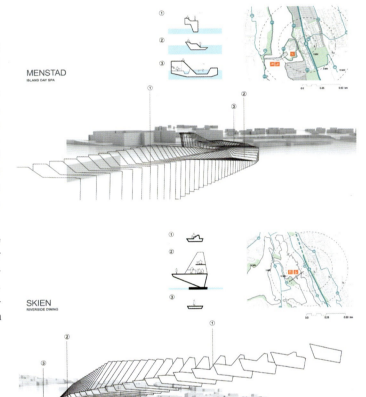

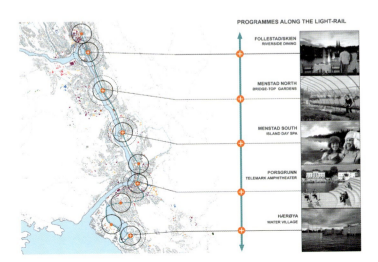

CONNECTIVITY
FROM PLACE TO TERRITORY

STAINS
(FR)

200

STAINS - QUARTIER DES BATÊTES
POPULATION: 34,900 INHAB. (CITY); 335,000 INHAB. (CONURBATION)
STRATEGIC AREA: 12 HA
PROJECT AREA: 7 HA
SITE PROPOSED BY: AGGLOMERATION COMMUNITY OF PLAINE COMMUNE, CITY OF STAINS
SITE OWNER: CITY OF STAINS, RATP (RÉGIE AUTONOME DES TRANSPORTS PARISIENS), CONSEIL GÉNÉRAL

Densification around a future multimodal hub

This site has the potential to become a genuine, town-scale multimodal centre. The Tangentielle railway, metro, bus, self-service bicycles, car sharing platform and day-to-day services and amenities will be grouped together, to provide a range of new services to the people of Stains and to visitors to George Valbon Departmental Park. Intermodality will entail a rich interweaving of programmes and functional mixes, with the opportunity to make greatly enhance the urban quality of the areas of transfer between transport modes. This site will be designed to offer qualities of use and landscapes on weekdays and weekends, day and night, winter and summer.

ELISE AVIDE (FR)
RAPHAËLLE BERNABEI (FR)
URBAN PLANNERS
BENJAMIN BOSSELUT (FR)
URBAN PLANNER, GEOGRAPHER
YOHAN DEMASSE (FR)
LANDSCAPE ENGINEER, URBAN PLANNER
PHILIPPE GAUDIAS (FR)
ENGINEER, URBAN PLANNER
OSCAR GENTIAL (FR)
ARCHITECT, URBAN PLANNER

RUNNER-UP

EUROPEAN RESULTS
FROM PLACE TO TERRITORY

STAINS (FR)

Stain's alive

Team point of view The territory of Stains was the scene of the urban paradigms of the past century. The most various programs have been realized here - from the garden city to the *grand ensemble*.
Instead of proposing a new absolute urban vision or a *tabula rasa*, the mutation of the voids left to the city is able to reinvent the urban life in Stains. At the time of the Greater Paris and its metropolitan network, we certainly don't have to look for the autonomy of the garden cities of the XIX century, but most of all hyper-connectivity. The site should therefore be thought as an entity interacting with all the components of the metropolis, following a logic of complementarity and not of self-sufficiency. The void is a conveyor of mobility. The void qualifies the programs. The void imposes upgradability.

Jury point of view By proposing as its principle the activation of public space around the lens, the project develops a relevant and economical strategy that allows for existing uses.
The question of crossings is clearly tackled and could act as a trigger for a long-term process coinciding with the creation of the station hub and the introduction of public spaces and high quality amenities…

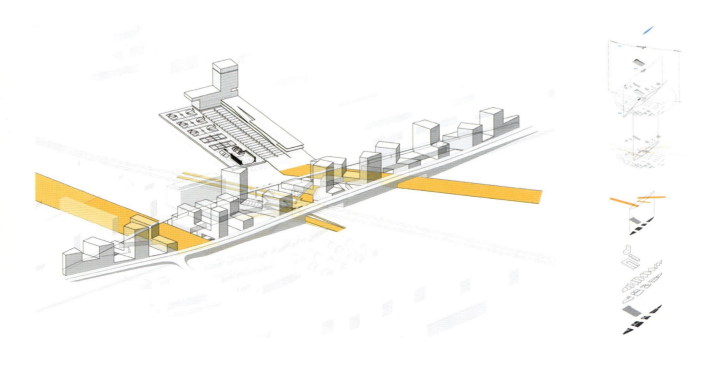

EUROPEAN RESULTS
FROM PLACE TO TERRITORY
STAINS (FR)

★ WINNER

ADÈLE CATHERINE (FR)
AURÉLIE FRANÇOIS (MU)
PIERRE-EMMANUEL LIMONDIN (FR)
ARCHITECTS
LAURA GIULIANI (FR)
ARCHITECT, LANDSCAPE ARCHITECT
EMMANUELLE KLINGER (FR)
ARCHITECT, URBAN PLANNER

202

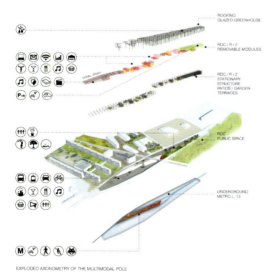

Effets de Serres

Team point of view Beyond the limits of the submitted reflexion area, our proposal for Stains is above all to be fitted in a larger territory that is nowadays weakened in terms of space and time connections. "Effets de Serres" calls for new ways of life towards a clear political and urban insertion within this loose metropolitan context, through the creation of an emblematic neighbourhood that will matter on this 'Grand Paris' scale.

Our project is a work of rhythm. It indeed "reconnections" different urban beats: the metropolitan mobilities' jerky tempo, the urban stroller's regular pace, the muffled and deep beat of soil labour. Our project is a work of harmony. Respecting the existing uses, it draws spatial, social, sensitive and evolutive connexions towards a renewed urbanity.

Jury point of view The project proposes a new kind of urban fabric based on an innovative approach to public space, which seeks to make existing and future mobilities clear and functional, along with their accompanying infrastructures. It is one of the few projects to take all forms of mobility into account and, in the way it irrigates the site from the multimodal hub, to recognise that transport time is also urban time…

Linked with the article *Cultural interferences*, p 256

203

EUROPEAN RESULTS
FROM PLACE TO TERRITORY

STAINS (FR)

RUNNER-UP

TANGUY MALLIER (FR)
CLAIRE KLINGER (FR)
ARCHITECTS

204

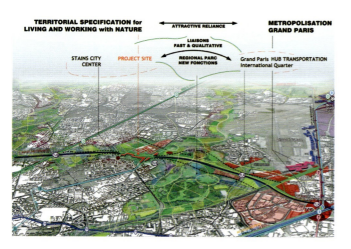

Linking live from earth to the city

Team point of view It's a meeting between city of Stains and Grand Paris, it's a project where soil impulse a metropolisation that makes sense and "reconnection" between economy, urbanity and nature.
Stain's station becomes the front door of Valbon Park for all the Ile-de-France. Its threshold is an attractive area in which companies, homes and fertile nature interact. A mixed building of 80 homes extends the city centre beyond the railroad. Workshops and car parks are noise barriers, their roof is a street. It stretches to the station, grip the existing surrounding, protects the gardens and bind them to the city. In this context, the area is a loam for some targeted companies, which shine here and densify the logistics area. The project illustrates the density of Ecocity, which calculation includes biodiversity, soil productivity and economic attractiveness, happiness… For huge cities with intense urbanity and close to the ground.

Jury point of view The project proposes a forceful urban intervention in the creation of a new gate to the park near the town centre. This new urban situation provides an opportunity to reinterpret the town of Stains and to bring nature into the city. The issue of crossings is particularly well tackled… and it is one of the few projects to work with and around the North tangential, by proposing an overhead network…

HONOURABLE MENTIONS

206

BELGIQUE/BELGIË/BELGIEN

MARCHE-EN-FAMENNE
Level Crossing

OLIVIER GOFFIN (BE), AURÉLIE MAES (BE),
JEREMY PLATEAU (BE), ARCHITECTS
LOÏC HERMANT (BE),
ICI ARCHITECTES SPRL, RUE FERNAND BERNIER 15
1060 BRUXELLES, BELGIQUE
T. +32 2 543 19 34 / CONTACT@NOUSSOMMESICI.BE /
WWW.NOUSSOMMESICI.BE /
WWW.FACEBOOK.COM/ICIARCHITECTES

ALLERØD
Flying ring

DAVIDE AGOSTINI (IT), MATTEO BATTISTINI (IT),
STEVE CAMAGNI (IT), FRANCESCO CECCARELLI (IT),
ARCHITECTS
LUCA LANDI (IT), ARCHITECT
STRADA MASSA CAPRELLO, 1
47025 MERCATO SARACENO, ITALY
T. +39 0547692305 / INFO@LPSARCHITETTI.COM /
WWW.LPSARCHITETTI.COM

CERDANYOLA DEL VALLÈS
The neighbourhood as a process

DIEGO CARRILLO MESSA (ES), EVA MORALES SOLER (ES),
RUBÉN ALONSO MALLÉN (ES), ELISENDA RIFÉ ESCUDERO (ES),
ARCHITECTS – MARIA JOSEP LÁZARO CASTRO (ES),
ARCHITECT, URBAN PLANNER
R. R. OLEAS (ES), INDUSTRIAL ENGINEER – C. SCHWARZ RODRI-
GUEZ (ES), M. BURGOS MARQUÉS (ES), ARCHITECTS – I. ROVIRA
CABALLERO (ES), STUDENT IN ARCHITECTURE – N. COLOMÉ
MONTULL (ES), ARCHITECT, URBAN PLANNER
OFFICE IN BARCELONA, SPAIN: INFO@GESTCIVIC.COOP
WWW.GESTCIVIC.COOP / OFFICE IN SEVILLA, SPAIN:
INFO@DESPACHODEPAN.COM / WWW.DESPACHODEPAN.COM

SAMBREVILLE
Prospectives

TEAM BOLEHORO: JULIEN BOIDOT (FR), MATHIEU
HOLDRINET (FR), ARNAUD LEDU (FR), EMILIEN ROBIN (FR),
ARCHITECTS
ISAAC STILLWELL (AU), PHOTOGRAPHER
WWW.BOIDOTROBIN.FR / WWW.MPLUS-ARCHI.EU /
CONTACT@ARNAUDLEDU.EU / WWW.BOIDOTROBIN.FR /
WWW.ISAACSTILLWELL.COM

KØBENHAVN
From O to X

RUTGER KUIPERS (NL), HENRY LACARCE (FR),
PEPIJN VAN VOORST (NL), KARHO YEUNG (NL), ARCHITECTS
STUDIO VY, ROSIER FAASSENSTRAAT 31E-F
3025GJ, ROTTERDAM, NETHERLANDS
T. +31 107850621 / INFO@STUDIO-VY.NL / WWW.STUDIO-VY.NL

GETARIA
Among vineyards

RAÚL ORTEGA CRESPO (ES), ARCHITECT
NATALIA IRAZUSTABARRENA OTEGUI (ES), ARCHITECT
DOPAMINE. SENSORY ARCHITECTURE, C/ VELETA, 2, 1ºB.
28231 LAS ROZAS DE MADRID, SPAIN
T. +34 644004406 / ESTUDIO@DOPAMINE.ES /
WWW.DOPAMINE.ES

DANMARK

ALLERØD
New Blovstrød Garden Suburb

SOPHIE SAHLQVIST (SE), LANDSCAPE ARCHITECT
FABIAN SAHLQVIST (SE), STUDENT IN ARCHITECTURE
SØNDER BOULEVARD 80, 2 TV
1720 KØBENHAVN V, DENMARK
T. +45 22956506 / S@SOPHIESAHLQVIST.COM /
WWW.SOPHIESAHLQVIST.COM

ESPAÑA

ALCALÁ DE LA SELVA
A Walk…

HÉCTOR DANIEL TORRES MATEO (ES), JULIO MUÑOZ
MOLERO DE ÁVILA (ES), JAIME TRASPADERNE VILA (ES),
MANUEL GALIÁN FERRER (ES), ARCHITECTS, ASSOCIATE
EQUIPO LAYERCAKE ARQUITECTOS:
LAYERCAKE.ES@GMAIL.COM / WWW.EQUIPOLAYERCAKE.COM

SAN BARTOLOMÉ
Moving doors

IÑAQUI CARNICERO (ES), LORENA DEL RIO (ES),
SILVIA FERNANDEZ (ES), ARCHITECTS
JOSE JAVIER GONZALEZ (ES), MIGUEL PALENCIA (ES),
MARIA VEGA (ES), STUDENT IN ARCHITECTURE
AVENIDA DEL RODEO 47
28250 MADRID, SPAIN
ICARNICERO@GMAIL.COM / WWW.INAQUICARNICERO.COM

FRANCE

SAN BARTOLOMÉ
ReCreation

MARTA HERRANZ MATESANZ (ES), ARCHITECT
CARLOS BAYOD LUCINI (ES), ARCHITECT

MART.HERRANZ@GMAIL.COM / CBLUCINI@GMAIL.COM /
WWW.MARTA-HERRANZ.COM

CLERMONT-FERRAND
Geological strata inhabited

JULIEN AVIGNON (FR), **JULIEN SALOM** (FR), ARCHITECTS
BAPTISTE MANET (FR), ARCHITECT

4, RUE DE LA GRANDE CHAUMIÈRE
75006 PARIS, FRANCE
T. +33 650639908 / AVIGNON.J@HOTMAIL.FR

NEUILLY-SUR-MARNE
Feasibility

MARINE MIROUX (FR), **CHRISTOPH HAGER** (AT), ARCHITECTS

WALDEMARSTR. 108
10997 BERLIN, GERMANY
T. +49 15775783738 / MIROUX@BERLINSUD.COM

SAN BARTOLOMÉ
Random occupation lines

BORJA GÓMEZ MARTÍN (ES), **ROBERTO LEBRERO LÓPEZ** (ES), ARCHITECTS

MARÍA AMPARO GONZÁLEZ MOYA (ES), ANA MAYOL GONZÁLEZ DE SUSO (ES), MARÍA LUISA DE MIGUEL GONZÁLEZ (ES), STUDENTS IN ARCHITECTURE

UNDEFINED OFFICE
T. +34 644064469 / OFICINA@UNDEFINEDOFFICE.COM /
WWW.UNDEFINEDOFFICE.COM /
WWW.FACEBOOK.COM/UNDEFINEDOFFICE

CLERMONT-FERRAND
The park of slaughterhouses

JENNY REUILLARD (FR), **BAPTISTE ROUGERY** (FR),
ALEXANDRA BLERET (FR), **LOÏC VEDEL** (FR), ARCHITECTS

ABJL.ARCHI, 128, BD DE CHARONNE
75020 PARIS, FRANCE
T. +33 672873947 / ABJL.ARCHI@GMAIL.COM

REIMS
Archipelago

THOMAS JOUFFE (FR), **MARIE LANG** (FR), **EMILIE MARX** (FR), **PAOLA PFENNINGER** (DE), **SÉBASTIEN POUPEAU** (FR), ARCHITECTS

ATELIERWORKSHOP, 34, RUE DE MONTMORENCY
75003 PARIS, FRANCE
T. +33 648749952 / CONTACT@ATELIERWORKSHOPEU /
ATELIERWORKSHOP.WORDPRESS.COM

SESTAO
Slow urbanism

JOSE LUIS MUÑOZ (ES), **ANNA TWEEDDALE** (AU), ARCHITECTS
CELIA MARTINEZ HIDALGO (ES), RAMIRO VILLEGAS ERCE (ES), ARCHITECTS – BEATRIZ QUINTANA VILLAR (ES), MARTA REGUERA GUTIEZ (ES), STUDENTS IN ARCHITECTURE

C/.BUENSUCESO, 40. LOCAL 4
18002 GRANADA, SPAIN
JLM.ESTUDIO@GMAIL.COM

NEUILLY-SUR-MARNE
Natural vs Artificial Flooding, you'd better think twice

RÉMY COINTET (FR), **ETIENNE ROUVERAND** (FR),
BENOIT STEHELIN (FR), ARCHITECTS
MATHIEU GONTIER (FR), LANDSCAPE ARCHITECT
SOUED YAHIAOUI (FR), ARCHITECT

ETIENNE ROUVERAND, 35 BOULEVARD BELLEVILLE
75011 PARIS, FRANCE
T. +33 699789109 / EROUVERAND@YAHOO.COM

TOULOUSE
Let's go for a walk...

DAMIEN VIEILLEVIGNE (FR), ARCHITECT
OLIVIER BOSCOURNU (FR), 3D DESIGNER

DVA.ARCHI@GMAIL.COM / RIOFRANKO@GMAIL.COM /
WWW.ATELIERDVA.COM

HONOURABLE MENTIONS

208

HRVATSKA

DUBROVNIK
Climath

ALISA ANDRASEK (HR), **ERMIS CHALVATZIS** (GR),
ANASTASIA LIANOU (GR), **IGOR PANTIC** (SRB), ARCHITECTS
JOSE MANUEL SANCHEZ (CL), KAROLY MARKOS (RO),
ARCHITECTS

BIOTHING, 29 THORNHILL BRIDGE WHARF
N1 0RU LONDON, UNITED KINGDOM
T. +44 7545338136 / AA@BIOTHING.ORG / WWW.BIOTHING.ORG

DUBROVNIK
Cable car parking

SASCHA GLASL (DE), **TJEERD HACCOU** (NL),
MARTHIJN POOL (NL), ARCHITECTS
EVA SOLLGRUBER (AT), ARCHITECT
MARINA VENDRELL (ES), ARCHITECT

SPACE&MATTER, KRAANSPOOR 36
1033 SE AMSTERDAM, NETHERLANDS
T +31 20 6306592 / INFO@SPACEANDMATTER.NL /
WWW.SPACEANDMATTER.NL

NEDERLAND

ALMERE
Het Huis Beiaard

JE AHN (GB), **MARIA SMITH** (GB), ARCHITECTS
GIJS LIBOUREL (NL), BUILDING ENGINEER

STUDIO WEAVE, 33 ST JOHN'S CHURCH ROAD
E9 6EJ LONDON, UNITED KINGDOM
T. +44 7903031976 / HELLO@STUDIOWEAVE.COM /
WWW.STUDIOWEAVE.COM

DUBROVNIK
Dubrovnik Pacemaker

JOSIP MIČETIĆ (HR), **MIRO ROMAN** (HR), **LUKA VLAHOVIĆ** (HR),
ARCHITECTS
IVA BALJKAS (HR), LUKA FRANJEŠEVIĆ (HR), NIKŠA LAUŠIN (HR),
ARCHITECTS – SANJA HORVATINČIĆ (HR), PETRA TOMLJANOVIĆ
(HR), IVAN VI EN (HR), ART HISTORIAN

WWW.ROMANVLAHOVIC.COM

MAGYARORSZÁG

SZEGED
Cultivating Rókus

LAURA BRADLEY (GB), **ISABELLA PERCY** (GB),
SARAH ROBINSON (GB), ARCHITECTS

239 UNDERHILL ROAD
SE22 0PB LONDON, UNITED KINGDOM
T. +44 2084252383 / INFO@CULTIVATING-ROKUS.EU /
WWW.CULTIVATING-ROKUS.EU

ALMERE
Natural history

DAVID DOMINGUEZ FUSTER (ES),
CHRISTIAN SINTES MIDMORE (ES), ARCHITECTS
MARÍA ALARCÓN (ES), MARCOS FEIJÓO (ES),
SUSANA FERNÁNDEZ (ES), MARC GISPERT (ES),
ALFONS TORNERO (ES), STUDENTS IN ARCHITECTURE

C/ MARIANA PINEDA 6, BAJOS 1ª
08012 BARCELONA, SPAIN
T. +34 934155685 / MODO@MODO.ST

DUBROVNIK
Local Microgrowth

GONZALO GUTIÉRREZ (ES), **GONZALO DEL VAL** (ES),
ARCHITECTS

INFO@GONZALOGA.COM / INFO@GONZALODELVAL.COM /
WWW.GONZALOGA.COM / WWW.GONZALODELVAL.COM

SZEGED
Linked integration

CSENGE CSONTOS (HU), **BORBÁLA GYÜRE** (HU),
AGRONOMY-LANDSCAPE ENGINEER
BARNABAS LARIS (HU), **ADAM VESZTERGOM** (HU),
ARCHITECTS
ANETT FARKAS (HU), STUDENT IN ARCHITECTURE

ADAM VESZTERGOM, VESZPREMVÖLGYI U. 42.
8200 VESZPREM, HUNGARY
T. +36 703699397 / VESZTERGOMADAM@GMAIL.COM /
WWW.VESZTERGOM.HU

AMSTERDAM
A Free Town

MARTTI KALLIALA (FI), **AUVO LINDROOS** (FI),
ALEKSI NIEMELÄINEN (FI), **TEEMU SEPPÄNEN** (FI),
ARCHITECTS

MARTTI KALLIALA C/O PRO TOTO, ISO ROOBERTINKATU 48-50 LH
00120 HELSINK, FINLAND
T. +358 503549649 / MARTTI.KALLIALA@GMAIL.COM

209

AMSTERDAM
Trading Futures

JELTE BOEIJENGA (NL), ARCHITECTURAL & URBAN THEORIST
JOOST BRANDS (NL), **CORINE ERADES** (NL),
NIELS TILANUS (NL), ARCHITECTS

T. +31652306933 / POST@CORADES.NL / WWW.CORADES.NL

LEEUWARDEN
Central lake

MATEUSZ ADAMCZYK (PL), ARCHITECT, URBAN DESIGNER

MARCELINA KOLASIŃSKA (PL), AGATA WOŹNICZKA (PL),
STUDENTS IN ARCHITECTURE

BUDCUD, BOSAKÓW 5A/28
31-476 KRAKÓW, POLAND
T. +48 607226706 / ADAMCZYK@BUDCUD.ORG /
WWW.BUDCUD.ORG

OSLO
Active edge

ANDREA ALESSIO (IT), **ILARIA ARIOLFO** (IT), ARCHITECTS
ALESSANDRO BUA (IT), URBAN PLANNER

2A+B, CORSO MARCONI 22
10125, TORINO, ITALY
T. +39 3498434730 / +39 0112734583 / 2APLUSB@GMAIL.COM /
WWW.PLA-C.EU

NORGE

CAPELLE AAN DEN IJSSEL
A day in the life

MICHALIS NTOURAKOS (GR), ARCHITECT

MOMFERATOU 103-105
114 75 ATHENS, GREECE
T. +31 61977950 / MNT.ARCH@GMAIL.COM

HAUGESUND
Gardenurbia

ANDREAS LYCKEFORS (SE), ARCHITECT

JONAS TJÄDER (SE), JOHAN ZETTERHOLM (SE), ARCHITECTS

HISINGSGATAN 30
41703 GÖTEBORG, SWEDEN
T. +46 709665090 / ANDREAS@BORNSTEINLYCKEFORS.SE /
WWW.WEAREYOU.SE / WWW.BORNSTEINLYCKEFORS.SE

OSLO
Tip Top Tip

VIRGINIE BLANCHARD (FR), ARCHITECT
ANTOINE DERRIEN (FR), **ORIANE PACALET** (FR),
ELVINA PIARD (FR), LANDSCAPE ARCHITECTS

L'ATELIER VOLANT, 27 RUE D'ANVERS
59000 LILLE, FRANCE
T. +33 361055819 / CONTACT@LATELIERVOLANT.FR /
WWW.LATELIERVOLANT.FR

EINDHOVEN
Samuel Josua

WULF BÖER (DE), **ALESSANDRO GESS** (DE),
MATTHIEU HACKENHEIMER (FR), ARCHITECT, URBAN PLANNER

THEVEN
T. +33 661267120 / INFO@THEVEN.EU / WWW.THEVEN.EU

HAUGESUND
Tales of the unexpected

MARIA MESTRES (ES), **MAGNUS WÅGE** (NO), ARCHITECTS
LEONOR MIGUEIS (PT), LANDSCAPE ARCHITECT

CARLES ALMOYNA (ES), ARCHITECT
ERLEND STRØNSTAD (NO) – ARCHITECTURE STUDENT

MESTRES WÅGE ARQUITECTES SLP. CALLE BONAVISTA 26.
PRINCIPAL 2
08012 BARCELONA, SPAIN
T. +34 932374683 / 34 680 502 993 / MWA@COAC.NET /
WWW.MESTRESWAGE.COM

OSLO
Do it

CHRISTIAN HJELLE (NO), ARCHITECT, URBAN PLANNER
FRØYDIS LINDEN (NO), AGRO ECOLOGIST, VISUAL ARTIST
CHRISTOFFER OLAVSSON EVJU (NO), LANDSCAPE ARCHITECT,
URBAN PLANNER – **ANDREA SPREAFICO** (NO), PHILOSOPHER,
VISUAL ARTIST

T. +47 93022477 / CHRISTIANHJELLE@YAHOO.NO

HONOURABLE MENTIONS

210

OSLO
Infrastructural archeology

RAMÓN ÁLVAREZ ROA (ES), JIMENA CAMPILLO GONZÁLEZ (ES), MARTA DOMÈNECH RODRÍGUEZ (ES), JUAN ENRÍQUEZ LAGE (ES), DAVID LÓPEZ LÓPEZ (ES), CRISTINA MAGRO BARONI (ES), MARÍA PALENCIA SERRANO (ES), MARIANA PALUMBO FERNÁNDEZ (ES), GONZALO PARDO ROQUERO (ES), PABLO SIGÜENZA GÓMEZ (ES), ANDRÉS VELARDE SANZ (ES), ARCHITECTS

C. ESTAÚN MARTÍNEZ (ES), A. R. CÁMARA (ES), ARCHITECTS

MAP13, C/ PJERTO NAVACERRADA 3, 3ºD
28220 MAJADAHONDA, SPAIN
MAP13.NET@GMAIL.COM / WWW.MAP13.NET

SKIEN-PORSGRUNN
Combinations

THOMAS LANDENBERG (SE), ARCHITECT

JENNY MÄKI (SE), MIKAEL STENQVIST (SE), ARCHITECTS

WHITE ARKITEKTER AB, MAGASINSGATAN 10, BOX 2502
40317 GÖTEBORG, SWEDEN
T. +46 31608732 / THOMAS.LANDENBERG@WHITE.SE

GUIMARÃES
Green Movements

SARA MOURA MARTINS (PT), ARCHITECT

ANA ROCHA (PT), ARCHITECT

MOURA MARTINS ARQ., AVENIDA DA BOAVISTA, 1015, 4º, S406
4100-128 PORTO, PORTUGAL
T. +351 226092389 / MAIL@MOURAMARTINS.COM /
WWW.MOURAMARTINS.COM

OSLO
Norwegian Rhapsody

BEATRIZ RAMO (ES), ARCHITECT, URBAN PLANNER

FRANCESCA RIZZETTO (IT), ALEXIA MARTHA SYMVOULIDOU (GR), ARCHITECTS

STAR STRATEGIES + ARCHITECTURE, KIPSTRAAT 7B
3011 RR ROTTERDAM, NETHERLANDS
T. +31 102135630 / STAR@ST-AR.NL / WWW.ST-AR.NL

POLSKA

WARSZAWA
Brochette

JOAN CABA (ES), MARTA MASFERRER (ES),
JORDI PERALTA (ES), JORGE PEREA (ES), ARCHITECTS

JORDI PERALTA, ARCHITECT
BAIXADA DE LES ESCALATES 7, 1 MATARÓ
08301 BARCELONA, SPAIN
T. +34 617005675 / JORDIPERALTA1982@HOTMAIL.COM

GUIMARÃES
Urban synergy

JOANA SEIXAS NUNES (PT), VANDA VISEU ALVES (PT), ARCHITECTS

RUA DAS FRANCESINHAS 23, 1º DTº
1200-675 LISBOA, PORTUGAL
T. +351 91 962 65 72

PORTUGAL

SKIEN-PORSGRUNN
Between the lines

HAN DIJK (NL), BORIS HOCKS (NL), URBAN PLANNERS
EMILE REVIER (NL), ARCHITECT

ANNA DIJK (N_), LUISA MOURA (PT), ARCHITECTS
TACO KUIJERS (NL), REGIONAL DESIGNER

POSAD SPATIAL STRATEGIES, BINCKHORSTLAAN 36
2516 BE DEN HAAG, NETHERLANDS
T. +31 703222869 / MAIL@POSAD.NL / WWW.POSAD.NL /
WWW.POSADLABS.COM

GUIMARÃES
Heritage vs Mutability

JOÃO PAULO ARAÚJO PEIXOTO (PT),
AMANDINE ANTUNES (FR), ARCHITECTS

REARQ, RUA CONSELHEIRO LOBATO
322 4705-089 BRAGA, PORTUGAL
T. +351 253215220 / REARQUITECTURA@HOTMAIL.COM

SCHWEIZ/SUISSE/SVIZZERA/SVIZRA

AIGLE
Superdensity

GIULIO RIGONI (IT), IRENE GARBATO (IT),
LEONARDO MURMORA (IT), ARCHITECTS

VIA AL TRODO 1
6572 QUARTINO - CANTON TICINO, SWITZERLAND
T. +41 762331228 / GIULIO.RIGONI@GMAIL.COM

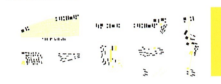

SUOMI-FINLAND

SVERIGE

AIGLE
Let's dense

CLAUDIO BONICCO (IT), **ANDREA LO PAPA** (IT), ARCHITECTS
ALBERTO MELLANO (IT), STUDENT IN ARCHITECTURE

STUDIO74, VIA CARLO EMANUELE III, 20
12100 CUNEO, ITALY
STUDIO74@STUDIO74.BIZ / WWW.STUDIO74.BIZ

PORVOO
In-forestation

THIBAUT BOURGADE (FR), **PAULINE BOURGADE** (FR),
ALEXANDRE DUBURE (FR), ARCHITECTS

17A, RUE DES MARGUETTES
75012 PARIS, FRANCE
T. +33 684677949 / THIBAUT.BOURGADE@GMAIL.COM /
WWW.SYN-APSES.COM

MALMÖ
Puzzling Holma

JOHN ANDERSSON (SE), **SIMON KLAMBORN** (SE),
ARCHITECTS
ELINOR ANDERSSON (SE), STUDENT ARCHITECTURE

VÄRNHEMSGATAN 7
212 15 MALMÖ, SWEDEN
ANDERSSON3000@GMAIL.COM

MONTHEY
Living cluster

LUCA BELATTI (IT), **MARIAGIULIA BENNICELLI PASQUALIS** (IT), **MILENA BLAGOJEVIĆ** (SRB), **ILARIA BROGI** (IT),
DARIA CARUSO (IT), **ROSARIO ANDREA CRISTELLI** (IT),
ALESSANDRO FLAMINIO (IT), **FRANCESCO FRAGALE** (IT),
FABIO MARCHESCHI (IT), **FRANCESCO MESSINA** (IT),
ARCHITECTS
GIUSEPPE MESSINA (IT), ARCHITECT

BODÀR_BOTTEGA D'ARCHITETTURA
VIA DR. PROF. LUIGI ZANCLA, 43 – 98051 BARCELONA PG (ME), ITALY
INFO@BODAR.IT / WWW.BODAR.IT

TURKU
'Janus'

WULF BÖER (DE), **ALESSANDRO GESS** (DE),
MATTHIEU HACKENHEIMER (FR),
ARCHITECTS, URBAN PLANNERS

THEVEN
T. +33 661267120 / INFO@THEVEN.EU /
WWW.THEVEN.EU

MALMÖ
Staging Holma

NADINE ASCHENBACH (DE), ARCHITECT
HELEN RUNTING (AU), URBAN DESIGNER
MAJA CLAESSON (SE), STUDENT IN ARCHITECTURE

LÅNGHALSVÄGEN 14
120 50 ÅRSTA, SWEDEN
T. +46 704244703 / NADINE_ASCHENBACH@GMX.DE

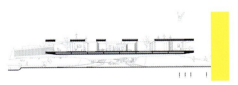

ROMAINMÔTIER
Close At hand

LAURE BOITEUX (FR), ARCHITECT

4 RUE JEAN JAURÈS
25500 MORTEAU, FRANCE
T. +33 675485276 / LAURE.BOITEUX@GMX.FR

TURKU
Our garden

ALESSANDRO FEA (IT), ARCHITECT, URBAN PLANNER
ROBERTO MANUELLI (IT), **GIANFRANCO ORSENIGO** (IT),
NICOLA RATTI (IT) ARCHITECTS – **ANNA MORO** (IT),
URBAN PLANNER

CARRER DE LA RIERETA 5, 1°-3°
08001 BARCELONA, SPAIN
T. +34 658696522 / WWW.DUESCENARIPERLALOMELLINA.IT

NORRKÖPING
Living in the infra villas

MARCELLO BONDAVALLI (IT), **NICOLA BRENNA** (IT),
VIRGINIA ORTALLI (IT), **CARLO ALBERTO TAGLIABUE** (IT),
ARCHITECTS

STUDIOWOK + ARCH. VIRGINIA ORTALLI
VIA SIMONE SCHIAFFINO 25
20158 MILANO, ITALY
T. +39 0294394473 / INFO@STUDIOWOK.COM

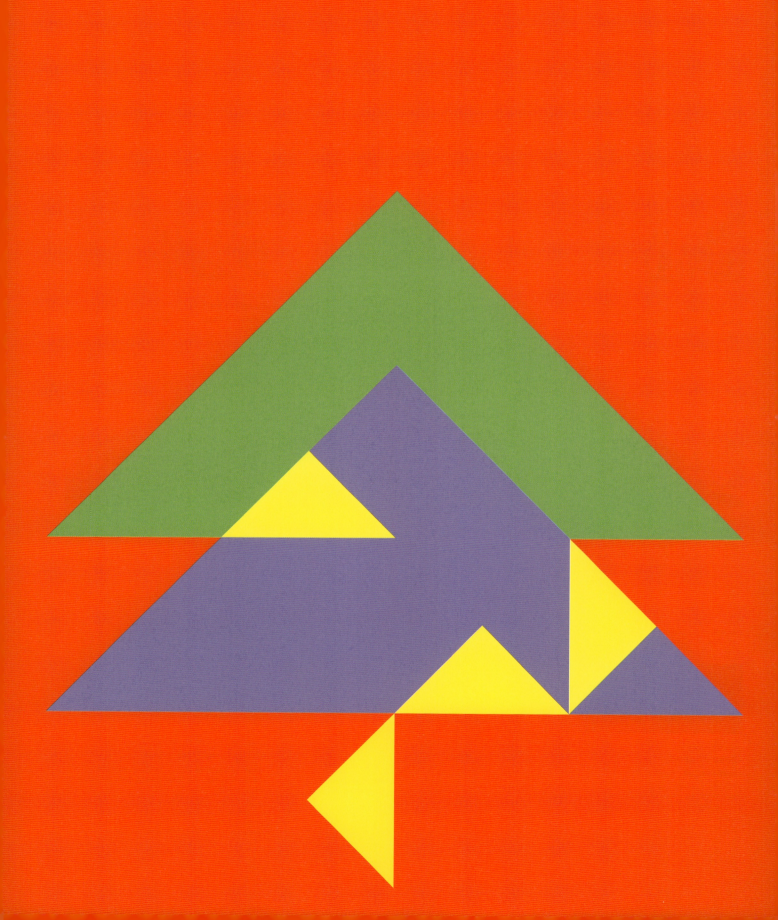

Backstage at a session

A Europan competition session could never happen without the active involvement of many partners, in particular the Europan national structures, the participating municipalities, the competitors and the experts (juries, analysts). It is the commitment of all these partners combined that gives the process meaning and ensures that the best proposals are selected, appreciated and in certain cases implemented. A look back at the high points of the Europan 11 session across Europe.

214

A preliminary topic for the site search

May 28 and 29, Neuchâtel: While the 56 winners and 67 runners-up of Europan 10 are talking to the municipalities and the organisers about the future of their ideas, and in between analyses of results, the members of the specially convened Scientific Committee discuss the theme of Europan 11 between two results analysis at the Results Forum in Switzerland.

On May 30, 2010, the day after the Forum, the organisers meets in General Assembly to vote on the timetable, the theme and the rules of the Europan 11 competition, which have already been explored through multiple e-mails and face-to-face discussions. As always at these Association meetings – which are essential to the proper operation of the structure, both in terms of democratic organisation and in finding adjustments between the sometimes different ideas defended by members of the network – the discussion is lively, in its own way reflecting the multiplicity of Europe's cultures. The final theme is adopted: **Resonance between territories and ways of life – what architectures for sustainable cities?**

This document specifies the content, but also the criteria for finding sites. Since the emphasis is on the relations between strategic thinking on a global territorial scale and local priorities, the idea of the perimeters is redefined, and the project site is no longer connected with a study site but with a strategic site, which incorporates all the parameters that govern municipal policies on mobility, uses and the relation to nature, which will influence the local site.

Digital submission

Another meeting, taking advantage of the presence in Switzerland of the representatives of the 22 member countries, focuses on the potential for greater use of online resources in competition submissions.

A compromise is found that reconciles the need for the juries to be able to look at physical panels in order to compare before judging, and at the same time for competitors to be able to submit their ideas online. Through these digital documents, the organisers and jury members will have access to all the project submissions on a restricted-access, fully anonymous, online platform.

A change of president

And finally, the Europan 10 Results Forum in Neuchâtel also marks the turning of an important page in the history of the competitions, since it sees the departure of Yvette Jaggi after eight years as a strongly committed President of Europan Europe, and the arrival of her successor at the head of the European Association, the German urbanist and theorist Thomas Sieverts, who is aware that his role will be far from purely honorary.

Looking for sites but funding as well

In summer 2010, during the search for new sites in the four corners of Europe, It quickly becomes clear that though European municipalities and developers are still keen to participate, in the light of the economic crisis it will not always be possible for their financial contribution to be as

high as in the previous session. Others decide to sit this one out and prepare to take part in Europan 12... In the different European and national structures, people are looking for ways to cut expenditure by 20%, without diluting the programme and while maintaining the quality of the competition... But we promise that there will be no reduction in the amount of the prize awards!

Setting the site themes

In October 2010, the experts on the Technical Commission and the Scientific Committee meet in Paris to discuss the first forty or so proposed sites, in order to identify transverse themes that can be used in tandem with the generic topic to generate debate and establish clarity through comparable elements common to several sites. However, no one doubts that new sites will arrive before January. The new President, Thomas Sieverts, has his baptism of fire, playing an active part in the discussions, which eventually identify three families of sites. After a day of analyses and discussions amongst themselves, then a second day with the organisers, a set of unifying themes emerge around which the sites can be grouped. At this meeting, three new members are welcome and onto the Scientific Committee: Chris Younès, French philosopher and urban anthropologist, Kristaan Borret, urbanist of the city of Anvers in Belgium and Frauke Burgdorf, director of an urban development foundation in Germany.

FORUM OF SITES TO REFINE STRATEGIES

Meeting of participating municipalities to refine strategies

On December 3 and 4, 2010, in Istanbul, Turkey, the first significant European event of the session takes place: the Sites Forum. The purpose here is to discuss, sometimes qualify, sometimes even change the programmes of the proposed sites (although others may still appear before the competition launch) through themed working groups and debates between experts and municipal representatives.

Starting with two introductory lectures by experts on two strategic topics for the Europan 11 session – the question of overlapping scales and the relationship between city and nature – on the Friday afternoon some twenty five representatives had the opportunity to discuss their locality's urban policies in these domains and their connection with the issues raised by the sites they entered in the competition.

So the subject of the first debate was **scales**, exploring the relations between cities' global sustainability strategy and the conception of local urban development, with the aim, beyond each participant's specific concerns, of launching potential avenues for transformation that reflect this relating of the global and local. **Thomas Sieverts, Europan's new President**, introduced this discussion with a lecture on current urban trends: "On the threshold of the third urban revolution, possible consequences."

The **second debate** explored the relations between city and countryside and what it means to live on the urban perimeter today. Neither separated by a hermetic boundary, nor diluted in diffuse urban sprawl, how can city and countryside coexist today and become dynamically interwoven? To situate the discussion within the context of Istanbul, **the Turkish architect and urbanist Ipek Akpinar**, Professor at Istanbul's Technical University's Faculty of Architecture, introduced the debate with a lecture on "Remapping a global city: dynamics, potentials, contradictions".

SITES' VISIT FOR THE COMPETITORS

The emphasis on the second day was on **small-scale discussions** through working groups. Experts and site representatives got together around the table to **explore in greater depth the future urban contexts of Europan 11** through common themes and comparative analyses. There were nine workshops in all, headed by members of the Technical Committee and the Scientific Committee, looking at the sites from the perspective of three main categories: Identity, Uses and Connectivity.

An **exhibition of the sites**, a space for more informal information sharing and discussion, and the Saturday **evening reception at Istanbul Modern**, a former warehouse converted to a Museum of Contemporary Art, gave the Forum a more recreational aspect.

Quite apart from the impassioned and fascinating discussions, the Istanbul atmosphere bodes well for the session, reconciling work, the production of meaning and a certain urban hedonism… an atmosphere exemplified by the closing reception at Istanbul Modern, on the shores of the Bosphorus…

Digital logistics

After the short end of year hiatus, beginning 2011, frenetic activity! Working with their municipalities, the national secretariats prepare their fact sheets and full site packs for competitors to download. The last few municipalities come on board. The European Secretariat finalises the competition website and compiles all the information from the national secretariats. Digitisation simulations are run with the European Webmaster and tests on the processes for printing A1 and A3 boards from 3 MB JPEGs… However, thanks to compression and the growing IT expertise of today's young professionals, nothing seems impossible and Europan Europe's enhanced servers are set up to handle the multiple downloads at the end of June…

A delayed launch, but in the right conditions

To ensure good preparation, it is decided to follow Switzerland's proposal to delay the launch by one month. It means that the only impact of the difficult economic context for the entrants will be the need to move fast in choosing their sites and designing their projects, since this time they will only have 4 months to finalise their submissions.

Thus, Monday, February 28, still a little under pressure because of the thousands of drawings, photos and documents of all kinds to upload to the competition website, the session is ready to start and there should be no outward sign of the somewhat increased efforts needed to meet the objectives of this eleventh session.

Some fifteen countries and around fifty municipalities across Europe propose urban scale sites for this session, and await innovative ideas and projects, including: Austria (Graz, Linz and

216

CITIES AND JURIES FORUM, DISCUSSION AROUND THE PRESELECTED PROJECTS. © L. Kjersheim

Wien); Belgium (Marche-en-Famenne and Sambreville); Croatia (Dubrovnik); Denmark (Allerød, København and Rødrove); Finland (Porvoo and Turku); France (Clermont-Ferrand, Neuilly-Sur-Marne, Reims, Savenay, Stains and Toulouse); Germany (Ibbenbüren, Ingolstadt, Selb, Wittstock and Würzburg); Hungary (Szeged; Ireland: Dublin); Kosovo (Pejë; Netherlands: Almere, Amsterdam, Capelle aan den IJssel, Deventer, Eindhoven and Leeuwarden); Norway (Haugesund, Oslo and Skien-Porsgrunn); Poland (Warszawa); Portugal (Guimarães); Spain (Alcalá de la Selva, Alcorcón, Cerdanyola del Vallès, Getaria, San Bartolomé and Sestao); Sweden (Malmö, Norrköping, Nynäshamn and Simrishamn); Switzerland (Aigle, Monthey and Romainmôtier).

The timetable gives a registration deadline of June 10, 2011 and submission deadline of June 30, 2011. The Juries will meet between September/November 2011. The Results will be announced on December 15, 2011

A good ratio between registrations and submissions

During the site choice and registration period, 3000 site packs are downloaded by teams from 63 different nationalities and 46 different countries, and 1826 projects submitted, making a good ratio of over 60%.

A time of intensive effort in the 17 participating country secretariats, which receive some 5486 panels to check and classify.

In each country, a technical committee made up of organisers, experts and very often site representatives, produces project analysis reports for their juries, but without eliminating any, since the juries will have to examine all the projects.

14 National juries each with a foreign component

Each participating country assembles the same jury structure, i.e. 9 members, at least 3 foreign, a majority of architects but also representatives of commissioning clients and from disciplines associated with the design process, landscape architects, historians, critics, artists, etc. The jury members include experts familiar with national priorities but also, in particular amongst the foreign members, figures of international repute.

2 substitutes attend the jury meetings to replace any absent members.

The juries follow the same rules and meet twice in the same period, on either side of a European event, the Cities and Juries Forum, where European scale discussion takes place on the shortlisted projects on each site before the winning and runner-up teams are chosen.

Municipalities involved in project assessment

The site representatives are not involved in the final jury that decides the winners and runners-up, to ensure that the choice of teams is based on the innovative nature of the projects, independently of local pressures. However, they are not excluded from the adjudication procedure, quite the contrary! They take part in the preliminary analysis of the projects, and present the priorities and their visions for the future of their sites to the juries, usually on-site; very often, after the jury vote, they hold a presentation of the results.

In certain countries, such as Austria and Germany, the site representatives are present at the first meeting to shortlist around 20% of projects that are perceived as credible in terms of the site priorities. And above all, in order to embed the jury within the Europan system between the national and European scales, a Cities and Juries Forum is held which, as its name suggests, is an occasion for meetings between the juries and the site representatives of all the countries taking part in the EUROPAN 11 competition.

Cities and juries forum, oslo (norway), november 4-5, 2011

For Europan 11, the Cities and Juries Forum takes place in Oslo in an urban regeneration area, in a magnificent industrial hall converted for this type of event.

It is structured as a series of **lectures, debates, working groups, exhibition, architectural excursions and informal meetings** to discuss solutions and focus adjudication of the entries shortlisted by national juries in their first meetings, where they analyse all the submissions and choose around 20% of the projects that contain an innovative idea in relation to the site's context.

MEETING OF A NATIONAL JURY

ARCHITECTURAL VISIT DURING THE CITIES AND JURIES FORUM

The International event is a collaboration between EUROPAN Europe, EUROPAN Norway, Oslo Municipality, Oslo School of Architecture and Design, Norsk Form and National Association of Norwegian Architects.

In fine, 326 projects shortlisted in the first round of jury meetings for the quality of their ideas are presented, discussed and compared anonymously on the basis of themed site categories, combining the views of experts and the strategic perspectives of the municipalities. For both site representatives and the jury members, the forum is a good opportunity for an exchange ideas about sites and projects shortlisted for them.

The Forum also plays an important role in organising comparative debates between different project sites that embody similar issues in order to broaden the discussions on the innovative nature of the projects, and it gives the juries wider assessment criteria which will be taken into account when the members of the 14 juries meet again after the Forum to choose the winning teams.

Certain countries hold this second series of jury meetings just after the Forum, in Oslo itself, in the School of Architecture. The others hold them at home during the month of November, for a final announcement in mid-December after verification that the winning projects comply with the competition rules.

Europan 11 results by numbers

43% of the europan 11 winning teams won in a country other than their own. 3000 site files downloaded by teams of **63 different nationalities** and **46 different countries. Among 1826 project submissions, 326 projects have been preselected** and debated in the Forum Of Cities And Juries in Oslo (Norway).

The 14 juries named **95 prize-winning teams – 41 winning teams, 54 runner-up teams –** and **54 honourable mentions**. The **95 winning teams are based in 19 different countries**. Of them, 57% won in their country of residence, hence 43% in a country other than their own, confirming the readiness of young professionals to tackle a context outside their experience. The teams that were most motivated to compete abroad come from Spain (9 of the 20 winning teams based in Spain won a prize on a foreign site), France (7 teams out of 17), Italy (7 teams) and the Netherlands (4 teams out of 12).

The winning and runner-up teams will respectively receive a prize of 12,000 and 6000 Euros. 816 000 euros awarded to young European architects!

The results forum

At the invitation of the City of Vienna and Europan Austria, a large closing Forum is held on May 17, 18 and 19. This Forum is based around three major sessions and an exhibition:

European workshop: reconnections

This strategic project workshop involves all the winning Europan 11 teams wishing to attend, with the objective of connecting the winning ideas with urban and architectural scenarios applied to the context of Vienna. The workshop is held in partnership with the City of Vienna from May 14-17, at the Vienna Technische Universitat. Over 4 days, mixed international teams of 6 or 7 architects from the members of the 95 winning teams present work is to produce a dozen alternative scenarios relating to 5 evolving urban contexts in Vienna, based around the five project classification topics: Common resources and change / Reconnecting through uses / Rhythms and timeframes / Remodelling shared spaces / Cultural interferences. The scenarios will be produced in collaboration with experts from the City of Vienna.

Debates, discussions

Debates open to everyone involved in Europan 11 – site representatives, winning teams and organisers from the 17 participating countries – in the form of one and a half days of talks and discussions, around the Results of the competition and the Project Workshop, then on in architectural practices, on the afternoon of May 18. Then throughout the day of May 19 the focus will be past and future implementation processes arising from Europan competitions.

Visits: views of vienna

Finally, there will be a panorama of urban changes in Vienna in the form of an introductory lecture followed on the morning of Sunday 20 May by guided bus tours of several recent urban productions representing the City's urban policy, including Europan implementation projects.

Europan 11 exhibition

The Forum coincides with an exhibition of the session results. In order to make it more attractive and interactive, Europan has asked the teams to produce it themselves.

CITIES AND JURIES FORUM © L. Kjersheim

LECTURES DURING CITIES AND JURIES FORUM © L. Kjersheim

European publications

The Forum also coincides with the publication of the European Catalogue of Europan 11 Results – RECONNECTIONS, and the publication on implementation processes developed during the previous two sessions –IDEAS IN MOTION (www.europan-europe.com online purchase)

And now beyond the competition of ideas...

Municipalities that have proposed sites have undertaken to follow up with commissions **in the form of urban studies and/or implementations**. Europan's goal is of course to award a "label" to the most talented teams of young European designers, but it is also to help them get involved in the design and implementation of their ideas in the urban contexts proposed in the competition. And although Europan is the central agency involved in the organisation and choice of the winning teams, in this new phase Europan can only play a facilitating and mediating role between the winning designers on the sites, the site representatives, the political and urban players, the users involved and, of course, at some point in the implementation processes, the developers responsible for construction.

So after the competition, events and publications take place to publicise the results, but Europan also encourages municipalities and winning teams to hold joint workshops to foster a better understanding of the winning project or projects among site agencies, and conversely a more in-depth familiarity with the site priorities by the design teams.

It is up to the site agencies to choose the team or teams with which to pursue the adventure, in different kinds of processes. These may take very different forms from one country to another. In the Netherlands, it is the winning team that has priority for the next stage; in Germany, the choice follows workshops between the parties concerned; in France, three winning teams on each site pursue the adventure in the form of scoping studies lasting a few months, after which the site representatives choose the operational team or teams. In certain cases, when the selected teams are foreign, at a certain stage they form a partnership with a local team, which may play different roles, varying from that of mentor and adviser to that of associate architect for the operational process based on the winning project.

219

Index

Europan 11, is :

49 sites
17 countries
14 national juries

95 winning teams :
41 winners
54 runners-up

WINNING TEAMS

222

BELGIQUE/BELGIË/BELGIEN

MARCHE-EN-FAMENNE – WINNER ★
The space of encounters

ANCA DIANA POPESCU (RO), **SORIN VLADIMIR POPESCU** (RO), ARCHITECTS

CALEA FLOREASCA NO. 68A, SECTOR1
14463 BUCHAREST, ROMANIA
T. +40 740383916 / ATELIERFORM@GMAIL.COM

DANMARK

ALLERØD – WINNER ★
When Nature Interferes with Everyday Life

METTE BLANKENBERG (DK),
EYRÚN MARGRET STEFANSDOTTIR (IS), ARCHITECTS

MAIL@METTEBLANKENBERG.DK / MAIL@EYRUNSTEF.DK /
WWW.METTEBLANKENBERG.DK / WWW.EYRUNSTEF.DK

KØBENHAVN – RUNNER-UP
The urban space and the spacious urbanity

RUNE BUNDGAARD JØRGENSEN (DK),
BJØRN MOGENSEN (DK), **MADELEINE SEMBRING** (SE),
LAURA WEDDERKIND BANK (DK), ARCHITECTS

TEGNESTUEVAERKSTEDET, EGILSGADE 1, 4TH
2300 COPENHAGEN, DENMARK
T. +45 26719299 / INFO@TEGNESTUEVAERKSTEDET.DK /
WWW.TEGNESTUEVAERKSTEDET.DK

SAMBREVILLE – RUNNER-UP
QCM

BENOIT COULONDRES (FR), **FLORENCE GAUDIN** (FR), ARCHITECTS

11 RUE DE THIONVILLE
75019 PARIS, FRANCE
T. +33 660773685 / +33 664946163 / E11BCFG@GMAIL.COM /
WWW.BENOITCOULONDRES.COM / WWW.FLORENCEGAUDIN.COM

ALLERØD – RUNNER-UP
Nest

JENNIFER GOMES (PT), **RAQUEL VIULA** (PT), ARCHITECTS

JORGE GIL (PT), LEE HWA-SEOP (KR), LAIA MULET (ES),
SEBASTIEN MULLER (PT), SUSANA OLIVEIRA (PT), ARCHITECTS

COWORKLISBOA - LX FACTORY, RUA RODRIGUES FARIA, 103
1300-501 LISBOA – PORTUGAL
T. +351 963195138 / JGOMES@OPENLABARCHITECTS.COM /
WWW.OPENLABARCHITECTS.COM

RØDOVRE – WINNER ★
Islev ID

SØREN LETH (DK), ARCHITECT, URBAN PLANNER
RASMUS THERKILDSEN (DK), ARCHITECT

SYLWIA BOGDAN (PL), ARCHITECT, URBAN PLANNER
JEPPE BONNE OLSEN (DK), INGRID EIDE (NO),
ANDRIUS ROPOLAS (LT), STUDENTS IN ARCHITECTURE

JÆGERGÅRDSGADE 152, 03E
8000 ÅRHUS C, DENMARK
T. +45 32111001 / POST@SLETH.DK / WWW.SLETH.DK

SAMBREVILLE – RUNNER-UP
Ville+Sambre+ville

GIOVANNI AURINO (IT), **DANILO CAPASSO** (IT), **LAURA FALCONE** (IT), **ANNA SIRICA** (IT), **BRUNA VENDEMMIA** (IT), ARCHITECTS

CARMINE CIUCCIO (IT), STUDENT IN ARCHITECTURE

DANILO CAPASSO, VIA ANNIBALE CACCAVELLO, 12
80129 NAPLES, ITALY
T. +39 3299613513 / INFO@DANILOCAPASSO.EU /
WWW.DANILOCAPASSO.EU

KØBENHAVN – WINNER ★
The last city quarter

FLEMMING RAFN THOMSEN (DK), **OLE SCHRØDER** (DK), ARCHITECTS

T. +45 40934309 / FRT@TREDJENATUR.DK / T. +45 25104460 /
OS@TREDJENATUR.DK / WWW.TREDJENATUR.DK

RØDOVRE – RUNNER-UP
Scenes from the suburbs

CÉDRIC CHAUSSE (FR), **CHARLOTTE PORTIER** (FR), ARCHITECTS, URBAN PLANNERS

OLIVIER MARQUET (FR), ARCHITECT, URBAN PLANNER
LUDOVIC POYET (FR) ARCHITECT

3 RUE GAMBEY
75011 PARIS, FRANCE
T. +33 687240776 / CONTACT@SCENESFROMTHESUBURBS.EU /
WWW.SCENESFROMTHESUBURBS.EU

223

DEUTSCHLAND

IBBENBÜREN – WINNER ★
Between the courtyards

MEHDI MOSHFEGHI (DE), ARCHITECT
LILIJA BARTULI (DE), ARCHITECT

KRAYENKAMP 15A
20459 HAMBURG, GERMANY
T. +494059370853 / MEHDI.MOSHFEGHI@GMX.DE

INGOLSTADT – RUNNER-UP
Dreaming/Awaking

LYDIA RAMAKERS (DE), **NORA WILDERMANN** (DE), ARCHITECT
KATRIN RHEINGANS (DE), ARCHITECT, URBAN DESIGNER

SANDERSTRASSE 6
12047 BERLIN, GERMANY
T. +49 1795482100 / NOKALY@HOTMAIL.DE

WITTSTOCK – WINNER ★
Bahnrad

STEFFEN BARNIKOL (DE), **STEFFEN BURUCKER** (DE), ARCHITECTS

NORDSTRASSE 50
99089 ERFURT, GERMANY
T. +49 1791460690 / EUROPAN.BB@GMX.DE

IBBENBÜREN – RUNNER-UP
Ianus

GIOVANNI SANTINI (IT), ARCHITECT
ANDREA KARIMKHAN (IT), ALEXANDROS LIASKOVITIS (GR), ROSA ROMANO (IT), ARCHITECTS

VIA DELLE CONCE 39/R
50122 FLORENCE, ITALY
T. +39 552001570 / MAP@MAPARCHITETTI.IT / WWW.MAPARCHITETTI.IT

SELB – WINNER ★
Dornröschen

ANDREAS BAUMER (DE), **THOMAS BERNHARDT** (DE), **GILLES-BENOIT TREVETIN** (FR), ARCHITECTS
TXELL BLANCO-DIAZ (ES), EGLE SUMINSKAITE (LT), STUDENT IN ARCHITECTURE – JOPPE KNEPPERS (NL), ARCHITECT

NAP - NETWORK OF ARCHITECTS & PLANNERS
GROENHOEDENVEEM 14
1019 BL AMSTERDAM, NETHERLANDS
T. +31 20 419 84 42 / INFO@NAP.EU / WWW.NAP.EU

WITTSTOCK – RUNNER-UP
Inner Gardens, Outer Gates

JANNA HOHN (DE), ARCHITECT, URBAN DESIGNER
JOSHUA JOHN YATES (GB), ARCHITECT
ANNA BUCHWALD (DE), LANDSCAPE ARCHITECT

SOLMSSTRASSE
1810961 BERLIN, GERMANY
T. +49 17632334959 / JANNAHOHN@GMX.DE

INGOLSTADT – WINNER ★
Ammerang

SEBASTIAN BALLAUF (DE), **FRANCESCA FORNASIER** (IT), **MAXIMILIAN OTT** (DE), ARCHITECTS

AM ISARKANAL 24
81379 MÜNCHEN, GERMANY
T. +49 1775758239 / SFMBFO@GMAIL.COM

SELB – RUNNER-UP
Selbland

ALEXA BODAMMER (DE), URBAN PLANNER, ARCHITECT **CHRISTOPH RICHTER** (DE), **JAN TRUTZ** (DE), **ROLAND ZÜGER** (CH), ARCHITECTS

S T U D I O Z + – KAMENZERSTRASSE 41
01099 DRESDEN, GERMANY
T. +49 3515634313 / T. +49 1782329341 /
MAIL@STUDIOZPLUS.COM / WWW.STUDIOZPLUS.COM /
WWW.SLETH.DK

WÜRZBURG – RUNNER-UP
Helianthus

DOMINGO MELENDO ARANCÓN (ES),
FRANCISCO PARRÓN ORTIZ (ES), ARCHITECTS
FERNANDO LÓPEZ BARRIENTOS (ES),
MIGUEL ANGEL SUÁREZ MORENO (ES), ARCHITECTS

CALLE MIRÓ
1341804 OLIVARES (SEVILLE), SPAIN
T. +34 954613493 / FPARRON@ARCO.INFONEGOCIO.COM

WINNING TEAMS

224

WÜRZBURG – RUNNER-UP
Le Nouveau Trianon

ANDREAS KROMPASS (DE), **VANESSA PHILIPP** (DE),
PHILIPP REICHELT (DE), **WERNER SCHÜHRER** (DE),
HEIKE UNGER (DE), **ANDY WESTNER** (DE),
CHRISTIAN ZÖHRER (DE), ARCHITECTS

VIERZUEINS, HESSSTRASSE 39
80798 MÜNCHEN, GERMANY
T. +49 8963852600 / INFO@VIERZUEINS.CC / WWW.VIERZUEINS.CC

ALCORCÓN – WINNER ★
Arbolópolis

DIEGO JIMÉNEZ LÓPEZ (ES), **JUANA SÁNCHEZ GÓMEZ** (ES),
ARCHITECTS
GONZALO ROLDÁN ÁLVAREZ (ES),
ANTONIO JESÚS TORRES SÁNCHEZ (ES), ARCHITECTS

DJARQUITECTURA, AVD. MARQUESA DE ESQUILACHE, 24
18600 MOTRIL, GRANADA, SPAIN
T. +34 958823130 / INFO@DJARQUITECTURA.COM / WWW.DJARQUITECTURA.COM

CERDANYOLA DEL VALLÈS – RUNNER-UP
The transparent city

JAVIER F. CONTRERAS (ES), **DINGTING CHEN** (CN),
ARCHITECTS

C/ BLASCO DE GARAY 34, 2ºD
28015 MADRID, SPAIN
T. +34 915933816 / CONTACT@CHCO.EU.COM / WWW.CHCO.EU.COM

ESPAÑA

ALCALÁ DE LA SELVA – WINNER ★
Productive landscape

CECILIA RODRÍGUEZ VIELBA (ES), **ARNAU SASTRE CUADRI** (ES), **POL VILADOMS CLAVEROL** (ES),
ARCHITECTS

C/DEGÀ BAHÍ 28-32 ENTL 2ª
08026 BARCELONA, SPAIN
T. +34 696006474 / INFO@POLVILADOMS.COM

ALCORCÓN – RUNNER-UP
Roundabout Profilactics

CRISTINA GOBERNA (ES), **URTZI GRAU** (ES), ARCHITECTS

FAKE INDUSTRIES ARCHITECTURAL AGONISM
170 TILLARY #103 BROOKLYN, NY
11201 NY, USA
T. +1 9172737414/+34 664279414 / INFO@ FAKEINDUSTRIES.ORG / WWW.FAKEINDUSTRIES.ORG

GETARIA – WINNER ★
The intrusive stairs

JOSE MANUEL CALVO DEL OLMO (ES), **GUILLERMO GOSALBO GUENOT** (ES), **JOSÉ LÓPEZ PARRA** (ES),
ARCHITECTS
ESTHER MUÑOZ MARTÍNEZ (ES), PHOTOGRAPHER
ANA PAGÁN APARICIO (ES), GRAPHIC DESIGNER

RONDA DE ATOCHA Nº3_ 4C
28012 MADRID, SPAIN
T. +34 637062237 / WWW.LAESCALERAINTRUSA.COM

ALCALÁ DE LA SELVA – RUNNER-UP
**Caminante, no hay camino,
se hace camino al andar (Traveller, there is no road, you make your path as you walk)**

JAVIER ACEDO ANDRÉS (ES), **PAULA ANASAGASTI GUTIÉRREZ** (ES), **LUCÍA MARTÍN LÓPEZ** (ES), ARCHITECTS

SANGENJO 25 8F
28034 MADRID, SPAIN
T.+34 615676507 / JAVIAC2@GMAIL.COM

CERDANYOLA DEL VALLÈS – WINNER ★
BLAT

JOSEP FERRANDO (ES), **MARC NADAL** (ES), **DAVID RECIO** (ES),
ARCHITECTS
ANNE-LISE ROUSSAT (FR), JORDI PÉREZ (ES),
BORJA RODRÍGUEZ (ES), STUDENTS IN ARCHITECTURE

C. MALLORCA 172 LOCAL INTERIOR
08036 BARCELONA, SPAIN
T. +34 931860183 / JFB_ARCH@COAC.NET / WWW.JOSEPFERRANDO.COM

GETARIA – RUNNER-UP
for Getaria and *of* Getaria

MARC BAJET MENA (ES), ENGINEER
PAU BAJET MENA (ES), **OSCAR LINARES DE LA TORRE** (ES),
ARCHITECTS

T. +34 610 839 864 / OSLITOR@HOTMAIL.COM /
T. +34 652 080 450 / PAU.BAJET@GMAIL.COM

SAN BARTOLOMÉ – WINNER ★
'Rurban' geology
P. BAQUERO MASATS (ES), **J. CASTELLANO PULIDO** (ES), **T. GARCÍA PÍRIZ** (ES), **L. M. RUIZ AVILÉS** (ES), **J. ANTONIO SERRANO GARCÍA** (ES), ARCHITECTS

J. BACHS RUBIO (ES), A. C. GALINDO DURÁN (ES), C. A. GARCÍA ALMEIDA (ES), J. E. INIESTA MOLINA (ES), M. DE LARA RUIZ (ES), A. P. LÓPEZ FERNÁNDEZ (ES), E. M. LUCENA GUERRERO (ES), ARCHITECTS

CUAC ARQUITECTURA – C/BUENSUCESO 40.
CP. 18002. GRANADA, SPAIN
T. +34 958992334 / CUAC.ARQUITECTURA@GMAIL.COM / WWW.CUACS.COM

SESTAO – RUNNER-UP
La Punta in state of transition
RAQUEL BÁSCONES RECIO (ES), ARCHITECT

MIGUEL JIMÉNEZ SÁNCHEZ (ES), ITXASNE LÓPEZ GOITI (ES), SUSANA RODRÍGUEZ JIMÉNEZ (ES), SARA ZUGASTI ROYUELA (ES), STUDENTS IN ARCHITECTURE

CALLE OCAÑA, 66 - 2ºB
28047 MADRID, SPAIN
T. +34 625529563 / RAQUELBASCONES@GMAIL.COM / EUROPAN11SESTAO@GMAIL.COM

FRANCE

REIMS – WINNER ★
Multitalented city
TADAS JONAUSKIS (LT), URBAN DESIGNER, ARCHITECT
JUSTINA MULIUOLYTE (LT), URBAN DESIGNER
LUKAS REKEVICIUS (LT), ARCHITECT

PUPA - PUBLIC URBANISM PERSONAL ARCHITECTURE, SPOORSINGEL 18
2613BE, DELFT, NETHERLANDS
T. +31 624943999 / INFO@PU-PA.EU / TADASJONAUSKIS@GMAIL.COM / WWW.PU-PA.EU

SAN BARTOLOMÉ – RUNNER-UP
Topographic activity
RUBÉN RAMOS JIMÉNEZ (ES),
HÉCTOR SALCEDO GARCÍA (ES), ARCHITECTS

JOSÉ JAVIER RODRÍGUEZ BARBUDO (ES), ARCHITECT

CALLE MAÍZ 12, 2º B
28026 MADRID, SPAIN
T. +34 686922597 / ESTUDIO@RARQ.ES / WWW.RARQ.ES / WWW.HSALCEDOGARCIA.BLOGSPOT.COM

CLERMONT-FERRAND – WINNER ★
Nudge City
PIERRE BAILLY (FR), **GÉRAUD SAFFRAY** (FR), ARCHITECT, URBAN PLANNER – **CHARLES DAUBAS** (FR), URBAN PLANNER

YANN EOUZAN (FR), ESTELLE PETIT (FR), GRAPHIC DESIGNER
THOMAS SÉRIÈS (US), DIGITAL PERSPECTIVES

RIO, 31, RUE DOUDEAUVILLE
75018 PARIS, FRANCE
T. +33 982483725 / CONTACT@RI-O.FR / WWW.RI-O.FR

REIMS – RUNNER-UP
Landscape beyond limits
AMÉLIE FONTAINE (FR), ARCHITECT, URBAN PLANNER
CÉSAR VABRE (FR), ARCHITECT

MADELEINE CLAVEL (FR), STUDENT IN ARCHITECTURE

ARCHITECTURE & URBANISME, 30 RUE DE TAISNIÈRES
59244 GRAND-FAYT, FRANCE
T. +33 671590932 / CONTACT@ATELIER-AMELIEFONTAINE.COM / WWW.ATELIER-AMELIEFONTAINE.COM

SESTAO – RUNNER-UP
Con la falda remangá
CARLES CROSAS ARMENGOL (ES), **JOAN SOLÀ FONT** (ES), ARCHITECTS

ÁLVARO PÉREZ OTÍN (ES), ARCHITECT
GUILLEM MARTÍNEZ PIERA (ES), STUDENT IN ARCHITECTURE

BERTRÁN 44 B3
8023 BARCELONA, SPAIN
T +34 9183848 / SFCA@COAC.NET

NEUILLY-SUR-MARNE – RUNNER-UP
Cartilaginous
ANDREA BELLODI (IT), **MICHELE PASCUCCI** (IT), **CARLOTTA MAZZI** (IT), ARCHITECTS

MARCO LOMARTIRE (IT), STUDENT IN ARCHITECTURE

OQ PROJECT, VIA VITTORIO VENETO N°19
44012 BONDENO, FERRARA, ITALY
T. +39 3283032631 / T. +39 0532896223 / INFO@OQPROJECT.COM / WWW.OQPROJECT.COM

SAVENAY – WINNER ★
"Mesures ligériennes"
THIBAULT BARBIER (FR), LANDSCAPE ENGINEER
LAETITIA LAFONT (FR), ARCHITECT

42 RUE D'AVRON
75020 PARIS, FRANCE
T. +33 675814551 / LETKA.CONTACT@GMAIL.COM / WWW.MILIEUX.FR

WINNING TEAMS

226

SAVENAY – RUNNER-UP
SB \ SH
LIONEL ROULLET (FR), **MATTHIEU THUILLIER** (FR),
ARCHITECTS

T. +32 497384655 / LIONEL.ROULLET@GMAIL.COM /
T. +33 685593218 / MATTHIEU.THUILLIER@HOTMAIL.FR

STAINS – RUNNER-UP
Stain's alive
ELISE AVIDE (FR), **RAPHAËLLE BERNABEI** (FR),
URBAN PLANNER
BENJAMIN BOSSELUT (FR), URBAN PLANNER, GEOGRAPHER
YOHAN DEMASSE (FR), LANDSCAPE ENGINEER,
URBAN PLANNER
PHILIPPE GAUDIAS (FR), ENGINEER, URBAN PLANNER
OSCAR GENTIAL (FR), ARCHITECT, URBAN PLANNER

1, CHEMIN DES VARINNES
69380 LES CHÈRES, FRANCE
T. +33 672751625 / OSCAR.GENTIAL@GMAIL.COM /
WWW.OSCARGENTIAL.BLOGSPOT.COM

TOULOUSE – RUNNER-UP
The Meta-Block: a model from Toulouse
L. BRENTERC'H (FR), ARCHITECT URBAN PLANNER – **E. MARIN**
(FR), ARCHITECT URBAN PLANNER, LANDSCAPE ARCHITECT
N. BUSSAC (FR), ARCHITECT URBAN PLANNER – G. MASSOT (FR),
ARCHITECT – T. STEPHAN (FR), STUDENT IN GEOGRAPHY

AGENCE COT, 17 RUE RAMPONEAU
75020 PARIS, FRANCE
T. +33 182281990 / AGENCE@AGENCECOT.FR /
WWW.AGENCECOT.FR

HRVATSKA

SAVENAY – RUNNER-UP
Dock life
XIANG WANG (FR), **WENMU TIAN (CN)**, ARCHITECTS
RAN SHE (CN), CHENGMEI ZONG (CN), ARCHITECTS

ATELIER WETTA, 50 RUE DU VERTBOIS
75003 PARIS, FRANCE
T. +33 177170512 / CONTACT@WETTA.FR / WWW.WETTA.FR

STAINS – RUNNER-UP
Linking live from earth to the city
TANGUY MALLIER (FR), **CLAIRE KLINGER** (FR), ARCHITECTS

ATELIER TMCK, 59, RUE DU FAUBOURG SAINT ANTOINE
75011 PARIS, FRANCE
T. +33 673149296 / INFO@ATELIER-TMCK.COM /
WWW.ATELIER-TMCK.COM

DUBROVNIK – WINNER ★
Back to citizens!
JAIME FONT FUREST (ES), ARCHITECT

MARCOS PARERA BLANCH (ES), JORDI ESPINET ROMA (ES),
JORDI PARCET COMAS (ES), STUDENT IN ARCHITECTURE

D311 ARCHITECTURE, CARRER DIPUTACIÓ 311
08009 BARCELONA, SPAIN
T. +34 670292440 / FONTFUREST@COAC.NET

STAINS – WINNER ★
Effets de Serres
ADÈLE CATHERINE (FR), **AURÉLIE FRANÇOIS** (MU),
PIERRE-EMMANUEL LIMONDIN (FR), ARCHITECTS
LAURA GIULIANI (FR), ARCHITECT, LANDSCAPE ARCHITECT
EMMANUELLE KLINGER (FR), ARCHITECT, URBAN PLANNER

CLIC ARCHITECTURE, 25 RUE DE LA BIENFAISANCE
75008 PARIS, FRANCE
T. +33 981759771 / CONTACT@CLIC-ARCHITECTURE.COM /
WWW.CLIC-ARCHITECTURE.COM

TOULOUSE – WINNER ★
Poetry of the random
ESTELLE BOURREAU (FR), **JEAN-BAPTISTE COLTIER** (FR),
AURÉLIE FABRE (FR), ARCHITECTS

15 RUE DES RÉGANS
31000 TOULOUSE, FRANCE
CONTACT@RNDMARCHITECTURE.COM /
WWW.RNDMARCHITECTURE.COM /
WWW.JBCARCHITECTURE.COM

DUBROVNIK – RUNNER-UP
Play Topography
ANTONIO BRAVO RINCÓN (ES), **MARÍA CARMEN RUIZ IBÁÑEZ**
(ES), ARCHITECT, URBAN PLANNER
SALVADOR APARICIO MASSÓ (ES), ARCHITECT
CLAUDIA CABALLERO MOYA (ES), STUDENT IN ARCHITECTURE

CALLE ABOLENGO, 1. LOCAL
28025. MADRID, SPAIN
T. +34 914284747 / ANTBRAVO@ARQUIRED.ES

227

IRELAND

DUBLIN – WINNER ★
CounterSpace
CAROLINE O'DONNELL (IE), ARCHITECT
LESLIE MIGNIN (US), STUDENT IN ARCHITECTURE

1310 E.SHORE DR.
ITHACA, NY 14850, USA
T. +1 9735191070 / COD@CO-DA.EU / WWW.CO-DA.EU

NEDERLAND

ALMERE – WINNER ★
Frame
TIMUR SHABAEV (RU), ARCHITECT
MARIA KRASNOVA (RU), ARTIST

GORDELWEG 92A-3
3037AL ROTTERDAM, NETHERLANDS
T. +31 639621566 / TSHABAEV@GMAIL.COM /
WWW.TSHABAEV.BLOGSPOT.COM

AMSTERDAM – RUNNER-UP
Basic City
MATTEO BETTONI (NL), **YONG CUI** (CN), **SARAH WOLFF** (DE), ARCHITECTS
MILENA ZAKLANOVIC (NL), **PETAR ZAKLANOVIC (NL)**, ARCHITECTS, URBAN PLANNERS

GROENINXSTRAAT 5C
3039TC ROTTERDAM, THE NETHERLANDS
T. +31 102735999 / INFO@BASICCITY.EU / WWW.BASICCITY.EU

DUBLIN – RUNNER-UP
East Wall Lot
JANE LARMOUR (GB), **PATRICK WHEELER** (GB), ARCHITECTS
HUGH MAGEE (IE), STUDENT IN ARCHITECTURE

50 PRETORIA STREET
BELFAST BT9 5AQ, NORTHERN IRELAND
T. +44 7900342036 / INFO@LARMOURWHEELER.COM /
WWW.LARMOURWHEELER.COM

ALMERE – RUNNER-UP
**Envisioning baucis,
observatory for an artificial wilderness**
OLAF JANSON (NL), **JOOST MAATKAMP** (NL), ARCHITECTS
KOEN LOOMAN (NL), BUILDING ENGINEER
RENS WIJNAKKER (NL), LANDSCAPE ARCHITECT

TULPSTRAAT 57
8012 BG ZWOLLE, THE NETHERLANDS
T. +31 611353515 / MAIL@ENVISIONINGBAUCIS.NL /
WWW.ENVISIONINGBAUCIS.NL

CAPELLE AAN DEN IJSSEL – WINNER ★
Polder Salad
ELENA CHEVTCHENKO (UA / NL), **ANDREW KITCHING** (GB), **KEN THOMPSON** (GB), ARCHITECTS
DAVE MORISON (AU), ARCHITECT

WALENBURGERWEG 19D
3039AB ROTTERDAM, THE NETHERLANDS
T. +31 614179736 / ELENA@ANDERSARCH.NET /
WWW.ANDERSARCH.NET

MAGYARORSZÁG

SZEGED – WINNER ★
The red balloon
GERGELY ALMOS (HU), **TAMAS KUN** (HU), **TAMAS MEZEY** (HU), ARCHITECTS

BARTOK BELA STREET 106-110. A/B IV/15
1115 BUDAPEST, HUNGARY
T. +36 303033827 / INFO@AMKSTUDIO.HU /
WWW.AMKSTUDIO.HU

AMSTERDAM – WINNER ★
I Amstel 3
SARA REICHWEIN (DE), ARCHITECT, URBAN PLANNER

T. +49 17610069091 / SARA.REICHWEIN@HOTMAIL.DE /
WWW.SARAREICHWEIN.DE

DEVENTER – WINNER ★
Planting havenkwartier
ERWIN SCHOT (NL), **BAS MEIJERMAN** (NL), **ELMAR HAMMERS** (NL), ARCHITECTS
ELOI KOSTER (NL), GRAPHIC DESIGNER

T. +31 573222180 / E.SCHOT@MAASARCHITECTEN.NL /
WWW.MAASARCHITECTEN.NL

WINNING TEAMS

228

DEVENTER – RUNNER-UP
DHK, a new history
FERDY HOLTKAMP (NL), **J-P WENINK** (NL), ARCHITECTS
KEVIN CLAUS (NL), STUDENT IN ARCHITECTURE

WENINK HOLTKAMP | ARCHITECTEN
ROOSTENLAAN 15
5644 GA EINDHOVEN, THE NETHERLANDS
T. +31-649925006 / JPWENINK@WENINKHOLTKAMP.NL /
FHOLTKAMP@WENINKHOLTKAMP.NL /
WWW.WENINKHOLTKAMP.COM

EINDHOVEN – RUNNER-UP
VOLT
TIBOR KIS (NL), **FLORIS VAN DEN BIGGELAAR** (NL), ARCHITECTS
DOROTA KOLEK (PL), THIJS VAN SPAANDONK (NL), ARCHITECTS

BLOEMSTRAAT 62-1
1016LE AMSTERDAM, THE NETHERLANDS
T. +31 61419705 / TIBOR.KIS@GMAIL.COM /
WWW.EINDHOVENVOLT.NL

NORGE

HAUGESUND – RUNNER-UP
Flotmyr is back on the postcard
KATJA ENGEL ZEPERNICK (DK), **ANETT GRØNNERN OLSEN** (NO), URBAN PLANNER
MERETE KINNERUP ANDERSEN (DK), **JONAS ROAR HANSEN** (DK), ARCHITECTS

STWWT, V/JONAS ROAR HANSEN, TONSBERGVEJ 60
4000 ROSKILDE, DENMARK
STWWT.ARCHITECTS@GMAIL.COM /
WWW.STWWT.WORDPRESS.COM

DEVENTER – RUNNER-UP
"Bricolage"
MARIEKE KUMS (NL), ARCHITECT
EUH YONG KIM (KR), YONG IL KIM (KR), ARCHITECTS
YUKA TAKEUCHI (NL), STUDENT IN ARCHITECTURE

MAKS, WILLEM BUYTEWECHSTRAAT 20
3024 BN ROTTERDAM, THE NETHERLANDS
T. +31 102264124 / MK@M-A-K-S.NL / WWW.M-A-K-S.NL

LEEUWARDEN – WINNER ★
nieuWATERgarden
P. BAQUERO MASATS (ES), **J. CASTELLANO PULIDO** (ES),
T. GARCÍA PÍRIZ (ES), **L. M. RUIZ AVILÉS** (ES), **J. ANTONIO SERRANO GARCÍA** (ES), ARCHITECTS
J. BACHS RUBIO (ES), A. C. GALINDO DURÁN (ES), C. A. GARCÍA ALMEIDA (ES), J. E. INIESTA MOLINA (ES), M. DE LARA RUIZ (ES), A. P. LÓPEZ FERNÁNDEZ (ES), E. M. LUCENA GUERRERO (ES), ARCHITECTS

CUAC ARQUITECTURA, C/BUENSUCESO 40.
18002 GRANADA, SPAIN
T. +34 958992334 / CUAC.ARQUITECTURA@GMAIL.COM /
WWW.CUACS.COM

HAUGESUND – RUNNER-UP
Hip-hubs
GONZALO COELLO DE PORTUGAL (ES),
MARTA GRANDA NISTAL (ES), ARCHITECTS
ANA MORIYON (ES), STUDENT IN ARCHITECTURE

BINOM ARCHITECTS, UNIT 3.1, 2-6 NORTHBURGH ST
LONDON EC1V 0AY, UNITED KINGDOM
T. +44 2032170025 / INFO@BINOM.CO.UK / WWW.BINOM.CO.UK

EINDHOVEN – WINNER ★
Composition IX, opus 18
DANIEL ZARHY (PL), ARCHITECT

STUDIOPEZ, 150 ARLOZOROV ST.
TEL AVIV 62098, ISRAEL
INFO@STUDIOPEZ.NET / WWW.STUDIOPEZ.NET

LEEUWARDEN – RUNNER-UP
Floating Blocks
ALINA LIPPIELLO (IT), **LEONARDO ZUCCARO MARCHI** (IT), ARCHITECTS
FAUSTO CUZZOCREA (IT), FABIO DE CIECHI (IT),
MANUELE MOSSONI (IT), FILIPPO ZORDAN (IT), STUDENT IN ARCHITECTURE
PIERRE BERTRAND GUYOT DE LA HARDROUYERE (FR),
ANNALISA ROMANI (IT), LANDSCAPE EXPERT-ARCHITECT
VESNA MARKOVIĆ (SRB), ARCHITECT

VIA JOMMELLI 33
20231 MILANO, ITALY
T. +39 3335931588 / ALINA.L@TISCALI.IT / WWW.LAPSTUDIO.EU

OSLO – WINNER ★
The gardens of Grønmo
SILKE VOLKERT (DE), **MAGNUS WEIGHTMAN** (GB), ARCHITECTS

MAASKADE 97C
3071 NG ROTTERDAM, THE NETHERLANDS
T. +31 619872530 / SILKEVOLKERT@GMX.DE

OSLO – RUNNER-UP
In return
JUAN BERASATEGI (ES), LANDSCAPE ARCHITECT
ELI GRØNN (NO), ARCHITECT

BERASATEGI-GRØNN, FREDENSBORGVEIEN 15A
0177 OSLO, NORWAY
T. +47 40059401 / ARK@ELIGRONN.NO

GRAZ – RUNNER-UP
Yeswebridge
JUAN PEDRO DONAIRE BARBERO (ES), ARCHITECT

IGNACIO NÚÑEZ BOOTELLO (ES), JESÚS NÚÑEZ BOOTELLO (ES),
DELIA PACHECO DONAIRE (ES),
PABLO BARUC GARCÍA GÓMEZ (ES), ARCHITECTS

CALLE VELARDE Nº 10 A
41001 SEVILLE, SPAIN
T. +34.954 546 286 / ESTUDIO@DONAIREARQUITECTOS.COM /
WWW.DONAIREARQUITECTOS.COM

LINZ – RUNNER-UP
Portrait of an Ensemble
SANDRA GNIGLER (AT), **GUNAR WILHELM** (AT), ARCHITECTS
LORENZ POTOCNIK (AT), URBAN PLANNER

RAINERSTRASSE 25
4020 LINZ, AUSTRIA
T. +43 6505673697 / LORENZ@POTOCNIK.NET / WWW.MIA.OR.AT /
WWW.POTOCNIK.NET

SKIEN PORSGRUNN – RUNNER-UP
Link+
PIERLUIGI D'ACUNTO (IT), ARCHITECT, ENGINEER
NORMAN HACK (DE), ARCHITECT

MAERZSTRASSE 9
1150 WIEN, AUSTRIA
NORMAN.HACK@GMX.NET

LINZ – RUNNER-UP
Urban Monolith
FRANCESCO FUSARO (IT), **MARCELLO GALIOTTO** (IT),
MARCO MONTAGNINI (IT), **NICOLA MONTINI** (IT), **ALESSANDRA RAMPAZZO** (IT), **GIAN LUCA ZOLI** (IT), ARCHITECTS

ALESSIA BARBIERO (IT), FRANCESCO DELLA MOTTA (IT), ENRICO NASCIMBEN (IT), LUDOVICO PEVERE (IT), PAOLA SCALVINI (IT), STUDENT IN ARCHITECTURE

MANGA – STUDIO C.SO, MAZZINI N. 68
48018 FAENZA (RA), ITALY
T. +39 0546680436 / INFO@MANGASTUDIO.ORG /
WWW.MANGASTUDIO.ORG

WIEN – WINNER ★
Dreiecksplatz
ARTUR BOREJSZO (PL), ARCHITECT

LEENA CHO (US), LANDSCAPE ARCHITECT, URBAN PLANNER
JASON HILGEFORT (US), URBAN PLANNER, ARCHITECT
ANDREAS KARAVANAS (GR), ARCHITECT, URBAN PLANNER

IMPRESSIVELY SIMPLE - URBANISM | LANDSCAPE | ARCHITECTURE
RODENRIJSESTRAAT 73A – 3037 PG ROTTERDAM, THE NETHERLANDS
T. +31 624182403 / INFO@IMPRESSIVELYSIMPLE.NET /
WWW.IMPRESSIVELYSIMPLE.NET

ÖSTERREICH

GRAZ – RUNNER-UP
Magnetic Urban Field
STEFAN GRUBER (DE), ARCHITECT

GILBERT BERTHOLD (AT), ARCHITECT
PHILIPP SOEPARNO (AT), STUDENT IN ARCHITECTURE

STUDIOGRUBER, GIRARDIGASSE 2/31
1060 VIENNA, AUSTRIA
T. +43 6765757222 / OFFICE@STUDIOGRUBER.COM /
WWW.STUDIOGRUBER.COM

LINZ – RUNNER-UP
Linzertus: Linzer Insertus
JULIO DE LA FUENTE (ES), **NATALIA GUTIÉRREZ** (ES),
ARCHITECTS

PAUL-ROUVEN DENZ (DE), STUDENT IN ARCHITECTURE

GUTIÉRREZ-DELAFUENTE ARQUITECTOS,
C/ PINTOR ROSALES, 9. LOCAL
28100 ALCOBENDAS, MADRID, SPAIN
T. +34 629529498 / JULIO@GUTIERREZ-DELAFUENTE.COM /
WWW.GUTIERREZ-DELAFUENTE.COM

POLSKA

WARSZAWA – WINNER ★
L-M-S URBAN SCALE
BARBARA SKRZYPCZYK (PL), **MARCIN SKRZYPCZYK** (PL),
ARCHITECTS

KATARZYNA CHABANNE (PL), ENVIRONMENTALIST

KOLONIA WIERZCHOWISKO, UL. POGODNA 49
42-233 MYKANÓW, POLAND
T. +48 660696942 / ARCHMAJSTER@YMAIL.COM /
WWW.ARCHMAJSTER.COM

WINNING TEAMS

230

WARSZAWA – RUNNER-UP
Taking from within
MATEUSZ HERBST (PL), ARCHITECT

UL. KICKIEGO 4A/34
04-369 WARSAW, POLAND
T. +48 601237334 / MATHERB@WP.PL

REPUBLIKA E KOSOVËS/REPUBLIKA KOSOVA

PEJË – WINNER ★
Fratres
HECTOR ARDERIUS SALVADOR (ES),
ROBERTO GARCIA FALLOLA (ES), ARCHITECTS

T. +34 630248905 / H.ARDERIUS@GMAIL.COM / T. +34 630288719 /
ROBERTO.GFALLOLA@GMAIL.COM

AIGLE – RUNNER-UP
Stage and squares
FAÏÇAL OUDOR (FR), **PAUL ROLLAND** (FR), ARCHITECTS
CYRILLE BEIRNAERT (FR), STUDENT IN ARCHITECTURE

2:PM ARCHITECTURES
75019 PARIS AND 33000 BORDEAUX, FRANCE
T. +33 954319844 / CONTACT@2PMA.COM /
WWW.2PMARCHITECTURES.COM

PORTUGAL

GUIMARÃES – WINNER ★
**270° Landscape,
regeneration of an urban sequence**
CÉDRIC-CLAUDE BOUTEILLER (FR),
FLORENT CHIAPPERO (FR), **MARIA JOÃO PITA** (PT),
OLIVIER MÉNARD (FR), **PHILIPPE-SERGE SEPULVEDA** (FR),
ARCHITECTS

COLLECTIF ETC, 50 RUE DU FAUBOURG SAINT DENIS
75010 PARIS, FRANCE
T. +33 659 05954 / CONTACT@COLLECTIFETC.COM /
WWW.COLLECTIFETC.COM

PEJË – RUNNER-UP
Diana's Ring
LAURA FABRIANI (IT), **GIOVANNI ROMAGNOLI** (IT),
SANTE SIMONE (IT), **ALESSANDRO ZAPPATERRENI** (IT),
ARCHITECTS

VIA TIBURTINA 98
00185 ROMA, ITALY
T. +39 3207034127 / SANTESIMONE@ME.COM

MONTHEY – WINNER ★
Three gates Three mobilities
MEHDI AOUABED (FR), **ALBERTO FIGUCCIO** (IT), ARCHITECTS

FIL ROUGE ARCHITECTURE, 114, RUE DE LYON
1203 GENÈVE, SWITZERLAND
T. +41 223450420 / INFO@FILROUGEARCHITECTURE.CH /
WWW.FILROUGEARCHITECTURE.CH

SCHWEIZ/SUISSE/SVIZZERA/SVIZRA

GUIMARÃES – RUNNER-UP
In between place's time
DANIEL DUARTE PEREIRA (PT), **FERNANDO FERREIRA** (PT),
ARCHITECTS
GABRIELA SILVA (PT), ARCHITECT
SARA FERREIRA (PT), DANIEL MACEDO (PT), STUDENTS
IN ARCHITECTURE

RUA POÇA DA BÁCORA, Nº2 TRANDEIRAS
4705-644 BRAGA, PORTUGAL
T. +351 916518411 / DANIELDUARTEP@GMAIL.COM

AIGLE – WINNER ★
White
FRÉDÉRIC MARTINET (FR), **VINCENT TRARIEUX** (FR),
ARCHITECTS
JULIEN BARGUE (FR), ARNAUD FAUCHER (FR),
HYDROLOGY AND ENVIRONMENTAL ENGINEER
SIMON PORTELAS (FR), STUDENT IN ARCHITECTURE

FMAU BRIVE, 4, RUE SAINT JEAN
19100 BRIVE, FRANCE
FMAU LA ROCHELLE, 20, AVENUE JEAN GUITON
17000 LA ROCHELLE, FRANCE
WWW.FMAU.FR

MONTHEY – RUNNER-UP
Line Code
JOSÉ MARÍA SÁNCHEZ GARCÍA (ES), ARCHITECT

MARTA CABEZÓN LÓPEZ (ES), RAFAEL FERNÁNDEZ CAPARRÓS
(ES), LAURA ROJO VALDIVIELSO (ES), MARILÓ SÁNCHEZ GARCIA
(ES), ARCHITECTS – ENRIQUE GARCÍA-MARGALLO SOLO
DE ZALDIVAR (ES), ENGINEER-ARCHITECT – JAIME GARCIA
DE OTEYZA (ES), ELENA GONZÁLEZ MENES (ES), ANA RIVERO
ESTEBAN (ES), STUDENT IN ARCHITECTURE

CALLE PRINCESA 27, 15º - 3
28008 MADRID, SPAIN
T. +34 915231885 / JOSEMARIA.SANCHEZ@JMSG.ES /
WWW.JMSG.ES

ROMAINMÔTIER – WINNER ★
Built edges / Garden-metropolis

VINCENT ARNÉ (FR), **AUDE MERMIER** (FR), ARCHITECTS

20 RUE DE LA PLAINE
75020 PARIS, FRANCE
T. +33 662559382 / +33 677963036 /
ARNEMERMIER@GMAIL.COM

PORVOO – RUNNER-UP
Diamonds

LAURA HIETAKORPI (FI), **SAANA KARALA** (FI),
JENNI POUTANEN (FI), ARCHITECTS

C/O TILANNE, ITSENÄISYYDENKATU 23
33500 TAMPERE, FINLAND
T. +358 407035786 / TILANNE.M3@GMAIL.COM /
WWW.TILANNE.ORG

SVERIGE

MALMÖ – RUNNER-UP
Greenish village

JOHAN AHLQUIST (SE), **CARLOS MARTINEZ** (US),
URBAN SKOGMAR (SE), ARCHITECTS

METRO ARKITEKTER, GUSTAV ADOLFS TORG 8 B
211 39 MALMÖ, SWEDEN
T. +46 406655952 / JOHAN.AHLQUIST@METROARKITEKTER.SE

ROMAINMÔTIER – RUNNER-UP
Terracement – Play Mobile

MOISÉS ROYO MÁRQUEZ (ES), ARCHITECT

MARCOS GARCÍA BRAVO (ES), JOAQUÍN RODRÍGUEZ PEÑA (ES),
ARCHITECTS – ANA JIMÉNEZ ROMERO (ES), JAVIER ROMERO
LOZANO (ES), STUDENT IN ARCHITECTURE

CALLE MARQUÉS DE SANTA ANA 32, 2ºPLANTA
28004 MADRID, SPAIN
T. +34 915220582 / +34 652438435 / MAIL@MOISESROYO.COM /
WWW.MOISESROYO.COM

TURKU – WINNER ★
Garden state

SAMI VIKSTRÖM (FI), ARCHITECT

ARKKITEHTITOIMISTO SAMI VIKSTRÖM, STURENKATU 40 H 96
00550 HELSINKI, FINLAND
T. +358 407204724 / SAMI.VIKSTROM@WELHO.COM /
WWW.SAMIVIKSTROM.TUMBLR.COM

MALMÖ – RUNNER-UP
Green grid

MALIN DAHLHIELM (SE), **ANNA EDBLOM** (SE), ARCHITECTS,
URBAN PLANNER
KARIN KJELLSON (SE), ARCHITECT

TJUSTGATAN 5
118 27 STOCKHOLM, SWEDEN
T. +46 707411467 / KARIN.KJELLSON@FYRA13.SE

SUOMI-FINLAND

PORVOO – WINNER ★
Embroidery

JOUNI HEINÄNEN (FI), LANDSCAPE ARCHITECT
VALTTERI HEINONEN (FI), **PIA SJÖROOS** (FI), ARCHITECTS

VESURIPOLKU 5 A
00760 HELSINKI, FINLAND
T. +358 400732829 / PIA.SJOROOS@IKI.FI /
WWW.LH5B.FI/VALTTERIHEINONEN

TURKU – RUNNER-UP
Orchard Avenues

MARK BALZAR (AT), **PETER STEC** (SK), ARCHITECTS

ANNA CSÉFALVAYOVÁ (SK), MARIANNA MACZOVÁ (SK),
DOMINIKA BELANSKÁ (SK), DANICA PIŠTEKOVÁ (SK),
STUDENT IN ARCHITECTURE

MEČÍKOVÁ 26
84107 BRATISLAVA, SLOVAKIA
T. +421 944223667 / INFO@PETERSTEC.NET /
WWW.PETERSTEC.NET

NORRKÖPING – WINNER ★
Delta-X

PELLE BACKMAN (SE), **EBBA HALLIN** (SE), ARCHITECTS

T. +39 3426310670 / PELLEBACKMAN@HOTMAIL.COM /
T. +46 702225686 / EBBAHALLIN@GMAIL.COM

WINNING TEAMS

NORRKÖPING – RUNNER-UP
Synapcity

M. BERNART (CZ), **G. BERRINO** (IT), **G. DE CASTRO** (IT),
R. DLESK (SK), **D. MAGRI** (IT), **V. M. MARINACCIO** (IT),
F. MAZZIOTTI (IT), **M. MORRONE** (IT), **R. E. NASH** (IT),
M. PARINI (IT), **P. F. PELANDA** (IT), **C. VENTURA** (IT),
ARCHITECTS

V. CHIAPPA NUNEZ (IT), M. PARINI (IT), M. SCARAVELLA (IT),
L. DE STASIO (IT), B. VALENTINI (IT), STUDENTS IN ARCHITECTURE

P-U-R-A PLATFORM FOR URBAN RESEARCH AND ARCHITECTURE
VIA ASELLI, 18 – 20133 MILANO, ITALY
T. +39 3929617999 / INFO.IT@P-U-R-A.COM / WWW.P-U-R-A.COM

SIMRISHAMN – WINNER ★
"Wear out"

MIGUEL HUELGA DE LA FUENTE (ES),
IRIA DE LA PEÑA MÉNDEZ (ES), ARCHITECTS

AVDA. DE LAS HUELGAS 17 -2
09001 BURGOS, SPAIN
T. +34 661786423 / INFO@SUKUNFUKU.COM /
WWW.SUKUNFUKU.COM

NYNÄSHAMN – WINNER ★
Skärscape

JAN DERVEAUX (BE), ARCHITECT – **RITA LEAL** (PT), **FRANZ RESCHKE** (DE), **ANNA VOGELS** (DE), LANDSCAPE ARCHITECTS

FREDERIK SPRINGER (DE), STUDENT IN LANDSCAPE ARCHITECTURE

FRANZ RESCHKE LANDSCAPE ARCHITECT, KOTTBUSSER DAMM 74
10967 BERLIN, GERMANY
T. +49 17621905517 / WWW.FRANZRESCHKE.DE

SIMRISHAMN – WINNER ★
Strädde

ANDERS ERIKSSON (SE), ARCHITECT

EGIL BLOM (SE), HANNES HAAK (SE), DANIEL LINDBERG (SE),
ARCHITECTS

LÖJTNANTSG 10A
21150 MALMÖ, SWEDEN
T. +46 703082396 / EGILBLOM@EGILBLOM.COM

NYNÄSHAMN – RUNNER-UP
Too big square

GAÉTAN BRUNET (FR), **ANTOINE ESPINASSEAU** (FR),
CHLOÉ VALADIÉ (FR), ARCHITECTS, URBAN PLANNER

19 RUE ANTONIN RAYNAUD
92300 LEVALLOIS PERRET, FRANCE
T. +33 647898635 / GAETANBRUNET@GMAIL.COM

JURIES

234

BELGIQUE/BELGIË/BELGIEN

National Members
PUBLIC AUTHORITY REPRESENTATIVE
MARTINE RIDIAUX, ARCHITECT, REPRESENTATIVE OF THE OPERATIONAL GENERAL DIRECTION OF TERRITORIAL PLANNING OF WALLONIA
CLIENT REPRESENTATIVES
BENOIT DISPA, MAYOR OF GEMBLOUX – **RENAUD KINET**, ARCHITECT DIRECTOR OF THE OF URBAN PLANNING OF LIÈGE
ARCHITECTS
PIERRE GOT, URBAN PLANNER, TOURNAI – **DIDIER LEPOT**, ARCHITECT URBAN PLANNER, LIÈGE (BE)/MAASTRICHT (NL)

Foreign Members
ARCHITECTS
RONAN ABGRAL-ABHAMON, ARCHITECT, EUROPAN 8 WINNER, PARIS (FR) – **PATRICK GENARD**, ARCHITECT, MADRID (ES)
PERSONALITIES
PHILIPPE PANERAI, ARCHITECT, TEACHER, URBAN PLANNING AWARD 1999, PARIS (FR) – **ALAIN PELISSIER**, ARCHITECT, URBAN PLANNER, PROFESSOR ENSA PARIS-VAL-DE-SEINE, DOCTOR ES-LETTRES, PARIS (FR)

Subsitutes
JOËL MATRICHE, JOURNALIST LE SOIR, BRUXELLES
JEAN MCHEL DEGRAEVE, ARCHITECT, HABITAT CONCEPT, MAISON DE L'URBANITÉ, RIXENSART

DANMARK

National Members
PUBLIC AUTHORITY REPRESENTATIVE
MIKALA HOLME SAMSØE, ARCHITECT MAA, INT. MASTER OF LEADERSHIP AND INNOVATION (LAICS), THE DANISH UNIVERSITY AND PROPERTY AGENCY, MINISTRY OF SCIENCE, TECHNOLOGY AND INNOVATION, COPENHAGEN
CLIENT REPRESENTATIVES
MAJ GREEN, DEPUTY DIRECTOR, URBAN AND ENVIRONMENTAL AFFAIRS, MUNICIPALITY OF GLADSAXE CHAIRMAN, THE DANISH TOWN PLANNING INSTITUTE
ARCHITECTS
ANDREAS KLOK PEDERSEN, ARCHITECT PARTNER BIG, COPENHAGEN – **MARTIN KEIDING**, ARCHITECT MAA AND EDITOR IN CHIEF, THE JOURNAL ARKITEKTUR DK, COPENHAGEN
PERSONALITIES
CHRISTIAN BUNDEGAARD, CONSULTANT, MA HISTORY OF IDEAS/ARCHITECTURE, COPENHAGEN – **TANJA JORDAN**, ARCHITECT MAA, RUBOW ARCHITECTS, EUROPAN 10 WINNER NORDHAVNEN, COPENHAGEN

Foreign Members
CLIENT REPRESENTATIVES
METTE SVENSEN, ARCHITECT, URBAN PLANNER AND PROJECT DEVELOPER, AGENCY FOR REAL ESTATE AND URBAN RENEWAL, MUNICIPALITY OF OSLO (NO)
ARCHITECTS
LUIS M. MANSILLA, ARCHITECT AND PHD. MANSILLA + TUÑON ARCHITECTS, MADRID (ES) – **RIENTS DIJKSTRA**, PRINCIPAL, MAXWAN ARCHITECT+URBANISTS, ROTTERDAM (NL)

Subsitutes
ANNE TIETJEN, ARCHITECT MAA, PHD, PROJECT MANAGER, HOUSE OF HERITAGE LTD, (DE)

DEUTSCHLAND – POLSKA (ASSOCIATED)

National Members
PUBLIC AUTHORITY REPRESENTATIVE
KARIN SANDECK, ARCHITECT, BAVARIAN STATE MINISTRY OF THE INTERIOR, MUNICH
ARCHITECTS
ULRIKE BÖHM, LANDSCAPE ARCHITECT, BBZL, BERLIN
ANDREAS GARKISCH, 03 ARCHITECTS, MUNICH
PERSONALITY
FRAUKE BURGDORFF, SPATIAL PLANER, DIRECTOR OF MONTAG STIFTUNG URBANE RÄUME GAG, BONN
PROF. CHRISTA REICHER, ARCHITECT, URBAN PLANER, AACHEN/DORTMUND

Foreign Members
CLIENT REPRESENTATIVE
HANS THOOLEN, COORDINATOR URBAN QUALITY, BREDA (NL)
ARCHITECTS
ROGER RIEWE, ARCHITECT, GRAZ (AT) – **MARIA AUBÖCK**, ARCHITECT, WIEN (AT)

Representative of poland
KATARZYNA FURGALINSKA, ARCHITECT, EUROPAN 10 WINNER, KATOWICE PL/OSLO (NO)

Subsitutes
MICHAEL RUDOLPH, ARCHITECT, EUROPAN 8 WINNER, STATION C23, LEIPZIG – **DR. IRENE WIESE-VON OFEN**, URBAN PLANER, ESSEN

ESPAÑA

National Members

PUBLIC AUTHORITY REPRESENTATIVE
GLORIA IRIARTE, ARCHITECT, BILBAO

CLIENT REPRESENTATIVES
JORDI BADIA, ARCHITECT AND PROFESSOR, ESTUDIO BAAS, BARCELONA – **JESÚS IRISARRI**, ARCHITECT AND PROFESSOR, LA CORUÑA

ARCHITECTS
JUAN DOMINGO SANTOS, ARCHITECT AND PROFESSOR, GRANADA – **JAVIER GARCIA-GERMÁN**, ARCHITECT, EUROPAN 10 WINNER, MADRID

PERSONALITIES
FÉLIX ARRANZ, ARCHITECT AND EDITOR, BARCELONA

Foreign Members

ARCHITECTS
GAIA REDEALLI, ARCHITECT, MILAN (IT)
KRISTINE JENSEN, LANDSCAPE ARCHITECT, COPENHAGEN (DK)

PERSONALITIES
NUNO RAVARA, ARCHITECT, HERZOG & DE MEURON, (CH)

Subsitutes

SEBATIÁ JORNET, ARCHITECT AND URBANIST, BARCELONA

FRANCE

National Members

PUBLIC AUTHORITY REPRESENTATIVE
FRANCK FAUCHEUX, DEPUTY CHIEF EXECUTIVE OF THE SUSTAINABLE DEVELOPMENT OFFICE, DEPARTMENT OF HOUSING AND NATURE PLANNING (MEDDTL), PARIS LA DÉFENSE
REPRESENTATIVE OF THE GENERAL DIRECTOR, DEPARTMENT OF HOUSING AND NATURE PLANNING (MEDDTL), PARIS LA DÉFENSE

CLIENT REPRESENTATIVES
CLAIRE MONOD, ELECTED MEMBER OF THE ILE DE FRANCE REGIONAL COUNCIL, PARIS – **LAURENT THÉRY**, DIRECTOR OF SAEM EURALILLE, LILLE

ARCHITECTS
JEAN-PIERRE PRANLAS-DESCOURS, ARCHITECT AND URBAN DESIGNER, PROFESSOR AT PARIS-MALAQUAIS SCHOOL OF ARCHITECTURE, ATELIER PRANLAS-DESCOURS, PARIS

PERSONALITIES
HENRI BAVA, LANDSCAPE DESIGNER, PROFESSOR AT KARLSRUHE UNIVERSITY (K.I.T), TER AGENCY, PARIS –
JEAN-MARIE DUTHILLEUL, CHIEF EXECUTIVE OFFICER OF AREP, PARIS

Foreign Members

ARCHITECTS
MIKE DAVIES, ARCHITECT AND URBAN DESIGNER, ROGERS PARTNERSHIP, LONDON (UK) – **MANUEL GAUSA**, ARCHITECT AND URBAN DESIGNER, PROFESSOR AT GENOVA SCHOOL OF ARCHITECTURE, GAUSA RAVEAU ACTARQUITECTURA AGENCY, BARCELONA (ES) – **MATHIS GÜLLER**, ARCHITECT AND URBAN DESIGNER, GÜLLER AND GÜLLER, ZURICH (CH)

Subsitutes

XAVIER BONNAUD, ARCHITECT AND URBAN DESIGNER, PROFESSOR AT CLERMONT-FERRAND SCHOOL OF ARCHITECTURE, MESOSTUDIO AGENCY, FONTENAY-SOUS-BOIS – **LAURENT PINON**, ARCHITECT AND URBAN DESIGNER, TEACHER AT PARIS-EST MARNE-LA-VALLÉE UNIVERSITY / LABORATORY GÉNIE URBAIN, ALPHAVILLE AGENCY, PARIS

HRVATSKA

National Members

PUBLIC AUTHORITY REPRESENTATIVE
KRUNOSLAV ŠMIT, ARCHITECT, PHD, ZAGREB

CLIENT REPRESENTATIVES
DAVOR BUŠNJA, ARCHITECT, DUBROVNIK ARCHITECT'S SOCIETY, DUBROVNIK – **SAŠA BRADIĆ**, ARCHITECT, VIENNA/ZAGREB

ARCHITECTS
SAŠA BEGOVIĆ, ARCHITECT, 3LHD, ZAGREB

PERSONALITIES
MARINA VICULIN, ART HISTORIAN, CURATOR IN KLOVIĆEVI DVORI ART GALLERY, ZAGREB – **SLOBODAN PROSPEROV NOVAK**, WRITER AND LITERATURE HISTORIAN, ZAGREB

Foreign Members

ARCHITECTS
CARME PINOS, ARCHITECT, BARCELONA (ES) – **MARIANNE SAETRE**, ARCHITECT, SNOHETTA, OSLO (NO) – **IVANA SRSEN**, ARCHITECT, BRUXELLES (BE)

Subsitutes

VANJA ILIĆ, ARCHITECT, ZAGREB – **DINKO PERAČIĆ**, ARCHITECT, SPLIT

JURIES

IRELAND

National Members
PUBLIC AUTHORITY REPRESENTATIVE
AIDAN O'CONNOR, PRINCIPAL ADVISOR, HOUSING DIVISION, DEPARTMENT OF THE ENVIRONMENT, HERITAGE AND LOCAL GOVERNMENT, DUBLIN
CLIENT REPRESENTATIVES
EDDIE CONROY, COUNTY ARCHITECT, SOUTH DUBLIN COUNTY COUNCIL – **GEETA KEENA**, SENIOR ARCHITECT, MAYO COUNTY COUNCIL
ARCHITECTS
PAUL KEOGH, PAUL KEOGH ARCHITECTS, DUBLIN – **SHEILA O'DONNELL**, PARTNER, O'DONNELL + TUOMEY ARCHITECTS, DUBLIN – **SEÁN MARTIN**, CITY ARCHITECT, SLIGO BOROUGH COUNCIL
PERSONAL TIES
FRANK MCDONALD, JOURNALIST, IRISH TIMES, DUBLIN

Foreign Members
ARCHITECTS
DAVID PRICHARD, PARTNER, METROPOLITAN WORKSHOP, LONDON (UK) – **ANNEMIEK RIJCKENBERG**, AMSTERDAM WELSTAND AMSTERDAM (NL)
PERSONAL TIES
MARIANNE SKJULHAUG, BERGEN SCHOOL OF ARCHITECTURE, BERGEN (NO)

Subsitutes
DAVID POWER, PARTNER, COX POWER ARCHITECTS, WESTPORT – **RONAN ROSE-ROBERTS**, PRINCIPAL, RONAN ROSE-ROBERTS ARCHITECTS, WICKLOW

NEDERLAND

National Members
CLIENT REPRESENTATIVES
MARIEN DE LANGEN, DIRECTOR HOUSING CORPORATION, AMSTERDAM – **ASTRID SANSON**, DIRECTOR URBAN QUALITY, MUNICIPALITY OF ROTTERDAM
ARCHITECTS
HANNEKE KIJNE, LANDSCAPE ARCHITECT HOSPER NL LANDSCAPE ARCHITECTURE AND URBAN DESIGN, HAARLEM – **KAREN VAN VLIET**, URBAN DESIGNER BGSV, ROTTERDAM
PERSONALITIES
HAN MEYER, PROFESSOR URBAN DESIGN TU DELFT

Foreign Members
ARCHITECTS
HELENA CASANOVA, ARCHITECT, EUROPAN 6 WINNER GRONINGEN AND EUROPAN 7 DEN HAAG, MADRID (ES)
MATTHEW TURNER, ARCHITECT AND JOURNALIST, LONDON (UK)
PERSONALITIES
KRISTIAAN BORRET, TOWN ARCHITECT ANTWERP (BE)

Subsitutes
FLOOR ARONS, ARCHITECT, EUROPAN 4 WINNER AMSTERDAM
JOOST GLISSENAAR, ARCHITECT, EUROPAN 5 WINNER AMSTERDAM

NORGE

National Members
PUBLIC AUTHORITY REPRESENTATIVE
KNUT FELBERG, CITY PLANNER, STATSBYGG, OSLO
CLIENT REPRESENTATIVES
METTE SVANES, DIRECTOR OF CITY PLANNING, BERGEN MUNICIPALITY
PERSONALITIES
TONE HUSE, URBAN GEOGRAPHER, RESEARCH FELLOW, TROMSØ

Foreign Members
CLIENT REPRESENTATIVES
AGNETA HAMMER, DIRECTOR OF CITY PLANNING, HELSINGBORG MUNICIPALITY (SE)
ARCHITECTS
LISA DIEDRICH, ARCHITECT, CO-EDITOR IN CHIEF OF SCAPE, (DE) – **JAN JONGERT**, ARCHITECT, 2012ARCHITECTEN, ROTTERDAM (NL) – **DEANE SIMPSON**, ARCHITECT, PROFESSOR BERGEN SCHOOL OF ARCHITECTURE/ THE ROYAL ACADEMY OF FINE ARTS, SCHOOL OF ARCHITECTURE COPENHAGEN (NZ)
BELINDA TATO, ARCHITECT, ECOSISTEMA URBANO, MADRID (ES)
PERSONALITIES
HELMUT MEYER, PRINCIPAL OF TRANSSOLAR ENERGIETECHNIK, STUTTGART (DE)

Subsitutes
ROSS LANGDON, ARCHITECT, WINNER EUROPAN 10 IN VARDØ, LONDON, NZ – **MARIANNA RENTZOU**, ARCHITECT, WINNER EUROPAN 10 IN TRONDHEIM, ATHENS (GR)

ÖSTERREICH – REPUBLIKA E KOSOVËS/ REPUBLIKA KOSOVA AND MAGYARORSZÁG (ASSOCIATED)

National Members
PUBLIC AUTHORITY REPRESENTATIVE
SABINE OPPOLZER, CULTURAL CRITIC, ORF, NATIONAL BROADCAST CORPORATION, WIEN

CLIENT REPRESENTATIVES
WOLFGANG SCHOEN, DIRECTOR OF HOUSING AGENCY WAG, LINZ

ARCHITECTS
KLAUS KADA, ARCHITECT AACHEN DE / GRAZ – **RUEDIGER LAINER**, ARCHITECT, WIEN

Foreign Members
CLIENT REPRESENTATIVES
PATRICK GMÜR, DIRECTOR OF THE DEPARTMENT OF URBAN PLANNING, ZÜRICH (CH)

ARCHITECTS
LIZA FIOR, ARCHITECT, MUF, LONDON (UK)
MIRZA MUJEZINOVICS, ARCHITECT, EUROPAN 8 WINNER, OSLO (NO)

PERSONALITIES
KAYE GEIPEL, ARCHITECTURAL CRITIC, BAUWELT, BERLIN (DE) – **ANGELIKA SCHNELL**, ARCHITECTURAL THEORIST, WIEN / BERLIN (DE)

Subsitutes
ROLF TOUSIMSKY / DANIELA HEROLD, ARCHITECTS, EUROPAN 7 WINNERS, SALZBURG

Representatives of Hungary
TAMÁS LEVAI, ARCHITECT, BUDAPEST (HU),
SUBSTITUTE: **BAROSS PÁL FRICS**, LANDSCAPE ARCHITECT, URBAN AND REGIONAL PLANNER, BUDAPEST (HU)

Representatives of Kosovo
LULZIM KABASHI, ARCHITECT, IVANIŠIN.KABASHI.ARCHITECTS, ZAGREB (HR)
SUBSTITUTE: **GEZIM PACARIZI**, ARCHITECT SIA, GENÈVE (CH)

PORTUGAL

National Members
PUBLIC AUTHORITY REPRESENTATIVE
MANUEL CORREIA FERNANDES, ARCHITECT, CHAIRMAN OF THE JURY, APPOINTED BY THE INSTITUTE OF HOUSING AND URBAN RENEWAL, O'PORTO

CLIENT REPRESENTATIVES
MANUEL FERNANDES DE SÁ, ARCHITECT, URBAN PLANNER, O'PORTO – **TERESA ANDRESEN**, LANDSCAPE ARCHITECT, PROFESSOR AT O'PORTO UNIVERSITY

ARCHITECTS
MARIA MANUEL OLIVEIRA, ARCHITECT, GUIMARÃES – **ANA ROXO**, ARCHITECT, URBAN PLANNER, LISBON

PERSONALITIES
JOSÉ MATEUS, ARCHITECT, PRESIDENT OF LISBON ARCHITECTURAL TRIENNIAL, TEACHER AT IST, LISBON

Foreign Members
ARCHITECTS
JOSÉ MARIA EZQUIAGA, ARCHITECT, TEACHER, MADRID (ES)
ULRIKE SACHER, ARCHITECT, MUNICH (DE)

PERSONALITIES
ANTONI REMESAR, URBAN DESIGNER & PUBLIC ART RESEARCHER, BARCELONA (ES)

Subsitutes
JOSÉ PEDRO LIMA DA SILVA, ARCHITECT, CCDRLVT, LISBON
PEDRO MENDES, ARCHITECT, TEACHER AT ISCTE, LISBON

SCHWEIZ/SUISSE/SVIZZERA/SVIZRA

National Members
PUBLIC AUTHORITY REPRESENTATIVE
FELIX WALDER, HEAD OF THE CONSTRUCTION DEPARTEMENT, FEDERAL ECONOMY DEPARTMENT (DFE), FEDERAL HOUSING OFFICE (OFL), GRANGES

CLIENT REPRESENTATIVES
CHRISTOPH COLONI, IMPLENIA REAL ESTATE, RENENS – **GEORGES-PHILIPPE MAYOR**, URBAN PLANNER, TERRITORY PLANNER REG A, 1RST DEPUTY COUNSELOR AT THE URBAN PLANNING DEPARTMENT OF THE CITY OF MONTREUX, GLION

ARCHITECTS
OLIVIER FAZAN MAGI, ARCHITECT, URBAN PLANNER, PRESIDENT OF THE JURY, LAUSANNE

PERSONALITIES
LORETTE COEN, JOURNALIST, LAUSANNE – **DR. PATRICK RÉRAT**, GEOGRAPHER, LECTURER IN CHARGE OF RESEARCH, GEOGRAPHY INSTITUTE & RESEARCH GROUP IN TERRITORIAL ECONOMY, UNIVERSITY OF NEUCHÂTEL, NEUCHÂTEL

Foreign Members
ARCHITECTS
AGLAÉE DEGROS, ARCHITECT, GUEST PROFESSOR TU WIEN, ARTGINEERING, ROTTERDAM (NL) – **KEES KAAN**, ARCHITECT, CLAUS EN KAAN ARCHITECTEN, ROTTERDAM (NL)

PERSONALITIES
ROBERT PROST, ENGINEER ENSAM, ARCHITECT, PARIS (FR)

Subsitutes
VANESSA GIANDONATI, ARCHITECT, EUROPAN 10 WINNER IN MONTREUX, MONTALE (IT) – **FRANÇOIS CHAS**, ARCHITECT, EUROPAN 9 WINNER IN DELÉMONT, NP2F, PARIS (FR) – **JULIEN DUBOIS**, ARCHITECT, LA CHAUX-DE-FONDS (CH) – **RODOLPHE LUSCHER**, ARCHITECT, URBAN PLANNER, VISARTE, PRESIDENT EUROPAN SWITZERLAND, LAUSANNE (CH)

EXPERT
BERNARD ZUMTHOR, ARCHITECTURE HISTORIAN, FEDERAL EXPERT FOR THE PRESERVATION OF HISTORIC MONUMENTS (FEDERAL OFFICE FOR CULTURE), MEMBER OF THE FEDERAL COMMITTEE ON HISTORIC MONUMENTS (CFMH), GENÈVE

JURIES

238

SUOMI-FINLAND

National Members

PUBLIC AUTHORITY REPRESENTATIVE
JUKKA NOPONEN, EXECUTIVE DIRECTOR, SITRA THE FINNISH INNOVATION FUND, HELSINKI

CLIENT REPRESENTATIVES
TUOMAS HAKALA, ARCHITECT, CITY OF HELSINKI, CITY PLANNING DEPARTMENT – **SALORANTA PÄIVI**, ARCHITECT, CITY OF HÄMEENLINNA, CITY PLANNING DEPARTMENT

ARCHITECTS
AARO ARTTO, APRT, HELSINKI – **SELINA ANTTINEN**, ANTTINEN OIVA ARCHITECTS, HELSINKI

PERSONALITIES
JUULIA KAUSTE, DIRECTOR, MUSEUM OF FINNISH ARCHITECTURE, HELSINKI, CHAIR OF THE JURY

Foreign Members

ARCHITECTS
HELLE JUUL, ARCHITECT, JUUL FROST ARKITEKTER, COPENHAGEN (DK) – **SIV STANGELAND**, ARCHITECT, HELEN & HARD, STAVANGER (NO)

PERSONALITIES
MARK ISITT, ARCHITECTURE CRITIC, STOCKHOLM (SE)

Subsitutes

KARI NYKÄNEN, ARCHITECT, M3 ARCHITECTS, OULU
LARS OLSSON, ARCHITECT, CITY OF KOTKA, CITY PLANNING DEPARTMENT

SVERIGE

National Members

PUBLIC AUTHORITY REPRESENTATIVE
ULF RANHAGEN, MEMBER OF THE SWEDISH DELEGATION OF SUSTAINABLE CITIES, PROFESSOR AT THE ROYAL INSTITUTE OF TECHNOLOGY, HEAD ARCHITECT AT SWECO, STOCKHOLM

CLIENT REPRESENTATIVES
OLLE FORSGREN, CITY ARCHITECT OF UMEÅ, PRESIDENT OF THE JURY – **KAROLINA KEYZER**, CITY ARCHITECT OF STOCKHOLM

ARCHITECTS
BOLLE THAM, ARCHITECT, THAM & VIDEGÅRD ARKITEKTER, STOCKHOLM

PERSONALITIES
MARIA HELLSTRÖM REIMER, ARTIST AND PROFESSOR IN DESIGN THEORY, SCHOOL OF ARTS AND COMMUNICATION, MALMÖ UNIVERSITY

Foreign Members

ARCHITECTS
MARKUS BADER, ARCHITECT, RAUMLABOR BERLIN (DE)
CELINE CONDORELLI, ARCHITECT, SUPPORT STRUCTURE, LONDON (UK) – **DORTE MANDRUP-POULSEN**, ARCHITECT, DORTE MANDRUP ARKITEKTER, COPENHAGEN (DK)

PERSONALITIES
KIERAN LONG, JOURNALIST AND ARCHITECTURAL CRITIC, LONDON (UK)

Subsitutes

LEIF BRODERSEN, HEAD OF THE SCHOOL OF ARCHITECTURE, ROYAL INSTITUTE OF TECHNOLOGY, ARCHITECT A1, STOCKHOLM
ANNICA CARLSSON, ARCHITECT, DIRECTOR OF EQUATOR STOCKHOLM, STOCKHOLM

239

RECONNECTIONS

ANALYSIS OF THE SESSION

ANALYSIS
OF THE SESSION

Reconnections

A "reconnection" re-links what has been isolated, separated, de-linked. So for "reconnection" to happen, there must first have been a "dis-connection" to repair. Thus Each site for the Europan competition can be understood as a situation of disconnection caused by now obsolete planning principles. Projects can bring about connections between different contradictory, even opposed elements, in order to create a meaning that overrides the division: between city and nature, between urban fragments, between an infrastructure and its context, between separated uses, etc. This second part of the catologue of Europan 11 Results formulates interpretations around the most emblematic winning projects, based on these 5 hypotheses of "reconnection", accompanied by the perspectives of a number of European experts.

Reshaping shared spaces — 242

POINT OF VIEW OF **OLIVER SCHULZE**, ARCHITECT, DI RECTOR OF GEHL ARCHITECTS IN COPENHAGEN DENMARK, TEACHER IN WASHINGTON UNIVERSITY IN ST-LOUIS UNITED STATES

Today a sustainable approach to city development demands the introduction of social and community spaces, where people can share qualities relating to space and time. These "shared spaces" evolve new features that do not necessarily correspond to those associated with the historical term "public space".

Linking with uses — 249

POINT OF VIEW OF **JOSÉ MARÍA EZ QUIAGA**, TEACHER, ARCHITECT AND URBAN PLANNER IN EZQUIAGA ARQUITECTURA SOCIEDAD Y TERRITORIO IN MADRID SPAIN

The dynamics of urban projects no longer arise only from their inherent spatial qualities but more often from their ability to potentiate a vibrant social life, introducing new activities that interact with existing programmes to re-establish new physical and social connections between the site and its context.

Cultural interferences — 256

POINT OF VIEW OF **ENRIQUE SOBEJANO**, ARCHITECT, NIETO SOBEJANO ARQUITECTOS, MADRID SPAIN/ BERLIN GERMANY

Cultural references act as generators that import elements into projects which can define strategies for reconnection to their environment. They can be based on the physical characteristics of the site or derived from more spiritual elements. They can be also narratives on social practices and local specificities.

Common resources and mutation — 263

POINT OF VIEW OF **MATHIEU DELORME**, ENGINEER, LANDSCAPE ARCHITECT, URBANIST, TEACHER AT THE FRENCH INSTITUTE OF URBAN DESIG N IN PARIS FRANCE

The finite nature of resources raises the question of scarcity and therefore of value. With the global environmental crisis, it is essential that designers should incorporate them into urban projects, treating them as shared resources not only to be preserved, but to be enhanced in a quest for a hybrid compatibility between city and nature.

Rhythms and timeframes — 269

POINT OF VIEW OF **CHRIS YOUNÈS**, PHILOSOPHER, ANTHROPOLOGIST, DIRECTOR OF THE RESEARCH LABORATORY GERFAU, TEACHER AT THE ENSAPLV AND ESA SCHOOLS OF ARCHITECTURE IN PARIS FRANCE

Generated by the multiple timeframes of activity in the contemporary city, urban rhythms have intensified to such a point that we now speak of 24-hour cities. The use of time should be taken into account in urban projects as a tool of reconnection, developing relations between citizens and urban and natural rhythms.

OLIVER SCHULZE

A CONVERSATION BETWEEN **BERND VLAY**, ARCHITECT, DIRECTOR OF EUROPAN AUSTRIA, MEMBER OF THE EUROPEAN TECHNICAL COMITTEE EUROPAN AND **OLIVER SCHULZE**, ARCHITECT, DIRECTOR OF GEHL ARCHITECTS IN COPENHAGEN, A DANISH OFFICE FAMOUS FOR CREATING OR INTENSIFYING SHARED SPACES IN CITIES ALL OVER THE WORLD. HE IS A TEACHER IN WASHINGTON UNIVERSITY IN ST-LOUIS US. (WWW.THELIVELYCITY.COM)

Reshaping shared spaces

Bernd Vlay: A sustainable approach to the development of cities requires introducing social and collective spaces, which we would like to call "shared spaces", suggesting that the term collective in this context is about people being able to share qualities relating to space and time. The word "shared" opens up the historically overloaded realm of "public space" which is strongly rooted in our history and therefore linked to multiple stereotypes about the meaning, appearance and performance of public space.

Our talk will explore the actual demands and potentials of shared spaces, and how they are articulated in the winning projects. What new forms can shared spaces take in the contemporary context of European cities?

Oliver Schulze: The topic has always been relevant: sharing space is something that has always happened and will always happen, and is therefore very important for architects to consider. It would be great if the understanding of shared spaces came into line with how our urban culture, our planning culture, and our design culture evolve.

I work as much in the US as I do in Europe. Different contexts, different buildings and different planning cultures crystallize sharing in different ways. There are some places where cities act as institutional 'patrons' that provide this platform. This could describe the European city which, for centuries, has provided an infrastructure of squares, parks, and streets, where people can meet. But it is just as interesting to look outside Europe, at cities like Los Angeles, which no longer perform that role. You need to start to look at things like transportation infrastructure, retail infrastructure, big mass entertainment centres, you need to look at providers of public activity that you can 'piggyback' and instrumentalize in providing these shared experiences. Because they will always happen.

They just happen in different environments. For a long time in the US, people have met in shopping malls and highly privatized environments. But they still meet and it still happens. It just takes an interesting and different form.

BV: Independently of the surviving institutional role, the "form" of the settled image of the European city is increasingly disappearing. Different urban cultures act simultaneously in quite different ways. They introduce new spatial practices that affects both planning tools and ways of life. More recently, the crisis has triggered the discussions. Institutions are short of money, new forms of coexistence are being considered, new authorships of shared spaces are appearing, affecting our urban experience. How do these transformations affect the practice of planning?

OS: What you just have described requires a fresh look at what spaces and places allow for this kind of intensified urban experience. It requires a certain de-stigmatizing of things like shopping environments and transportation infrastructure as purely utilitarian experiences. We will have to form new synapses and new synergies between things that were previously not considered "high culture". Things that have been working for millenia, like markets, marketplaces where people move – this is the kind of stuff where you still have a kind of base-flow, a kind of base-momentum of life to tap into.

BV: The first subtopic, **Linking proximity to territorial landscapes,** might generate new perspectives for this momentum: Both projects I propose to discuss suggest an interesting link between neighbourhood scale and territorial scale. They enrich the quality of a place by reconnecting it to a large-scale landscape, giving the site a new "geography", a new meaning. At the same time, they deal with places that lacked urban substance, lack intensity. A lack of urban substance meets an abundance of landscape-quality. The Ibbenbüren (DE) (fig. 1) project *Between the courtyards* (fig. 1) shows housing-islands floating within a large territorial continuum, a riverside-landscape. The project *Ville+Sambre+Ville* in Sambreville (BE) (fig. 2), somehow does the same, promoting the riverside as an ecological park, which would appeal

1 – **IBBENBÜREN** (DE), WINNER – *BETWEEN THE COURTYARDS* > SEE MORE P. 44

RECONNECTIONS
ANALYSIS OF THE SESSION

to the whole province. The architectural project is just a particle framed by this huge park. Bearing in mind the archetypal ingredients of shared spaces, such as markets in dense areas, these projects go in a completely different direction, linking a neighbourhood directly to an extended, stretched out landscape, the new public territory. Is the concept of interlinking the macro with the micro scale promising for dynamizing public space in marginal areas with "low urban intensity"?

OS: The macro-and-micro approach shows a clear role for cities and regions in identifying larger spatial networks that could be transformed to provide new experiences, new life forms, new places to meet and engage with others. On the micro-scale, both projects put a lot of effort into the creation of courtyards. But the question is, what will happen in these courtyards? Their idea of larger regional spatial networks is interesting: they could actually become a landscape amenity, not just for the people who live there, but for the city as a whole – new networks in the mental map of citizens and visitors.

But how can it actually become part of a living network? Let us look at the Ibbenbüren project: What really happens to the green spaces up to the water? What are the physical means used to make them a green network, which you can experience in smaller and larger segments, inviting other people from outside to use this amenity? You have to create spaces for a mix of people who live here and who come here for other purposes. This is a great opportunity for leadership by the cities! They need to think differently: Where can we recycle existing landscapes, which might move from being utilitarian landscapes to ecosystems which people find desirable?

And there is another important point: an empty courtyard, which is hard-landscaped and not occupied by anybody, imposes a certain burden on the space. Whereas a larger landscape provides lively points and tranquil areas for individual recreation as well – this is an asset, a value, a positive thing.

BV: Isn't the main ingredient of these projects the idea of relating a place to the territorial landscape, introducing a new challenge for cities, such as how they might exchange with elements of nature? Seen in this light, if we replaced the courtyard type-housing with a carpet-type-housing, the urbanistic concept of a macro-micro-configuration would work the same way.

OS: I agree. The focus on form might be quite misleading here. There are other factors, which are far more important to pursue. If we want to create intensity and liveliness, aspects of creating social stuctures are far more important and significant than urban morphology. Suburbia is teaching us a lesson here.

3 – **MALMÖ** (SE), RUNNER-UP – *GREEN GRID* > SEE MORE P. 102

2 – **SAMBREVILLE** (BE), RUNNER-UP – *VILLE+SAMBRE+VILLE* > SEE MORE P. 92

RESHAPING SHARED SPACES
OLIVER SCHULZE

BV: The second group, **Diversifying the street networks**, deals more with the city's system than with its form. The projects extend the role of the street as a place that generates options for diverse activities and encounters: spatial enrichment, the creation of landscapes, new textures, and various public facilities not only transform the street space but introduce new patterns for sharing urban situations.

We all know that the grid is one of the paradigmatic methods of organizing urban space. The projects focus on working with the paradigm of the "grid". *Green Grid* for example in Malmö (SE) (fig. 3) uses the grid as an inclusion manoeuvre, integrating an existing housing development, making its dead in-between-spaces vanish in a new spatial integrity.

The project for Eindhoven (NL) (fig. 5) deals with an existing campus whose buildings are linked by a suspended network of bridges. How can this big campus area be revitalised? Shared programmes inside the vertical building-cores flip the horizontal web of bridges to the third dimension.

OS: This subtopic shows one of the most impressive ideas. Just take Malmö: the concept is fantastic! We live in this region, and I have looked at some of the city extension projects south of the city of Copenhagen, and I compared them with older grid models close to central Copenhaguen, like in Frederiksberg.

Part of the dullness of these extension zones, organised mostly around a central artery, arises from this precise arrangements of streets, few intersections, and blocks. Inherent in the grid, by contrast, is a very simple mathematical component concerning the quantum of possible movement options, the different ways of getting around. People can experience the sense of encountering the unexpected. You will not always meet everybody in your district on your route from A to B. People can take many routes, there is a hierarchy, and there are different things going on. This is one of the things I really like about certain American cities, which do work very well. I would always prefer a city district with a lot of intersections, a lot of points where you might have to choose whether to turn left, right, or go straight on. The more, the better. *Green Grid* uses this as a strategic device to transform an existing area. And I am more excited about the project's next century. How you can see, over a century, how pockets will be rebuilt and redensified? This is pointing in a very important direction.

The project for Eindhoven is quite different: the idea of activating the vertical cores is interesting because it demonstrates that the circulation spaces in buildings can be used as corridors of interaction. But do these vertical spaces have enough contact with daylight? There is some green colour on the wall, but are there also substantial environmental qualities?

BV: The campus is pretty much spread out. The horizontal programme is only one of connecting buildings, in which the uses are vertically organized. Proximity and density work vertically. The project responds very simply, saying, if density follows the vertical line, we just flip the streets to the third dimension. This provides more interface between uses and access. Then, the most important question is whether the new Campus' programmes are powerful enough to feed and activate all these spaces?

5 – **EINDHOVEN** (NL), WINNER – *COMPOSITION IX, OPUS 18* > SEE MORE P.66

4 – **CERDANYOLA DEL VALLÈS** (ES), RUNNER-UP – *TRANSPARENT CITY* > SEE MORE P.168

RECONNECTIONS
ANALYSIS OF THE SESSION

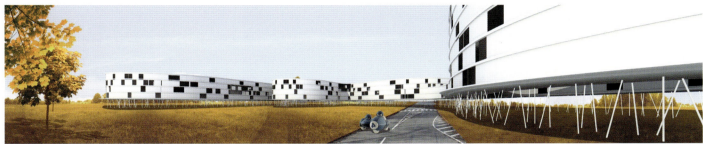

6 – WÜRZBURG (DE), WINNER – *HELIANTHUS* > SEE MORE P.107

OS: The basic idea is clear and I do follow this logic. There are excellent examples of office buildings that do create these types of environments. But in this specific case, we have to assume that the reasons why the skywalks did not work are quite complex. The project would have to promote environmental qualities, which should go hand in hand with meeting places like this.

BV: The third subtopic, **Changing hierarchy to explore new cohabitation**, suggests strong typological transformations, on the urban as well as on the architectural scale. These transformations introduce a different perception of inside/outside relations, rearranging the spatial order. Familiar hierarchies disappear so that new modes of coexistence and interaction can be explored. Why do the projects consider this exploration to be necessary today?

OS: This group provoked strong reactions in me. Whereas *Helianthus* for Würzburg (DE) (fig. 6), seems to repeat the historical idea of an internalising megastructure that leaves the ground floor of the city completely free, the project for Cerdanyola (ES), *The transparent city* (fig. 4), provides an interesting response to the organization of the urban floor: the Kasbah-idea as a complex world of voids and inhabited components. It relates to our desire to have an individual blueprint for our lives. Is this something that can be created as part of a big development? In Copenhagen there are entire new city districts where all the apartments are pretty much the same. Without interference, it is very rare that the market would create such a complex world. But this is in fact what makes Cerdanyola an important proposal: today we do build cities on a large scale, and we do have the opportunity, in terms of capital and planning power, to actually develop entire city districts. The way Cerdanyola reflects this important issue is quite playful.
The project's configuration – independently of the plans of the single units – does create a believable platform for a population of diverse composition: different kinds of family structures, different kinds of lifestyle preferences, and this is often missing in today's city extensions.

BV: Red Balloon for Szeged (HU) (fig. 7) extrapolates the inherent hierarchy of a city block: the perimeter-block-building becomes a frame, which activates another space and time. What does this strategy produce urbanistically?

OS: I really like Szeged, the *Red Balloon*. It suggests reconfiguring part of an existing city which has historical building components. It uses new building mass strategically to frame something that exists, putting it on a platform. It allows us to romanticize it, turning the industrial structure into an industrial relic. The pure fact of being older than the new has a value. This is often missing in city extension projects. Just the virtue of having something around that is older will, at subconscious levels, work for the people who are in the area and open up many opportunities.

BV: The projects in our final subtopic, **Establish a linear intensity**, create a central link that attracts diverse local developments. This link provides an activated public ground which, as a programmatic and structural driving force,

7 – SZEGED (HU), WINNER – *THE RED BALLOON* > SEE MORE P.94

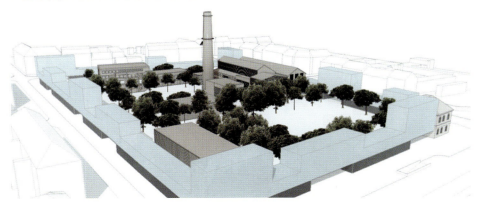

RESHAPING SHARED SPACES
OLIVER SCHULZE

8 – NORRKÖPING (SE), RUNNER-UP – *SYNAPCITY* > SEE MORE P.176

gives coherency to a variety of developments. The concept of linear urbanity relates to historical urban figures such as streets, bands, strips, sequences of squares. Can the re-invention of this concept offer a successful intensification strategy within a low-density sprawl area?

OS: This subtopic certainly strikes a chord with me. I am naturally drawn to this kind of intensification. Our research and work in non-central parts of urban regions tells us that it is indeed very difficult to create lively settings in suburban conditions. We have to be a little less naive in assuming that everything can be vitalised. We have to understand how that limited potential for life can be concentrated, rather than being spread out thin like Nutella on a slice of bread. One of the important skills for an urban designer is to make choices. We have to selectively deactivate some areas, and activate others. I do like the spine as an idea of selective activation that can still provide a spatial continuum: a sequence of spaces that a person can experience in part or in whole, something that is suggestive of an urban narrative.
I like also the idea of an evolutionary spine, like the one that the project Synapcity (fig. 8) suggests: a linear sequence of spaces with different activities, where people and functions start to overlap in time and space. These spines have a logical relationship with the transportation infrastructure, the multiple options of getting around, the retail structure, the supermarkets... I would always throw everything that can generate life at these spines!

BV: In one of the perspectives of the project for Norrköping (SE), *Synapcity*, we can see a modest situation with a housing development and some groundfloor activities, a low key urban situation that goes beyond the stereotypes of ubiquitous urban vibrancy. Instead, the project suggests that the spine as such can also provide qualities that are not dependent on an excess of urban programmes, but rely on spatial issues such as the quality of connectivity.

OS: I appreciate that very much. If we are not in a city centre with a location which has evolved over centuries, then it takes more than the local residential population to create active urban environments. No opportunity to tap into urban life should be missed – this is what I mean when I say "throwing programmes at the spine"!
Where are the bus stops? Where do the bikes go? Where do people walk, drive, shop? These very mundane and pragmatic questions need to be considered, if you want to maximise the life that can be generated by the local group of people who live here anyway. You have to ask, "Does it invite other people to actually spend time here?" This is where the landscape you were talking about might come in. This snow landscape with ice-hockey might be suggestive.

BV: The project *Flotmyr* for Haugesund (NO) (fig. 9) inserts a loop in an existing grid, creating a sequence of different ambiences – activity band, cultural hub, etc. The architetcs introduce a conscious polarization within a sea of indifference.

OS: Life and vitality in urban environments are a limited commodity, you have to be very mindful of where you can make it happen. Even when you polarize and concentrate: if you just counted the number of people placed in the drawn section on bridges and elevated structures, it seems to be suggestive of the quantum of people you expect to find in a central metropolitan area. Outside such compact metropolitan settings, it is best not to try to create multilevel platforms for shared living. As far as vibrant conditions and outdoor spaces are concerned, I would try to squeeze as much as possible into the ground plane.

BV: On the other hand, the diagrams of the plan show a quite modest proposal, suggesting a design that can evolve due to specific conditions.

OS: I agree that there are a lot of good things in this proposal specifically. It is very compact and it has this wonderful spine and polarization. If you conceive the "park bridge" as a "park plaza", it would even be fabulous!

BV: During our talk you have hinted several times at an important point: shared spaces will always be around. We just need to detect them under contemporary and future conditions. To do this, we need to "de-traumatize" our world, be more open to a re-evaluation of things and situations, for example to accept shopping venues as cultural grounds for sharing. What would your final advice be to (a) the municipalities/clients, (b) the architects?

OS: The bottom line is: You can't say that municipal leadership and administration are dead and that, in the future, public space will be left to institutional clients, like real estate owners, or shopping malls or transportation authorities. There is an important role for civic leaders to play in providing leadership and vision for what their city should be like in the future. Even if we have to accept that we won't be rolling out endless numbers of squares and hardscapes, areas that need to be maintained and individually designed. Just take a cycle ride on our new bicycle infrastructure in Copenhagen and you will get a very handsome experience of a city that has a very clear vision, a city that wants to be the number 1 cycle-city in the world, having identified clear performance goals, enshrined in policy. The city is committed to realizing projects that in turn realize this vision. Municipal need to be more astute in understanding the role of transportation infrastructure, of retail, of private developments. What are their impacts on our experience of the city? How can they contribute to what I have described as "concentrating" life rather than dispersing it. This would be the agenda for municipal clients.

For architects and urban designers it is different. In Europan in particular, we deal with a problem, which the topic of "shared spaces" communicates clearly: form is only a small part of the answer. Creating lively urban environments has so much to do with the evolution of social structures, and all the processes that feed into it. It is not just a "bonanza" of shapes. Architects and building environment professionals need to become much more astute in understanding that form is only the vehicle of good city development. We all have it. We all have city extension projects in our big cities where we were thinking that we can just simulate, through large scale planning and design, the complexities and richness of urban environments. But even with "Schlümpfe"-cities or Smurf towns, which emulate historical structures, it is not that easy. Form will not be the only dimension required in order to actually create a shared city

BV: These topics demonstrate that Europan is not looking for a "bonanza" of shapes. In the winning Europan 11 projects form, in most cases, is not understood as shapes. Instead, the projects strongly address forms of relationship between things. How do configurations of buildings relate to the landscape? How do typological developments suggest new forms of coexistence?

9 – **HAUGESUND** (NO), RUNNER-UP – *FLOTMYR* > SEE MORE P.164

OS: I agree with you. The reason I like *Green Grid* for Malmö (SE) is because the most basic concept of this scheme is to set up a framework that can evolve over time. You see how you can develop a phasing and time-strategy that just works with what is there and enhances the opportunities for encounter. It is a very simple way to increase the complexity of the environment. At the moment I still think of Europan as a platform where you construct teams from different design professions. For example, an architect would find a landscape architect to work with, and together they would do a design project. It would be wonderful if Europan 12 was actually a bit more directive in soliciting proposals that also have a clear attitude to evolution, to something over time. How do you actually build a Kasbah? Should you just sell it through a gigantic private public partnership? How do you sell off individual components of land? In Seestadt Aspern there are some interesting ideas about "Baugemeinschaften", there are excellent examples in Malmö as well. They have realized that you can increase the complexity of urban environments significantly if you make sure that multiple lifestyles can find a home, that no block should ever be built by a single brain, that designers have to engage with each other, work less autistically. City planning is all about time, exchange and negotiation.

JOSÉ MARÍA EZQUIAGA

A CONVERSATION BETWEEN **DAVID FRANCO**, ARCHITECT, MADRID, MEMBER OF EUROPAN'S EUROPEAN TECHNICAL COMMITTEE AND **JOSÉ MARÍA EZQUIAGA**, TEACHER, ARCHITECT AND URBAN PLANNER IN EZQUIAGA ARQUITECTURA SOCIEDAD Y TERRITORIO IN MADRID. HE HAS BEEN INVOLVED IN PROJECTS RELATING TO THE CITY AND REGION SINCE THE BEGINNING OF HIS PROFESSIONAL ACTIVITY, HOLDING IMPORTANT URBAN RESPONSIBILITIES IN LOCAL AND REGIONAL ADMINISTRATIONS IN MADRID. HE HAS BEEN AN INTERNATIONAL ADVISOR IN THE DEVELOPMENT OF COLOMBIA'S ZONING LAW AND THE URBAN PLANS FOR BOGOTÁ AND MEDELLÍN, AND ALSO BID CONSULTANT IN THE DEVELOPMENT OF THE REGIONAL STRATEGY FOR BUENOS AIRES METROPOLITAN REGION. HE IS PROFESSOR OF URBANISM AT THE HIGHER TECHNICAL SCHOOL OF ARCHITECTURE OF MADRID.

RECONNECTIONS
ANALYSIS OF THE SESSION

Linking with uses

David Franco: When we analysed the Europan 11 winning projects, we were impressed by the many which introduce new activities that interact with existing programmes in order to reestablish new physical and social connections on the site. Could you give us your general view on how adding uses or activities in different urban contexts is enough to connect spaces that had been disconnected or lacked social intensity?

José María Ezquiaga: I would like to start with a short introductory point. Recently, the municipalities participating in Europan have been increasingly interested in submitting sites that that have no easy solution within standard urban planning practices. Just as there was a moment when the ideas of urban decay, recycling or revitalisation gave the competition its first impetus, now we increasingly see problems associated with the reorganization or revision of peripheries. Especially in metropolitan areas, low-density peripheries, which are not only confined to big cities, but also include the magma that fills the space between small cities and the transitions between the rural and the urban. These types of space have become characteristic of European territorial identity. In all European cities we find a mixture of low-density urban growth, crammed with activities usually linked with mobility nodes and infrastructures. The laws of spatial organization that were useful for Europan's early days, in the historical city, are no longer valid for dealing with these types of spaces. In the first place, the idea of connection no longer has the same meaning. In the traditional city, continuity is the essential element. Continuity is structured by density, by the presence of routes and by a sequence of stimulations that structure those routes. In general, we call these stimulations activities. In the low-density suburban periphery, this approach is no longer valid.

DF: What are the usual strategies or methods of reconnecting isolated urban areas by introducing new uses?

JME: What is interesting here is the distances between the different pieces, the role of infrastructure, and the presence of voids, which means that connecting by in-filling is not always the most suitable solution. The connection has to be more subtle, syntactic rather than structural. At the metropolitan scale, the usual tendency of urbanism is to solve the problem by a very abstract approach: only very large elements are taken into account, such as highways or train infrastructures, or big uses, such as commercial hubs.
These big infrastructures and hubs hide the possibility of working with a multiplicity of elements that occur at ground level. When we see this territory from high above, it seems relatively clear, and you can easily read the large-scale structures, and that can be comforting for planners, because it creates an illusion of coherence. But when we get down to ground level, we see that this territory that seemed empty from above is full of different things. And these things are precisely the source of inspiration for many Europan participants, who can look at the problem with fresh eyes, from a perspective where the lack of experience can be an advantage.

DF: In a first subtopic, we put projects that **Reconnect urban fragments by programming the ground**. Like the Scenes from the Suburbs project in Rødovre (DK) (fig. 1), which proposes a new linear shared space to provide pedestrian access to all the site's different common areas and amenities, introducing a unifying identity with a distinctive pavement for all the dispersed urban spaces along the main street. Or the 270° landscape, regeneration of an urban sequence

1 – RØDOVRE (DK), RUNNER-UP – *SCENES FROM THE SUBURBS*
> SEE MORE P. 129

project in Guimarães (PT) (fig. 2) in which a new structure for the periphery emerges through the creation of a collection of programmed public spaces of different scales and types, which link the unconnected areas of the periphery: the infrastructure, the built fragments and the landscape.
Can connected uses create a continuity of urban spaces and what type of connection is introduced by this continuity? Does it have to be just physical or there are other ways?

JME: We need to be aware that in these peripheral sites we cannot achieve continuity merely by filling them with uses, and even the concept of continuity itself has a different meaning. Physical continuity in these cases has to be replaced by the notion of distance and the concept of relation. Not just with reference to flows, but to those visual and conceptual elements that can be understood by a walker on the ground. In this sense, these projects exploit micro opportunities, such as voids, as alternatives to introducing new uses that may enrich and create more complexity. The void introduces the agricultural environment, the green, where we are not talking

LINKING WITH USES
JOSÉ MARÍA EZQUIAGA

about crop production or a high-value ecological zone, but about the interrelation between the void and the occupied. Not only voids to which we give a specific public meaning, but simply those that have a meaning just because they are empty spaces, intertwined with built ones. And we can use these new ingredients not to repair, because that would imply that the entire periphery is pathological, but to improve, to enhance and to transform into something even more complex.

But we still don't have the right tools for this approach, neither in architecture nor urbanism. That is why we need to retain the syntactic view from the macro scale, the value of the relations between things, but translate it into the language of the architectural object, as is characteristic with Europan. In Europan, the projects usually deal with relations, but always with an architectural result, and this restores the idea that architects essentially deal with things, something that differentiates us, but also makes us complementary, for example, to sociologists or economists.

On the other hand, it's clear that we don't trust monumental architecture anymore, since in the outskirts, iconic language is swallowed up by the suburban magma that consumes any identity. This is a dialectic, in which we work with things but syntactically, by producing architectures but remembering that its value lies more in the relation with other architecture than in itself.

2 – **GUIMARÃES** (PT), WINNER – *270° LANDSCAPE, REGENERATION OF AN URBAN SEQUENCE* > SEE MORE P.188

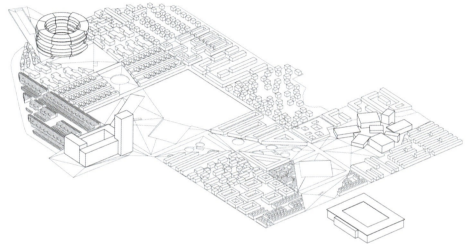

3 – **INGOLSTADT** (DE), WINNER – *AMMERANG* > SEE MORE P.84

This is already a very significant change. We can see this very clearly in the Rødovre project, where a nuclear structure produces a number of architectures that will trigger different social events, none of them really decisive. The ability of these architectures to produce these social events is more important than their iconic or plastic value. The transformations proposed are more open, and both the Rødovre and the Guimarães projects can be seen as open code projects. Though we can see in both of them how, to a certain degree, they still trust in the linear sequences, in routes. These are maybe the last attachments to the past.

These projects could probably work even better if they were not just physical continuities or promenades – since the distances are quite long for just walking – but rather as sequences that can structure the space in the sense of creating mental maps, like those of the inhabitants of the old city. It is no longer a chaotic magma, without any higher rules of perception, but an organizational proposal.

DF: So the role of the programme in this kind of ground requalification process would be perceived at the pedestrian scale, more a programme of micro-transformations than big areas. Would these programmatic strategies be relational? I mean, not imposing specific brands or uses, but introducing flexible combinations of programmes into these empty spaces.

JME: That's what I call syntax, since up to now we have been interested in the big meanings, in the semantics; this approach would lead us to deal more with the relations between things than with the things themselves. The syntax of the periphery exists beyond architects or other agents and, although it's a very reductive and poor syntax, the seeds of innovation are right there. These Europan projects try to pick up anything innovative in these architectures, to enrich the basic programme of the peripheries.

They work from a vision of things, rather than from architectural objects, and the idea of things is better because there they are already there, like an electric pylon or a water treatment plant, or like an environment for new activities which, as we can see in the Rødovre project, reinforces interaction and sociability.

A final point is that we need realism. The growth rules of these peripheries in Europe are very simple but extremely powerful: the presence of

RECONNECTIONS
ANALYSIS OF THE SESSION

infrastructures, fabric structured from maximum simplicity. It's probably in the mistakes that we can find the most potential: places where we see a bad encounter between a garden city and pre-existing countryside or infrastructures. It's in these mistakes that we can find new strategies for transformation, because in huge low-density continuities there are fewer possibilities of reusing space. Though both in Guimarães and Rødovre we can see that there are voids, mistakes and transitions. There is enough space to introduce the virus that might lead to transformation.

DF: The second subtopic includes winning projects **Creating shared spaces by introducing polarities**. For example, in the *Ammerang* project in Ingolstadt (DE) (fig. 3), the polarities of three large, multi-functional buildings, placed on a generic empty grid, create a polygonal strip of public landscape, which will connect the different urban fabrics that will gradually grow over the frame formed by the grid. Or the project *Hip-Hubs* in Haugesund (NO) (fig. 4) proposes a series of sheltered public hubs that combine public spaces and shared use buildings, and introduce a new structure of focal points on the site that activate three main connective axes in the existing urban fabric.
Can densification of uses in focal points be a strategy for creating dynamic urban spaces?

JME: The methods we see in Haugesund and in Ingolstadt are part a very clear tradition in the history of urbanism. If we look back to the Rome of Sixtus V, some objects – monoliths, churches… – were linked virtually through visual connections reinforced by the dimensions of the monument. These are the starting points of the syntactic relationships which, as the connections are merely visual, are formalized as streets. And the origin of a grid is also there: a fabric that gets filled in a way that produced the dialectics of ancient Rome, the loss of the connective tissue that constitutes the city itself and its reconstruction. But not directly from a grid, as Cerdá did some centuries later, but from events.
On the one hand, I still maintain that the grid is not to blame for the monotony we find, for instance, in contemporary Spanish suburbs. This monotony is due to uniformity of programme, density and typology. On the other hand there is no doubt that a more qualitative understanding of the city, through its focal points, generates a richer fabric. If Spain's peripheral extensions had been planned, for example, like the Ingolstadt project, with three big components, the resulting fabric would have been very different from what we know, where they started simply with a grid. When we start with a grid, even if some of the compartments are occupied by different uses, the programmes are unable to infect the rest because they are locked inside the geometry of the grid, so they can't effectively generate itineraries or other urban values. That is why I believe that this method via focal points is an effective way to rebuild the fringe between the rural and the urban, as in Ingolstadt.

DF: What type of densification can function as a focal point and how can the concentration of different uses or urban intensities function as poles of attraction?

JME: It is essential to define what density means today. The idea to some degree emerged from recognition that low density is very costly, that the low density of those enormous garden city extensions was a huge waste of land and infrastructure. There is no doubt that the solution in the future will be to occupy less land, which means increasing density, but also to reuse and transform the existing fabric by changing uses.
It is important to understand that density doesn't necessarily mean more volume or area. The highest density comes with intensity of events, so the density that should interest us is density with the greatest variety of programmes. So, first we can generate density by increasing the intensity and variety of the programme. Second, we enrich social structure, since one of the main reasons for typological monotony is that typologies are repeated because they embody the same residential programme and therefore attract the

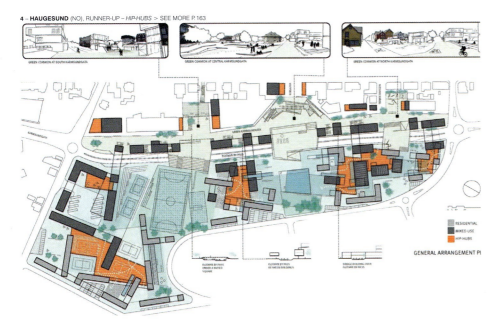

4 – **HAUGESUND** (NO), RUNNER-UP – *HIP-HUBS* > SEE MORE P. 163

LINKING WITH USES
JOSÉ MARÍA EZQUIAGA

same type of residents. So another way to densify is by increasing population variety, with different family models, ages and income levels.

And third, a variety of architectural types is crucial and in this case there is a clear correlation between typological uniformity and the impoverishment of the social fabric. What is the alternative? At territorial level it is the creation of poles, even though within the dominant system these poles are usually interpreted on the larger scale. So again it's interesting to work on the variety and polarization of the focal points themselves, as we can see in the Haugesund project, where a pole is structured by micro polarities. This is about fractal structure, a technique we see a lot in Europan projects, where a bigger piece is scaled down into smaller pieces with the same structure, and on so down to the architectural scale.

This solves the problem of the relations between the poles and their environment, because the biggest disadvantage of these focal points is that they are alien to the growth of the other fabric, and that they don't encourage variety of access but are usually only connected via the main infrastructures. By contrast, in the Haugesund project, we can see how pedestrians can coexist with vehicles, and the poles themselves are programmatically specialised. They don't seek grandiose architectural expression, but rather concentrate on generating public spaces very casually, just by the placement of the architectural components. This is an example of how effective it is to deal with interstitial spaces not through a homogenizing strategy, but by means of complexity and innovative handling of the existing structures.

DF: Renewing identities with programmatic infills is the third approach adopted by winning projects in this topic. This is the approach of the *Dornröschen* project in Selb (DE) (fig. 5), which proposes a new mix that includes cultural, commercial, recreational and housing uses, introduced into the existing urban fabric through small-scale operations like infills or new buildings or just by reprogramming, with the result that the old identity of the "porcelain city' is revitalized with a contemporary atmosphere. Or the *Linzertus* project in Linz (AT) (fig. 6), which reactivates an old tobacco factory by introducing a sequence of programmatic additions, implemented progressively on a step-by-step strategy in the form of different infills that respond to the specific conditions of the existing structures. Can an acupunctural injection of uses be a way of transforming a monofunctional space into a living area?

JME: The projects that develop smaller scale reprogramming strategies have the quality of being more helping us read and understand

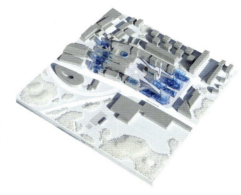

6 – **LINZ** (AT), RUNNER-UP – *LINZERTUS* > SEE MORE P.113

questions that are also relevant on a territorial scale. In the territorial realm, the syntax has to be understood from knowing rather than seeing. The difference between these new territories and historical urbanism is that perceptive relations always played an important role in traditional urbanism. At the territorial scale, these visual relations won't be always possible, so we need to give greater importance to the arrangement of the filling than to visible itineraries, which at this scale are clearly theoretical. In the urban realm, however, the anthropomorphic relations and visual distances between objects are much more apparent at the medium scale, where new architecture is the main instrument for enhancing the existing structure.

DF: What is the role of the existing fabric in this process and what type of connection is established between this and the new?

JME: Both the Selb and Linz projects are generalizable, since these situations are very frequent in European cities, and they should become a standard response, what we might call urban recycling. An intelligent combination of rehabilitation and substitution without expressly choosing any of the standard options, the simplest of which is total replacement and its opposite, idolisation of what is there. The notion of recy-

5 – **SELB** (DE), WINNER – *DORNRÖSCHEN* > SEE MORE P.134

cling raises the possibility of combining these strategies in a natural way, understanding what is best for the city, and not only from a financial perspective or out of architectural conservatism.

DF: With regard to the specific role of programmes and understanding a complementary approach to existing uses, what kind of activities can be introduced inside these existing fabrics?

JME: The programme is essential. In today's city, reprogramming processes can't be permanent; indeed, it will become increasingly appropriate to create open processes where programmes can be reinterpreted differently over time. So the idea of architecture following function needs to be inverted; it will be functions that follow the increasingly open possibilities of architecture. I also believe that some openness should be left for residents, since architects and municipalities tend to overdefine programmes, and more open programming can trigger citizen participation.

As regards facilities, I believe that the future management model should include a more active role for the user, so the uses and other characteristics of public buildings won't necessarily be defined by a third party. It will be the users themselves who will take the leading role, allowing buildings to evolve in step with community history, adapting to different priorities at different times. Communities have a biography over time, in which, for instance, the proportions of the different populations change. So the reprogramming strategies that we can see in these projects have to be open code operations.

On the other hand, it's essential in these urban scenarios that the focal point should express complexity, by which we mean a wide variety of possibilities. Given that the main problem in our cities is not habitability, but functional and therefore social monotony, injecting complexity like in the Linz and Selb projects is always a smart strategy.

DF: The last category for uses as a design strategy is projects **Introducing new social dynamics by programmatic diversity**. This is the standpoint of the *Nudge City* project in Clermont-Ferrand (FR) (fig. 7), which considers the spatial outcomes of a new flexibility in introducing a mix of uses in built-up areas and public spaces that can merge individual desires with communal necessities. Or the *Planting havenk-*

7 – CLERMONT-FERRAND (FR), WINNER – *NUDGE CITY* > SEE MORE P.110

LINKING WITH USES
JOSÉ MARÍA EZQUIAGA

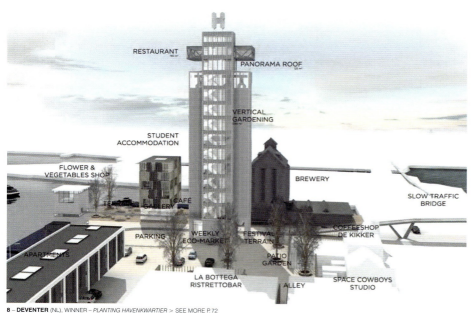

8 – DEVENTER (NL), WINNER – *PLANTING HAVENKWARTIER* > SEE MORE P.72

wartier project in Deventer (NL) (fig. 8), where the strong productive identity of the existing buildings, especially the Hoge silo, is reinterpreted in a contemporary way by introducing new programmes, such as vertical gardening or an eco-market in the tower or different residential types in the other buildings, producing a new, cohesive mixture of uses that will activate the ground level public spaces.

How can we revitalize public spaces by introducing new varieties of uses at district scale?

JME: The main question you are asking is whether multifunctionnality is possible at district scale. Not only is it possible, but it is the natural context for a multifunctional approach, because here, at district scale, as in the project of Clermont-Ferrand, is where it is needed most.

After a certain time, there is a tendency to fractality at metropolitan scale. Initially, the pieces of a metropolitan environment are created as very simple components, but tend to become more complex as time passes. And the individual fragments often reproduce the complexity of the metropolitan area as a whole. In this way, a small town is like a huge metropolitan area in miniature, including the infrastructure, the green areas, the garden city, the historical core, etc...

It is also important to consider the programmatic focal points, and here the district is the key scale at which we can generate collective identities through programmatic combinations that do not necessarily have to be public. Some of the components that function best as focal points are, indeed, private. The lack of attractive elements that create a sense of community is one of the problems in European social cohesion. It is revealing that the Deventer project refers explicitly to this idea of social cohesion, a term that draws on standard European union terminology and reflects the aspiration to generate a new paradigm of pluralistic coexistence.

DF: Finally, can we make a more general point, through the idea of reconnecting or re-linking, which refers to the reactivation of a connection that doesn't have to be strictly physical. Do you think that strategies that embody this idea of re-linking or reconnecting mean a step back for the architect and a step forward for society? Are you thinking more about open frames where people can self-organise rather than introducing predetermined programmatic combinations in neighbourhoods?

JME: These deterministic architecture-based mixtures of uses reflect strong municipal influence. If, against a background of uncertainty, the question is opened up and society is given a greater role, architectural expression still remains, but in a less determining capacity. It has to be more dialectical, so we could start thinking about architecture as a process: buildings capable of mutating and reprogramming themselves over time, facilitating reuse over time.

Social cohesion is very difficult to achieve as a top-down process, from government. Instead you need to engage civil society, which takes us to the great debate in Europe right now about our democracy's need to reconnect (re-link). For we need to reinforce the links among citizens and between citizens and government, and to understand that democracy is civil society's pact to share common instruments.

Just as it's very difficult to derive small fabrics and micro elements from the urbanism of infrastructures, it is very difficult for macrosocial programmes to understand idiosyncrasies and small problems. And ultimately the big social problems that we now see don't arise from macropolitics or big issues, but from very small questions, some of which haven't even been formulated yet. The architectural expression of this reality has to be an open code architecture, a long way from monumental architecture, and this is yet another lesson we can learn from Europan.

ENRIQUE SOBEJANO

A CONVERSATION BETWEEN **JENS METZ**, ARCHITECT, BERLIN, MEMBER OF EUROPAN'S TECHNICAL COMMITTEE AND **ENRIQUE SOBEJANO**, ARCHITECT, MADRID/BERLIN. TOGETHER WITH HIS PARTNER FUENSANTA NIETO, HE HAS BEEN RUNNING AN OFFICE IN MADRID SINCE THE LATE 1980S. ARCHITECTURE GRADUATES FROM ETSA MADRID AND THE UNIVERSITY OF COLUMBIA, NEW YORK, THEY EDIT THE SPANISH ARCHITECTURAL REVIEW ARQUITECTURA AND CURRENTLY TEACHES AT THE EUROPEAN UNIVERSITY IN MADRID AND THE UDK IN BERLIN. AMONG THEIR MOST PROMINENT ACHIEVEMENTS ARE THE MORITZBURG IN HALLE, THE CENTRO DE CREACIÓN CONTEMPORÁNEA AND THE MADINAT AL-ZAHRA MUSEUM IN CÓRDOBA, THE PALACIO DE CONGRESOS IN ZARAGOZA AND THE SAN TELMO MUSEUM IN SAN SEBASTIAN. (WWW.NIETOSOBEJANO.COM)

Cultural interferences

Jens Metz: Cultural references are an important generator of project strategies, sometimes based on the physical characteristics of the site or its surroundings, sometimes derived from more spiritual elements such as abstract figures or mental images, or even grounded in social practices and local specificities. The proposed exemplary projects seem to explore solutions that go beyond the traditional sense of cultural reference by incorporating different interpretations, turning it into "Cultural Interferences". How far can these interferences be used to connect a project to its surroundings on a cultural level?

Enrique Sobejano: I see a very interesting game in your introduction between the terms reference and interference, which is probably a key question, because it deals with the fact that an architectural project is always nourished by different points of view, multiple influences. I think that we can distinguish between interferences that are objective and those that are subjective – within the limitations of those words. Perception of the outside world is objective: it relates to landscape, topography, orientation, climate or programme, whereas the thoughts in our inner world are subjective: they reflect our own background, memory and culture, something that differs for each one of us. There are different ways to respond to topography, climate or other physical conditions, but it is always a problem that can be addressed clearly, an objective question that every project has to consider. On the other hand, subjective interferences are more personal, and in that sense may refer to remote issues that interest an architect in one place but maybe not necessarily in others. I think that these two perspectives, the perceptual and the mental, or the objective and the subjective, constantly connect different facts, establishing a net of associations where a project at some point becomes something unique and specific.

JM: These interferences can be seen as a remix of different cultural contexts, reconstructing a fragmented but recognisable identity based on more than one culture, reflecting current social discourses. How can these influences be translated into architecture?

ES: Architecture is the outcome of multiple apparently unconnected circumstances, which end up resembling one another and finally crystallising in a building. I believe in architecture's influence and capacity to transform places and cities as well as people's lives. It may not be able to change the world as was claimed by the 1920s avant-garde, but I am still convinced that a single building or even a small intervention can bring about a profound transformation, in the same way that a good book can change the way you think. A project is always a choice that begins by recognizing and establishing limits, which means that you focus your attention on some points and ignore others. In other words, I think that the different cultural influences – interferences – cannot be considered methodologically. There is not a single linear path, but rather an aggregation of fragments. There is no single starting point, an original and unique moment, but rather every conscious architectural concept resides in the ties between apparently unrelated events.

1 – ALCORCÓN (ES), RUNNER-UP – *ROUNDABOUT PROFILACTICS*
> SEE MORE P.183

JM: If we look at the first group of projects, **Revisiting an archetypical figure**, they seem to take an archetype and then deliberately transform it into something hybrid to raise cultural questions.

In Alcorcón (ES) (fig. 1), the *Roundabout Prophylactics* project emphasises the existing conditions as a locus of freedom on the edge of the town, reinforcing its status by building an inhabited wall around it, thus protecting the informal or marginal uses of popular culture frequent in peripheral areas.

In Leeuwarden (NL) (fig. 2), the juxtaposition of built structures, farmland and water forms the three key elements of the *NieuwatergardeN* proposal, creating a somewhat hybrid picture, part familiar traditional skyline, part a modern scale urban structure.

And the *Too Big Square* in Nynäshamn (SE) (fig. 3) deliberately confronts two opposite void systems, the traditional European city's spatially demarcated square and the floating spaces of suburbia, to create friction between them.

How far can a project develop its identity from a familiar archetype?

ES: The archetype is a very deep concept, quite different from type. Whereas typologies are rational and serial, archetypes on the contrary are

RECONNECTIONS
ANALYSIS OF THE SESSION

emotional and form part of our collective memory. They are not part of a particular culture, but rooted in an archaic universal civilization. The principle of the archetype is rather vague, which is what makes it a very interesting concept in establishing the origin of a project. An archetype – the platform, the tower, the wall or the roof – is always wide and open, it can be a sort of a playground out of which a specific project may develop.

In Alcorcón, the project is a strange Arcadia, I suppose. The archetype of the inhabited wall is used as a gesture, to give the project impetus. The wall becomes the boundary, as I said before, a statement that whatever happens outside is denied, reflects a problem – the banal, repetitive and speculative urbanism that the city suffered – which no single project can solve. It's a sort of anti-Utopia, a reaction to something that they expect to happen. In that sense it is a clear political statement, also with ambiguities, that opens a discussion on the city, the current economic crisis, and the future process of development.

In Leeuwarden, I think the project deals more with a typological concept. The house-type is

2 – LEEUWARDEN (NL), WINNER – *NIEU WATER GARDEN* > SEE MORE P. 14

used as a system, as the combinatorial repetition of a single unit. It plays on series, part of a combinatorial way of understanding a house type, which is a quite different way of tackling the topic.

And in Nynäshamn, the project raises the question of whether an archetype can simply be a tool or instrument that can be used directly as a project concept. Actually, making the square "too big" renders the original archetype unrecognisable. And that is a very interesting point, which relates to the archetype as a starting point, which has no other possibility than to be transformed into something else in order to deal with the complexities of a place.

JM: Another group of projects called **Reactualising vernacular traces** seek their inspiration in the past or in surviving visible traces.
The *Geologia Rurbana* project in San Bartolomé (ES) (fig. 4), transforms its rurban spirit into a straightforward morphology and a contemporary architectural language, with a structure derived from the island's distinctive geology.
In Capelle aan den Ijssel (NL) (fig. 5), the *Polder Salad* project rejects continuity and erases the traces of Modernism; it paradoxically repeats the tabula rasa of the 1960s by demolishing the existing structures to reinstall a polder landscape with row-house-like urban typologies.
How can a project find its foundation in a narrative reinterpretation of memory?

ES: In a way every project tells a story or stories. Architecture is simply narrative, whatever the designing architect intends. The main question is not whether those projects are narratives, because personally I could argue that most of them

3 – NYNÄSHAMN (SE), RUNNER-UP – *TOO BIG SQUARE* > SEE MORE P. 125

CULTURAL INTERFERENCES
ENRIQUE SOBEJANO

4 – **SAN BARTOLOMÉ** (ES), WINNER – «RURBAN» GEOLOGY > SEE MORE P.152

can be, but whether narrative is what the architects choose as their main argument. A narrative concept is usually linked to a linear path following steps or layers that lead to an end. A non-hierarchical approach, on the other hand, would be the opposite, with different approaches eventually perhaps establishing a net of non-linear associations. Every project fluctuates between memory and invention: it is a reinterpretation of our own memories.

In the project in San Bartolomé the most attractive expression resides in the drawing of the layers, which reflect topography and climate – objective – but also cultural issues interpreted by the architects – subjective. They deal with an additive concept: culture as an accumulation of layers, ultimately incorporating their own new housing proposal. They also clearly establish a link with the island's traditional houses – cubic, simple, additive and white – which may look like a reference to modern architecture, but is really embedded in the culture of Lanzarote, a centuries-old tradition.

In Capelle aan den Ijssel, I wouldn't say that the project goes back only to the pre-1960s status. They return to the agricultural traces, but also, in a way, to 1960s architecture. They deny this model as an urban proposal, but they don't deny it so much as an architectural expression, and this ambiguity makes the project more complex to interpret. The cultural interferences reside essentially in the geometric pattern of the former water channels, but in the row housing the architectural language accepts a well-known modern model.

JM: So this would also be a concept to do with updating a place, like the projects in the group that we called **Reinventing an emblematic image**.

If we look at the *Garden state* project in Turku (FI) (fig.9), it aims to create common spaces in the semi-public yards and a landscaped open space around them, employing the metaphor of the farm. The aim is to make the image of

RECONNECTIONS
ANALYSIS OF THE SESSION

259

the farm as a self-sufficient organism a model for a commuter town. There is a comparable concept in Deventer (NL) (fig. 6), where *Bricolage* projects the structure of an artist's village onto the harbour area, re-branding the site with a Mediterranean image to create a new polarity. How can a project that is based on the transposition of a somewhat generic emblematic image as an abstract metaphor avoid being considered artificial?

ES: Metaphor has been always a difficult concept in architecture. It has been used many times, in a way we all talk in metaphors, and consciously or not, every building can represent something other than itself. Metaphors are images we use to understand our surroundings. Every project, even those that arise from the most abstract concepts, originates wittingly or unwittingly in a metaphor. The key issue is to avoid getting trapped by it, to avoid pastiche, and to understand that architecture is always more complex than a single image.

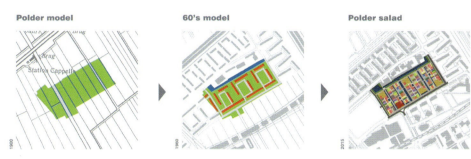

5 – **CAPELLE AAN DEN IJSSEL** (NL), WINNER – *POLDER SALAD* > SEE MORE P. 104

In Turku, the concept refers to a farm, therefore the cluster of constructions becomes the way of tackling the project: the metaphor of a village conceived as a farm. But you always have to go deeper in, to understand what the idea means, like the space in-between and the type of relations among them.

In Deventer I have more doubts. It is not that you can't borrow references where you want, of course you can. In this case the project is in the Netherlands but recalls Indian and Mediterranean motifs, with other references interfering, even recent Japanese architectural examples. Excessive eclecticism carries the risk of the value of the cultural interferences in architecture being lost.

JM: So, moving from small metaphors to larger ones, we will shift to projects that we classified as **Revealing the collective memory**. The main question here is about the symbolic value of architecture in constructing an identity, for example in the young states of Croatia and Kosovo or in the faceless suburbs of Paris.

For instance in Dubrovnik (HR) (fig. 7), the *Back to citizens!* project elegantly resolves the programmatic demands and the challenge of scale by dispatching the new squares with a Modernistic architectural language along the promenade, while still trying to deal with the historical legacy. In Pejë, the *Diana's Ring* (fig. 8) project refers to the entire region as a cultural entity, creating a sort of imaginary landscape based on the ancient myth of Diana, goddess of hunting. Here, the architecture still seems to act as a symbol for a cultural identity.

Identifying the specificities of a place is the attitude of the architects of the *Effets de serres* project in Stains (FR) (fig. 10), where a soft programme of winter gardens redevelops the local identity and economy, to give the place identity in the urban disaster of the Paris suburbs.

In what ways can a strong collective memory be useful in developing a project strategy?

6 – **DEVENTER** (NL), RUNNER-UP – *BRICOLAGE* > SEE MORE P. 71

CULTURAL INTERFERENCES
ENRIQUE SOBEJANO

7 – **DUBROVNIK** (HR), WINNER – *BACK TO CITIZENS!* > SEE MORE P. 40

ES: Recently, there has been much emphasis on the importance of the process, and less on the value of the architectural object itself. In other words, the important question is the process, not the final result. I think that if you take this concept too far, you lose a key issue: the perceptual value of architecture. Some projects work only on very open questions or strategies. They rely on establishing a couple of rules, on the assumption that people's social needs will eventually establish a good community. I still believe that it is the architect's role – and that's why we are architects – to understand these inputs, and to transform them into architectural space, construction, meaning, which in the end is not simply process.

ES: Collective memory also refers to the concept of archetypes. It is also very personal, but connected to many other people who share similar feelings. It doesn't refer to a particular form, but to a feeling, a perception, or to landscape or social relations. It represents a memory that is common to a group of people or to a society. And in that sense it opens up a lot of possibilities that can be dealt with in architecture.

When you work in a historical place like Dubrovnik, it is somehow easier to recognize the clues. There is an immediate tendency to react to the existing structures, to understand them and to refer to the memory of the place, something that is clear in this project. It is also an open strategy where a modern language establishes a sort of dialogue with the architecture of the past.

The use of national symbols is often propagated by politicians, on nationalist grounds, but I don't believe that architecture should aim to promote political symbols. I don't believe in the grand gestures that represent countries. On the other hand, I believe much more in buildings that really give identity and try to respond to a place and a culture. I am more interested in this project as a proposal linked to a town – Pejë – than to a state – Kosovo. Collective memory belongs to people who share similar references and experiences, ultimately filtered by their own way of understanding a place. Here in Stains, in a project like this, these feelings are filtered through the architects' view of the landscape, typology or sustainability issues, and they developed their project from their own interpretation.

JM: On the subject of filters, and by extension, of the questions that Europan projects raise, we notice that there is a shift of attention from spatial organisation to social imagination that we called Recounting social practices.
Refine this approach in *The gardens of Grønmo* project in Oslo (NO) (fig. 11), where the gradual transformation of the former landfill site into an ecological park takes into account the expectations and spatial needs of the different users, but does not propose a specific architecture.
Does this sort of "social engineering", focusing on the process, mark the launch a new "social trend" in architecture?

8 – **PEJË** (KO), RUNNER-UP – *DIANA'S RING* > SEE MORE P. 21

9 – **TURKU** (FI), WINNER – *GARDEN STATE* > SEE MORE P. 160

RECONNECTIONS
ANALYSIS OF THE SESSION

10 – STAINS (FR), WINNER – *EFFETS DE SERRES* > SEE MORE P.202

ES: I think a change is happening in the new generation of young architects, where this idea of the architect being in sole charge is changing. More and more architects present their projects as groups, not only for practical reasons, but rather because they think that this has a social implication, and also as an ideological statement, the idea that architecture should not, especially after the crisis, be determined by the specific object-quality of the project.
I have the impression that there has been something missing in the past decade, a lack of deeper architectural debate. And Europan has played an important role, as an expression of the transformations in architecture in the last 20 years.

You previously mentioned Arcadia: the Oslo project is probably more like Arcadia than Alcorcón project. This is also a project in the form of a statement, reflecting the modern Nordic architectural tradition, like certain works by Ralph Erskine, and the idea of participative architecture. This attitude promulgates an architecture that is not at all interested in the quality of the object but in the social processes that transform it.

JM: This shift is very visible in the recent sessions of Europan, not only in the projects, but also in the questions addressed by the different site briefs. To conclude and to return to the introduction and the topic of Cultural Interferences, to what extent do the Europan competitions and the debates they create support this change?

ES: Europan is part of a change that I hope will not end with the crisis. It started 20 years ago, as with other European programmes such as Erasmus, which helped to transform the younger generations' perceptions of Europe. Europan is and has been a way for young architects to look up and travel around Europe, to learn from each other, and this is incredibly positive. And I think that this is the way we would like to see Europe go.
It's also interesting to see how young people react in different cultures within the European culture. I would say that this is one of Europan's more interesting values: how these different cultures or societies within Europe address the problems of architecture. I think many of these young architects know they are talented, but have difficulty transforming their ideas. I can see that in recent years, they have been shifting to more social problems. It is not that these questions didn't exist ten years ago, but they were not so hard, and not so visible. And now they are.

JM: So this means not only that the context has changed, but also the way in which architects act in this context?

11 – **OSLO** (NO), WINNER – *THE GARDENS OF GRØNMO* > SEE MORE P.62

MATHIEU DELORME

CONVERSATION BETWEEN **EUROPAN** AND **MATHIEU DELORME**, ENGINEER, LANDSCAPE ARCHITECT, URBANIST, GRADUATE OF THE BLOIS HIGHER NATIONAL SCHOOL OF NATURE AND LANDSCAPE. HE TEACHES AT THE FRENCH INSTITUTE OF URBAN DESIGN IN PARIS. HE IS PARTICULARLY INTERESTED IN THE EMERGENCE OF LANDSCAPE AS A DEVELOPMENT TOOL, IN PARTICULAR ITS ECONOMIC DIMENSION. HOW CAN A DEVELOPMENT STRATEGY PRODUCE NEW USES, NEW FORMS AND THEREFORE NEW LANDSCAPES? HE WORKS AT THE INTERLAND AGENCY: "DESIGN ME TOMORROW'S BASQUE COUNTRY" (ATLANTIC AND PYRENEES URBAN PLANNING AGENCY), THE FUTURE OF PLAINS AGRICULTURE IN FRANCE, DRAFTING OF THE MANTES-EN-YVELINES 2030 DEVELOPMENT SCHEME AND A STUDY ON THE DEVELOPMENT AND MANAGEMENT OF COASTAL EROSION IN AULT EN BAIE DE SOMME.

RECONNECTIONS
ANALYSIS OF THE SESSION

Common resources and mutation

Europan: This session of Europan marks the growing role of nature in urban project design. The inclusion of natural (biotic, abiotic) elements is more refined, more complex, to the point that they are becoming key factors. We now know that natural resources are limited, but this awareness of the finite world is not obvious, we don't see it directly, it is abstract at the scale of human life and scarcely perceptible at the scale of urban sites. And yet, it is very easy to understand on a large scale, as Kenneth Boulding wrote in "Spaceship Earth", we are all on a spacecraft somewhere in the Universe, it is up to us to divide up the rations, but how?

Mathieu Delorme: the finiteness of resources raises the question of scarcity and therefore value: resources have always been a core concern of civilisations in the quest for an optimum relation with nature. Every culture, every political system defines its own value system. The utility attributed to water reserves, soil fertility, wind properties, the diversity of flora and fauna, depends on common beliefs and practices: the Greeks, for example, were highly attentive to demographic control, keeping a balance between population size and available resources. New York City was long concerned about its drinking water supply and began a policy to acquire land with water reservoirs in the Catskill Mountains a long way from Manhattan. This protected area, a filtration ecosystem of almost 400,000 ha, supplies 90% of the city's drinking water needs. This example illustrates one of the values attributed

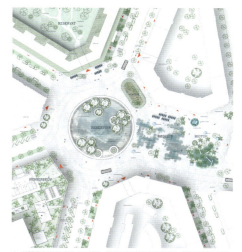

1 – KØBENHAVN (DK), WINNER – *THE LAST CITY QUARTER* > SEE MORE P. 122

to natural elements: service value. Bees pollinating plants, wetlands naturally purifying water, animals like pigeons that act as urban garbage collectors,... There is no shortage of examples, infinite combinations…

So it is interesting to see the current attempt to estimate the service value provided by a natural element, for example wetland capacity for self-purification. The economic value of flows of ecosystem materials and energy was estimated in 1997 at 33,000 billion dollars a year. A 2010 study valued the services performed by bees for British farming at 487 million euros. The wish to include natural elements in economic choices reflects a significant change and has direct consequences for urban projects. However, we should not forget the option value of nature, i.e. its value in the future. New species are discovered every day. One of them might be a cure for an as yet unknown illness. Measuring the biomass in natural ecosystems, the US empirical ecologist Robert Ulanowicz has shown that totally optimised systems are not sustainable. So the challenge is to find the right balance between efficiency at a given moment and resilience, the capacity to adapt after an event. It is all a question of thresholds and regulation.

2 – NEUILLY-SUR-MARNE (FR), RUNNER-UP – *CARTILAGINOUS* > SEE MORE P. 69

COMMON RESOURCES AND MUTATION
MATHIEU DELORME

264

Europan: The question of thresholds inevitably raises that of the compatibility between the need for urban development and the optimum use of existing resources, whether visible or not.

MD: It is essential for designers to develop a close understanding of natural features and their problems: the greater our understanding of natural processes, the more it will be possible to place natural elements at the heart of the project approach. Too often, they are merely preserved, like museum pieces, when we should use them as levers, sources of inspiration that can directly influence form but also long-term urban strategy. Ecosystems are complex and it is regrettable that the modern world had little time for ancient empirical knowledge. Certain writings, like those of Vidal de la Blache, father of human geography, deserve rereading because they still have value today. Water management as the fundamental factor in projects is largely accepted today, in particular rainwater storage. Public water storage systems are designed and operated to match rainfall conditions. However, other areas remain under-exploited, for example soil, in its formation and evolution, its pedological and agronomic dimension, but also in its economic facets such as land values and sharing.

Europan: The first family of Europan 11 projects in this shared resources group is called **Preservation/Creation**. The response to resource sharing in this session reveals a diversity of choices from the different winning teams, ranging from preservation, to total hybridisation, through to the pure creation of a new resource. The runner-up project in Neuilly-sur-Marne (FR) (fig. 2) opts for conservation, redefining the boundaries of municipal territory to retain a continuous and porous system of unbuilt fabric. Conversely, in order to minimise an existing district's environmental footprint, the winning project in København (DK) (fig. 1) recreates nature and proposes using the public domain as a vehicle for a new ecological system that connects existing fabric to artificial biotopes. Considering these two extremes, can both preservation and inventing a resource be foundation elements in an urban strategy?

MD: To raise the question of creating or preserving a resource is to raise the question of the human role. Through modernity, we have moved from a spontaneous process where the organisation and operation of ecosystems is governed by natural cycles, to a process dominated, constructed and managed by human beings.
The winning project in Neuilly-sur-Marne (FR) forms part of an ancestral system that places the town in an updated nature, with the ecological goal of minimising the human footprint on the natural environment. In response, the project here adopts the posture of a semi-detached observer: human and natural flows pass through the natural spaces, but separately, somewhat as pedestrian walkways used to be placed above roads in former urban planning systems.
The project in København (DK) reflects a more recent trend: placing nature in the city. Here,

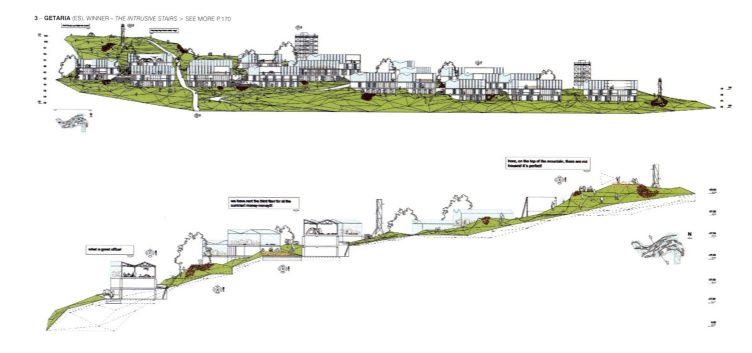

3 – GETARIA (ES), WINNER – *THE INTRUSIVE STAIRS* > SEE MORE P.170

RECONNECTIONS
ANALYSIS OF THE SESSION

265

4 – **SAVENAY** (FR), WINNER – *MESURES LIGÉRIENNES* > SEE MORE P.180

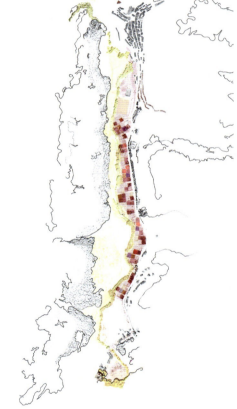

5 – **ALCALÁ DE LA SELVA** (ES), WINNER – *PRODUCTIVE LANDSCAPE*
> SEE MORE P.140

obviously, we think about the work by Alphand and Barillet-Deschamps in Haussmann's Paris, which takes a more modern form here marked by environmental concerns. The project thus takes an engineering perspective, conceiving public space as an infrastructure that gives a scientific response to an urban problem.

Developing use with nature, in a remote or integrated urban form, raises the question of the tolerance threshold of milieus in their interactions with the city. This requires the identification of natural dynamics: flooding, plant engineering, phytoremediation… through the development of an in-depth knowledge of the milieu. And behind it a key question: do human beings have a place in the natural milieu or should it be designed independently of human activities?

Europan: True, many projects seek to propose hybrid solutions that sketch a possible understanding and coexistence between nature and urbanisation. A first series of projects, entitled **Juxtaposition**, proposes putting urbanisation and existing resources side-by-side. The two entities interact, but at the same time each retain their own characteristics. This is true of the winning projects in Getaria (ES) (fig. 3), Allerød (DK) (fig. 6) and Savenay (FR) (fig. 4). Remaining with this question of a critical threshold, is it possible to juxtapose urban and natural fragments without one threatening the other?

MD: Becoming part of a place, part of a system without "breaking it", while preserving its specific character, is a tricky conceptual feat. The three projects in this family share the same meticulous observation, sensitivity to the properties of the site. Whilst in Getaria (ES), a single parameter – topography – is carefully studied in the project, in order to establish the right urban form, the Allerød (DK) project goes further and reimagines a scenario: the milieu outlined does not separate

COMMON RESOURCES AND MUTATION
MATHIEU DELORME

human beings from nature but draws the interactions, the tensions, seeks a balance between pieces of nature and built spaces.

In the Savenay (FR) project, the focus is on the quest for meaning by reference to the problematic dimension of scale. With each question asked, with each strategic issue, a problematic scale broadens the spectrum of analysis by linking the construction of the project's local dimension to a territorial dynamic.

These projects see the territory as a resource, as a toolbox. They are founded in and develop ancient skills – techne in Martin Heidegger's sense – in the search for a new relation between man and nature.

Europan: In the category called **Valorisation**, the natural resource, reinforced and activated, is used in the projects to create a link between heterogeneous urban elements, communities with different rationales (e.g. residents and tourists), but also to restore clarity to an area whose full potential is no longer perceived.

Can the valorisation of a natural resource restore meaning to a changing area?

MD: The example of America's parks, recently cited as a model by the French landscape architect Michel Desvigne, is very interesting in this respect. It is not about designing opportunistic linear parks, meaningless "ecological corridors",

6 – ALLERØD (DK), WINNER – *WHEN NATURE INTERFERES WITH EVERYDAY LIFE* > SEE MORE P.148

"parkways" in which thick plantings divide and conceal rather than structuring. The attempts that have worked well and still work are those that have a strong geographical and historical relation with the site, which give the projects enduring value. Which means that "valorising" is not that simple!

The Alcalá de la Selva (ES) (fig. 5) project sees the resource as a way of leveraging local economic development, by means of a respectful balance between reactivating long-standing agricultural production and tourist appeal. Social connection entails the creation of a new farming and management ecosystem based on and respectful of the soil as a resource (agro-tourism). The Romainmôtier (CH) (fig. 7) project is founded on the sensitivity of the relationship between an individual and a place. The choice of the urban form around which communal life is organised arises from a gentle, curious and constantly changing way of looking at the site's spatial and cultural patterns. This approach is interesting because it triggers an unending dynamic that constantly recomposes, repairs and develops the relationship between human beings and their "environs", their living milieu. It does not draw the town but the town's project.

Europan: In this final category **Transformation**, the resource is perceived as a tameable and mutable element. This series of projects proposes modelling natural elements as urban features, in order to create a sort of inhabited fringe, a hybrid between town and resource, a

7 – ROMAINMÔTIER (CH), WINNER – *BUILT EDGES / GARDEN-METROPOLIS* > SEE MORE P.196

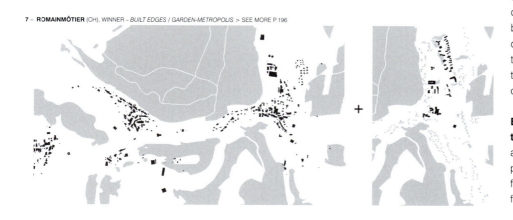

RECONNECTIONS
ANALYSIS OF THE SESSION

267

8 – NYNÄSHAMN (SE), WINNER – *SKÄRSCAPE* > SEE MORE P.126

solution for their coexistence. Can transforming, modifying a natural resource be a solution for creating hybrid landscapes, that coexist effectively and lastingly?

MD: The question of transformation is first about tackling the relation between the time of the resource, its life-cycle, and what one could call human time, the duration and durability of a project. These two projects work on two very different timeframes.
In Sambreville (BE) (fig. 9), it is the time of human settlement over multiple generations, which perpetually reinvent a new connection with the river, a new accord between people and the resource. Drawing inspiration from a past culture of wetlands drainage skills to make the site habitable, the project also seeks an equivalence between nature and buildings, trying to find a similar relationship and to show that it has always been there: it is a spatial transcription.
Whereas in Nynäshamn (SE) (fig. 8), the winning team works in geological time, proposing to sculpture, to scarify the site by reinterpreting the different, somewhat violent, movements that animate the millennial bedrock of this territory. The proposed transformation thus creates a bridge where human time and the time of human habitable space resonates with the slow transformation of geological time: a timeframe beyond us, a project that is powerful in its urban impact without lapsing into superfluous monumentality. So what we see here are two conceptual processes of resource transformation: human time linked with culture and geological time with nature.

Europan: In what way is hybridising urban artificiality and nature today a relevant design response?

MD: The word "relevant" is too weak. Achieving synergy with life, the climate and the earth, that is tomorrow's challenge! The time for anthropocentric thinking is gone, we need to think systems, i.e. making links between available resources and ways of inhabiting. Far from having a merely picturesque or ornamental role, landscape is increasingly becoming a strategic planning tool, because it allows us to think in a way that no longer opposes nature and culture, town and country, centre and periphery, the natural and the artificial.
1- clients especially need to ask different questions, but designers also have a role to play. Like the landscape architect Michel Desvigne, who heads the urban and landscape design schemes for the new Saclay International cluster, focusing on the concept of amplified geography. Or like the town that is looking for people with the skills to introduce a maintenance system for a new neighbourhood using animals…
2- However, this hybridisation should not be done simply through ecological engineering, but by involving things that are already there, a respect for urban memory, in short the construction of a new public space to support the perpetual – and necessary – evolution of the "natural" human milieu: the city.
3- Urban development raises the question of property rights. There is a debate about this: does private property protect natural resources (overgrazing on municipal land)? Elinor Ostrom, the American economist and political scientist, Nobel Prize for economics 2009, has shown that, historically and all over the world, communities have managed and can still manage public property in an economically viable way through the creation of "institutional arrangements". Alongside private or State management, there is a third effective institutional framework whereby communities can collectively manage common property, for example ecosystems, without causing their collapse.

9 – SAMBREVILLE (BE), RUNNER-UP – *QCM* > SEE MORE P.91

CHRIS YOUNÈS

CONVERSATION BETWEEN **STÉPHANE BONZANI**, ARCHITECT AND TEACHER, MEMBER OF EUROPAN'S EUROPEAN TECHNICAL COMMITTEE AND **CHRIS YOUNÈS**, PHILOSOPHER, ANTHROPOLOGIST, TEACHER AT THE ENSAPLV AND ESA SCHOOLS OF ARCHITECTURE IN PARIS AND MEMBER OF EUROPAN'S SCIENTIFIC COMMITTEE. SHE IS DIRECTOR OF THE RESEARCH LABORATORY GERPHAU. (WWW.GERPHAU.ARCHI.FR)

RECONNECTIONS
ANALYSIS OF THE SESSION

Rhythms and timeframes

Stéphane Bonzani: Taking account of urban rhythms and the multiple timeframes of activity in the project is an issue that arises in a certain number of winning ideas in Europan 11. In this group, all the projects use the dimension of "time" as an instrument of reconnection. The proposals aim to develop relationships between people, or between urban and natural rhythms. Integrating conceptions and rhythms leads to the question: how can we give «hospitality» to urban spaces so that they are appropriated by users of the city? How can we link the challenge of integrating different uses at different times with the spatial metamorphosis of the city?

Chris Younès: From an ecological perspective, the question of the metamorphoses of urban habitat to make it more hospitable has become critical. This term metamorphosis, whose Greek prefix "meta" means "beyond" or "what comes after", and which refers to a succession of forms in a phenomenon, a person or an environment, is particularly relevant to the need to transform a modernist heritage of separation and monofunctionalism, which do not make a city. So recreating legacies, being open to encounters, is about committing to a future that includes or rejects the past, in a dynamic reinvention of forms of life. And this includes adjusting them to reflect passing time or, conversely, in terms of mutations, transmutations.

In inhabited environments, which are complex, self-organised, sequenced systems, all the links are interconnected and yet within this interconnection each can take its own initiative. Of course, a system orders its own constituent elements, but not mechanically. Between one link and another, there is always a possibility of variation, of change, although the constituent elements exist in a synergistic relation. Such an environment is in no way a fixed spatial object, but is animated by a multitude of shifting links. We are talking about an urbanism of reconnection rather than fracture. The aim is not to imitate models but to invent scenarios that reflect the resistances and resources specific to each situation, and the contextual conditions of a project. This process requires us to decode the already-there and identify its strengths, but also to imagine other possible relations, passages and porosities. These connections contribute to an interlinking of scales, through which space and time, macro and micro, human and nonhuman work rhythmically together. Which is a way of seeing oneself in the world and configuring it, in particular through projects that propose metamorphoses that take the form of hybridisations between natures and cultures, which lead one to imagine other revaluations and intertwinings between long and short times, between fast and slow, between permanences and instabilities.

SB: The first subtopic on which we would like your views is what we have called **Coflowing**. How the restructuring of networks and transport modes – to adapt them both to fast citywide flows and gentler local flows – leads to new spatial systems where the city is designed "with" flows, through overlapping systems and tailored types of spaces.
Three projects have been chosen to illustrate this approach: *Magnetic urban field* in Graz (AT) (fig. 2), *Con la falda remangá* in Sestao (ES) (fig. 1) and *Bahnrad* in Wittstock (DE) (fig. 3). These projects propose to intensify and enrich urban life by combining and interweaving the

1 – **SESTAO** (ES), RUNNER-UP – *CON LA FALDA REMANGÁ* > SEE MORE P.47

2 – **GRAZ** (AT), RUNNER-UP – *MAGNETIC URBAN FIELD* > SEE MORE P.54

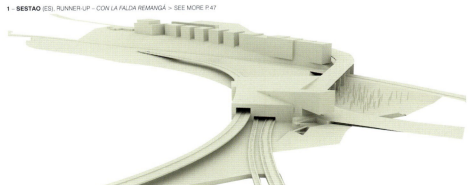
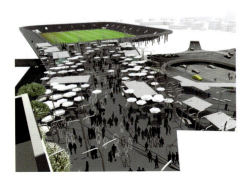

RHYTHMS AND TIMEFRAMES
CHRIS YOUNÈS

3 – WITTSTOCK (DE), WINNER – *BAHNRAD* > SEE MORE P.50

city's various flows: inhabitants, visitors, commuters, tourists, young and old people,... Most of them create a public space as a complex mobility system. Sometimes they use existing infrastructure. In your view, how do these projects deal with mobility in urban space? What kind of dynamic can be given to the city? Does it create a new type of urban space?

CY: You can't conceive the city as static, since it's in motion. The complexity of different elements and also different rhythms needs to be integrated into urban design. Changes in lifestyle have triggered the bipolarity between static and dynamic, here and there, fixity and mobility, local and global. This dual polarisation wards off the pitfalls of vagabondage or reclusion. Home is the place we leave and return to. This embeddedness in space and time has only ever worked because of the lines of motion that pass through it and to which it belongs. The anthropologist Radkowski stressed the transition, in urban living, from sedentariness to a nomadism very different from traditional nomadism. The possible connections between home, district, city, network, world, trace other reconfigurations by polarisation and extension that accelerate and intensify movement, altering the notion of proximity. Today's debates on the "walkable city", combining different types of mobility, are a significant facet of this tension between near and far, and of their inseparability in the hospitality of places. Habitability now faces new complexities from the exacerbation in the speed, intensity and diversity of movement. At a time of a generalised fragmentation of geographical space between work, leisure and home, there is a resurgence of embeddedness in the district, the neighbourhood. These ways of life require systems of travel and intensity that permit changes of rhythm and articulation between fast and slow, lively and relaxed. So the winning *Bahnrad* project in Wittstock seeks to connect local and global through infrastructures, and to regenerate the urban by reactivating green mobilities through a territorial scale conversion of railway lines to cycle tracks.

Let me say something about the other two projects, which opt instead for polarising systems. In Sestao, *Con la falda remanga* is based on the coexistence of different flows and a programmatic mix, combining metropolitan transport and intermodalities with other kinds of services to create public space where they intersect. In the outskirts of Graz, there is a similar quest for a system that will condense the ingredients of a fragmented landscape and generate a "Magnetic urban field" by orchestrating an intertwined choreography of public transport, roads, bicycles and pedestrians. The proposal seeks to create this kind of urban field to absorb variations, and in particular to maintain urban vitality when the crowds of spectators have quit the stadium.

4 – ALCALÁ DE LA SELVA (ES), RUNNER-UP – *CAMINANTE, NO HAY CAMINO, SE HACE CAMINO AL ANDAR* > SEE MORE P.139

RECONNECTIONS
ANALYSIS OF THE SESSION

5 – **LINZ** (AT), RUNNER-UP – *PORTRAIT OF AN ENSEMBLE* > SEE MORE P.114

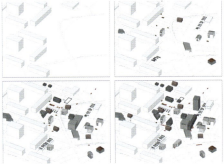

6 – **NORRKÖPING** (SE), WINNER – *DELTA X* > SEE MORE P.174

SB: The second sub-topic is about **Regenerating inhabited environments through ecorythms**. Urban rhythms (like the city's growth process, the movements of people in public spaces, uses, social development, economic development…) and natural rhythms (the cycle of days and seasons, flooding, plant growth,…) are synchronized to achieve more sustainable development and good quality of life. Nature plays the role of guide, a timeline for human life, as in the four selected projects *Caminante, no hay camino, se hace camino al andar* in Alcalá de la Selva (ES) (fig. 4), *Wear out* in Simrishamn (SE) (fig. 9), *Nest* in Allerød (DK) (fig. 8), *Arboropolis* in Alcorcón (ES) (fig. 7). How do these projects mould the ecological dimension of the city?

CY: The multiplication of human techniques for modifying the environment forces us to rethink the distinction between man and nature. Nature can no longer be seen simply as something subordinate to the desires and power of human beings, but in terms of its inherent properties. Capable of self-generation and self-movement (Aristotle), it enfolds humanity in the constantly renewed power of generation that defines it. The importance of this relationship with a nature of perpetual change and stupefying diversity, seems all the more precious in developing new urban, architectural and landscape forms to counter urban encroachment and the fragility of ecosystems. The references to geological, tectonic, biological and climatic nature are in counterpoint to the purely human timeframe. Moreover, the desire of urbanites for closeness to water, air, sunlight, wind, flora and fauna, daily and seasonal rhythms, also reflects the emergence of significant changes in attitudes to the importance of a nature that is both domesticated and wild. All this helps to revitalise representations and metamorphoses that may take specific forms, but each time seek to find approaches, such as the *Caminante, no hay camino, se hace camino al andar* project in Alcalá de la Selva, that reconnect natural and urban environments and thereby reactivating social and productive lines of force. Or else like *Wear out* in Simrishamn, which responds to the risk of flooding by creating an urban fabric that is a hybrid of public space, housing and wetlands, a coexistence with water and natural life. And also "Nest" in Allerød which proposes an urban structure that interacts with the natural elements with which day-to-day life is closely entwined, bringing forests, fields, lakes and gardens within range. Or else *Arboropolis* in Alcorcón where the tree becomes the resource element of a residual enclave site. Indeed, here a grove of different tree varieties offers a strong natural component in an industrial zone and provides a way of reconnecting the future landscape and the existing town and also introducing timeframes into the urban fabric.

7 – **ALCORCÓN** (ES), WINNER – *ARBOLÓPOLIS* > SEE MORE P.184

RHYTHMS AND TIMEFRAMES
CHRIS YOUNÈS

272

9 – SIMRISHAMN (SE), WINNER – *WEAR OUT* > SEE MORE P.26

SB: We called the third sub-topic **Co-evolution** or how to transform a territory by a shared process. And we selected three corresponding projects: *Dreaming/Awaking* in Ingolstadt (DE) (fig. 11), *I Amstel 3* in Amsterdam (NL) (fig. 10) and *Portrait of an ensemble* in Linz (AT) (fig. 5). In these proposals, the most important dimension is the process of implementation. They seek to invent another way to produce urban fabric, working through various partners and very often expecting strong participation by the inhabitants. They set a system of rules, a framework, as a starting point for the future development. Time, in these strategies, is the rich dimension of unexpected events, co-creation, and collective production. How do you think that the paradox can be resolved of defining an evolution that will take several years to implement in an unstable environmental and economic context with changing uses?

CY: The transformation of the city on its own fabric is a new challenge for a sustainable development policy. Many urban projects seek to combine evolution and mutation by stressing the importance of process, in order to reconcile different, opposing and even conflictual approaches to a constantly disputed common good. Creative inspiration seems to be nothing like enough to determine the desirable sapiences in the face of complex and uncertain situations with long timeframes. To counter unsustainable development, other scenarios and other engagements are being sought by repositioning the relations between nature and culture, technology and society, but also the relations between actors. These are new ways of setting conditions for sharing and adaptation not by positing illusory solutions, but by promoting transitions and leaving open the capacities of environments to mutate to accommodate the future. Self-destruction and self-regeneration are powerful metamorphic forces that entail both creative ferment and local initiatives. And it is true that several Europan 11 winning or runner-up projects reflect this perspective. *Dreaming/Awaking* in Ingolstadt bases urbanisation on an open development strategy. In a sort of game of consequences or collage, a festive interpretation of the existing structure is initiated in theatrical form, offering an alternative to an authoritarian system or a finished design. *I Amstel 3* in Amsterdam (fig. 10) looks to transform a monofunctional sector into an animated urban space through a strategy of gradual colonisation that focuses on three triggers designed to send pulses throughout the neighbourhood and initiate a dynamic of reclamation by new types of inhabitants – pioneers as it were – who would participate in the evolution of their en-

8 – ALLERØD (DK), RUNNER-UP – *NEST* > SEE MORE P.147

RECONNECTIONS
ANALYSIS OF THE SESSION

10 – **AMSTERDAM** (NL), WINNER – *I AMSTEL 3* > SEE MORE P.32

vironment. In Linz, the *Portrait of an ensemble* team has responded not with a form but with a narrative in which they imagine eight characters playing different but interactive roles in the evolution of brownfield site. This vision, which sets the rules of the game, becomes a medium for discussion and debate.

Still with the idea that we cannot program the future but should rather try to work on the possibility conditions of a future, one winning project, *Delta-X* at Norrköping (in Sweden) (fig. 6), proposes a series of urban rules relating only to land divisions and a hyper-connected system of flows, with the aim of restoring the initiative in appropriation and self-organisation to citizens. As a result, the regeneration of the neighbourhood is based on the inhabitants' own dynamics, rather than financial speculation or a design proposal.

SB: In this interview, you have introduced the notion of metamorphosis in an original way in speaking of the evolution of city, precisely because it involves time. But what systems do these metamorphoses follow specifically for modern cities in the era of sustainable development?

CY: Broadly speaking, thinking about rhythms and timeframes in architecture means thinking about the incessant metamorphoses of inhabited environments, it means rediscovering the underlying naturo-cultural energies or vibrations and the articulations of space and time, the importance of cycles and recurrences. But it also means remembering that man is a being in motion and one needs to leave room for the unpredictable in designing living spaces. It is a central challenge for architects and urban designers to introduce this new paradigm and particularly in Europan, in its role as a platform of innovation for Europe's cities.

11 – **INGOLSTADT** (DE), RUNNER-UP – *DREAMING/AWAKING* > SEE MORE P.83

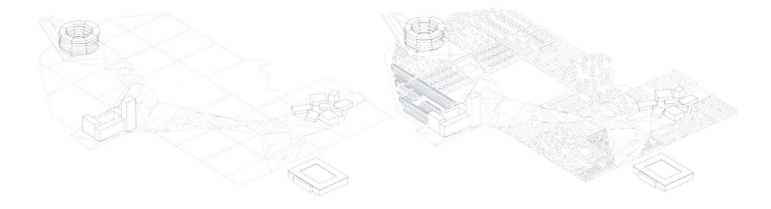

EUROPAN SECRETARIATS

EUROPAN BELGIQUE/BELGIË/BELGIEN
143, RUE DE CAMPINE
4000 LIÈGE
TEL + 32. 4. 226 69 40 / FAX + 32. 4. 226 47 35 /
SECRETARIAT@EUROPAN.BE / WWW.EUROPAN.BE
FRENCH, ENGLISH
9:30 A.M. TO NOON / MONDAY, WEDNESDAY, FRIDAY

EUROPAN DANMARK
DAC (DANISH ARCHITECTURE CENTRE), STRANDGADE 27B
1401 COPENHAGEN K
TEL + 45. 3257 1930 / FAX + 45. 3254 5010 /
EUROPAN@DAC.DK / WWW.DAC.DK/EUROPAN
DANISH, ENGLISH
9 A.M.-5 P.M. / MONDAY TO FRIDAY

EUROPAN DEUTSCHLAND
LÜTZOWSTRASSE 102-104
10785 BERLIN
TEL + 49. 30. 262 01 12 / FAX + 49. 30. 261 56 84 /
MAIL@EUROPAN.DE / WWW.EUROPAN.DE
GERMAN, ENGLISH
10 A.M.-5 P.M. / MONDAY TO FRIDAY

EUROPAN ESPAÑA
PASEO DE LA CASTELLANA, 12.
28046 MADRID
TEL + 34. 91. 575 74 01 / + 34. 91. 435 22 00 /
FAX + 34. 91. 575 75 08 / EUROPAN.ESP@ARQUINEX.ES /
WWW.EUROPAN-ESPES
SPANISH, FRENCH, ENGLISH
10 A.M.-2 P.M. / MONDAY TO FRIDAY

EUROPAN EUROPE
GRANDE ARCHE DE LA DÉFENSE, PILIER SUD
92 055 PARIS-LA-DÉFENSE CEDEX
TEL + 33. 1. 40 81 24 47 /
CONTACT@EUROPAN-EUROPE.COM /
WWW.EUROPAN-EUROPE.COM
ENGLISH, FRENCH
10 A.M.-5 P.M. / MONDAY TO FRIDAY

EUROPAN FRANCE
GRANDE ARCHE DE LA DÉFENSE, PILIER SUD
92 055 PARIS-LA-DÉFENSE CEDEX
TEL + 33. 1. 40 81 24 54 / FAX + 33. 1. 40 81 94 75 /
STEPHANIE.DE-MONTGOLFIER@DEVELOPPEMENT-DU-
RABLE.GOUV.FR / WWW.EUROPAN-FRANCE.ORG
FRENCH, ENGLISH
9 A.M.-1 P.M. / MONDAY, TUESDAY, THURSDAY, FRIDAY

EUROPAN HRVATSKA
C/O MINISTRY OF ENVIRONMENTAL PROTECTION, PHYSI-
CAL PLANNING AND CONSTRUCTION, ULICA REPUBLIKE
AUSTRIJE 20
10000 ZAGREB
TEL + 385. 1. 6101 852 / FAX + 385.1. 3782 155 /
EUROPAN-HRVATSKA@ZG.T-COM.HR / WWW.EUROPAN.HR
CROATIAN, ENGLISH
9 A.M. TO NOON, 1 P.M.-3 P.M. / MONDAY TO FRIDAY

EUROPAN IRELAND
ROYAL INSTITUTE OF THE ARCHITECTS OF IRELAND (RIAI),
8 MERRION SQUARE
DUBLIN 2
TEL + 353. 1. 676 1703 / FAX +353. 1. 661 0948 /
INFO@RIAI.IE
ENGLISH
10 A.M.-1 P.M. / MONDAY TO THURSDAY

EUROPAN MAGYARORSZÁG (ASSOCIATED WITH ÖSTERREICH)
HUNGARIAN SOCIETY FOR URBAN PLANNING,
LILIOM UTCA 48
1094 BUDAPESTI
TEL 36. 1. 215 5794 / FAX 36. 1. 215 5162 / MUT@MUT.HU /
WWW.EUROPAN-HUNGARY.HU
HUNGARIAN, ENGLISH
10 A.M.- 1 P.M. / MONDAY TO THURSDAY

EUROPAN NEDERLAND
MUSEUMPARK 25, P.O. BOX 2182
3000 CD ROTTERDAM
TEL + 31. 10. 440 12 38 / FAX + 31. 10. 436 00 90 /
OFFICE@EUROPAN.NL / WWW.EUROPAN.NL
DUTCH, ENGLISH
9 A.M.-5 P.M. / MONDAY TO FRIDAY

EUROPAN NORGE
C/0 0047, SCHWEIGAARDSGATE 34 D
0191 OSLO
TEL + 47. 24 20 11 47 / FAX + 47. 21 56 39 78 /
POST@EUROPAN.NO / WWW.EUROPAN.NO
NORWEGIAN, ENGLISH
10 A.M.-4 P.M. / MONDAY TO FRIDAY

EUROPAN ÖSTERREICH
HAUS DER ARCHITEKTUR, PALAIS THINNFELD,
MARIAHILFERSTRASSE 2
8020 GRAZ
TEL + 43. 664. 350 89 32 / FAX + 43. 316 83 21 51 /
OFFICE@EUROPAN.AT / WWW.EUROPAN.AT
GERMAN, ENGLISH
9 A.M.-2 P.M. / MONDAY, WEDNESDAY, THURSDAY

EUROPAN POLSKA (ASSOCIATED WITH DEUTSCHLAND)
PALAC KULTURY I NAUKI, BAIPP (BIURO ARCHITEKTURY I
PLANOWANIA PRZESTRZENNEGO), FL. XVII, R. 1716
PLAC DEFILAD 1
00-901 WARSZAWA
TEL + 48. 22 656 77 87 / FAX + 48. 22 656 64 88 /
EUROPAN@EUROPAN.COM.PL / WWW.EUROPAN.COM.PL
POLISH, ENGLISH
10 A.M.-1 P.M. / MONDAY TO THURSDAY

EUROPAN PORTUGAL
TRAVESSA DO CARVALHO 23, 1200
097 LISBOA
TEL + 351. 21. 324 11 30 / FAX + 351. 21. 347 23 97 /
EUROPAN@EUROPANPORTUGAL.PT /
WWW.EUROPANPORTUGAL.PT
PORTUGUESE, ENGLISH
10 A.M.-1 P.M., 2 P.M.-6 P.M. / MONDAY TO FRIDAY

**EUROPAN REPUBLIKA E KOSOVËS/REPUBLIKA KO-
SOVA (ASSOCIATED WITH ÖSTERREICH)**
C/O CHWB, RR. R. ZOGOVIQ NR. 8
10000 PRISHTINE, KOSOVE
TEL +377. 44. 758 510 / FAX +377. 38. 243 918 /
CONTACT@EUROPAN-KOSOVO.ORG /
WWW.EUROPAN-KOSOVO.ORG
ENGLISH, FRENCH, SPANISH
9 A.M.-12,30 A.M., 2 P.M.-5,30 P.M. / MONDAY TO FRIDAY

EUROPAN SCHWEIZ/SUISSE/SVIZZERA/SVIZRA
P/A LUSCHER, BOULEVARD DE GRANCY 37
1006 LAUSANNE
TEL + 41. 21. 616 63 93 / FAX + 41. 21. 616 63 68 /
CONTACT@EUROPAN.CH / EUROPAN@BLUEWIN.CH /
WWW.EUROPAN-SUISSE.CH
FRENCH, GERMAN, ITALIAN, ENGLISH
2 P.M.-5 P.M. / MONDAY AND THURSDAY

EUROPAN SUOMI - FINLAND
SAFA, RUNEBERGINKATU 5
00100 HELSINKI
TEL + 358.45 1393665 / FAX + 358. 9. 58444222 /
EUROPAN@EUROPAN.FI / WWW.EUROPAN.FI
FINNISH, SWEDISH, ENGLISH
9 A.M.-4 P.M. / MONDAY TO FRIDAY

EUROPAN SVERIGE
C/O SVERIGES ARKITEKTER, BOX 5027
SE-10241 STOCKHOLM
TEL + 46.8.50557700 / FAX + 46.8.50557705 /
EUROPAN@ARKITEKT.SE / WWW.EUROPAN.SE
SWEDISH, ENGLISH
9 A.M.-12 A.M., 1 P.M.-3 P.M. / MONDAY TO FRIDAY

CREDITS

276

EUROPAN 11 RESULTS

This book is published in the context of the eleventh session of Europan

HEAD OF PUBLICATION
DIDIER REBOIS, EUROPAN EUROPE GENERAL SECRETARY

EDITORIAL SECRETARY
FRANÇOISE BONNAT, EUROPAN EUROPE RESPONSIBLE OF EUROPAN PUBLICATIONS

THEMATIC ANALYSIS
STÉPHANE BONZANI, ARCHITECT, TEACHER, PARIS FRANCE
DAVID FRANCO, ARCHITECT, TEACHER, MADRID SPAIN
JENS METZ, ARCHITECT, URBAN PLANNER, TEACHER, BERLIN GERMANY
DIDIER REBOIS, ARCHITECT, TEACHER, EUROPAN EUROPE GENERAL SECRETARY, FRANCE
BERND VLAY, ARCHITECT, GENERAL SECRETARY OF EUROPAN ÖSTERREICH, VIENNA AUSTRIA

AUTHORS
MATHIEU DELORME, ENGINEER, LANDSCAPE ARCHITECT, URBANIST, TEACHER AT THE FRENCH INSTITUTE OF URBAN DESIGN IN PARIS FRANCE
JOSÉ MARÍA EZQUIAGA, TEACHER, ARCHITECT AND URBAN PLANNER IN EZQUIAGA ARQUITECTURA SOCIEDAD Y TERRITORIO IN MADRID SPAIN
OLIVER SCHULZE, ARCHITECT, DIRECTOR OF GEHL ARCHITECTS IN COPENHAGEN DENMARK, TEACHER IN WASHINGTON UNIVERSITY IN ST-LOUIS UNITED STATES
ENRIQUE SOBEJANO, ARCHITECT, NIETO SOBEJANO ARQUITECTOS, TEACHER, MADRID SPAIN/ BERLIN GERMANY
CHRIS YOUNÈS, PHILOSOPHER, ANTHROPOLOGIST, DIRECTOR OF THE RESEARCH LABORATORY GERFAU, TEACHER AT THE ENSAPLV AND ESA SCHOOLS OF ARCHITECTURE IN PARIS FRANCE

ENGLISH TRANSLATION
JOHN CRISP

GRAPHIC DESIGN AND LAYOUT
GENERAL DESIGN
MAROUSSIA JANNELLE WITH MORGANE REBULARD

PRINTING
UAB BALTO PRINT (VILNIUS, LITHUANIA)

EDITED BY
EUROPAN EUROPE
LA GRANDE ARCHE, PILIER SUD
92055 PARIS LA DÉFENSE CEDEX
FRANCE
WWW.EUROPAN-EUROPE.COM

ISBN N° 978-2-914296-22-9
LEGALLY REGISTERED
SECOND QUARTER 2012